**Justice for Our Children**

# Justice for Our Children

An Examination of Juvenile Delinquent
Rehabilitation Programs

Dennis A. Romig

**Lexington Books**
D.C. Heath and Company
Lexington, Massachusetts
Toronto

**Library of Congress Cataloging in Publication Data**

Romig, Dennis A.
 Justice for our children.

 Includes index.
 1. Rehabilitation   of   juvenile   delinquents.   2. Juvenile   justice.
Administration of. I. Title.
HV9069.R65        364        77-9154
ISBN 0-669-01787-6

Second printing, October 1978.

Published simultaneously in Canada.

Printed in the United States of America.

International Standard Book Number: 0-669-01787-6

Library of Congress Catalog Card Number: 77-9154

To Dr. Grandma

May Catherine Mitchell Wilder Gates
A World Changer!
Whose process is to focus on people,
Whose technique is objective love,
Whose system is education,
Whose effects are far-ranging,
Whose reward is her own joy in Life.

# Contents

# List of Figures

# List of Tables

# Preface

Justice for our children implies that delinquent youth receive, in fact, what our laws mandate: rehabilitation. Justice for our children then requires that we study our treatment approaches, that we discard what is ineffective and secure, and that we foster what is successful. This book is a study of what rehabilitates, what does not, and why in each case. Rehabilitation of juvenile delinquents is possible. But it is contingent upon the attainment of certain standards of quality. Approaches and programs that are successful with normal teenagers and with other treatment populations do not work with delinquent youth.

The book draws from a review of the literature of over 825 books and articles on the treatment of juvenile delinquents. Only about 170 of the studies met the primary criteria of having a matched or randomly assigned control group. These studies were intensely investigated, and from them principles for the rehabilitation of juvenile delinquents have been formulated. Recommendations are made in every area of delinquency programming for the upgrading of existing treatment approaches. In addition to specifying needed improvements in present methods, an ideal program is developed and offered for consideration. The prediction is that when the principles articulated in this book are utilized in treatment programs, there will be justice for our children.

# Acknowledgments

One of the greatest pleasures in completing a work of this magnitude is the opportunity thus presented to acknowledge all those who meant so much in its development. I am fortunate to have had my life touched by literal giants from the field of behavioral science. It began with Dr. Warren Baller, back at the University of Nebraska. He was and still is for many people, Mr. Educational Psychology for Nebraska and the Midwest. He showed me how rigorous and strict intellectual pursuits could be combined with warmth and compassion.

Dr. Angelo Bolea taught me that important breakthroughs in psychology can only be made over authentic Italian pizza after a vigorous workout on a handball court. Angelo is made of the same toughness that I am sure Freud had, to get in and look at life in ways that are off limits to others.

My doctoral program, like many university programs, was at times boring, irrelevant, and pedantic. Dr. Charles Cleland, in addition to being one of the most productive researchers at the University of Texas, served as a one-man Red Cross station for graduate students with downtrodden spirits. He injected life and humor into all aspects of research and teaching, as well as serving as my mentor.

Dr. Paul Liberty is another professor who was a lighthouse on the dark plains. He is partially responsible for the impetus of this book, because he taught his students always to do their "homework" for any job undertaken. By *homework* he meant study the literature and find out what works. The first job I took when I finished graduate school was as a psychologist working with juvenile delinquents at a state training school. It was at that point in 1972, as part of my "homework," that the research for this book began.

For the past four years I have been closely involved with Dr. Bob Carkhuff, whose consulting firm aided the Texas Youth Council in its post-Morales reorganization. The influence of Bob's Human Resource Development Model upon my life and this book is gratefully acknowledged.

Other individuals who were helpful in the preparation of this book are Dr. Charles D. Saddler; Craig Sommer; Dr. John Cannon; James Eugene Wilder, Jr.; Catherine Wilder Gates; and Dr. David Berenson. Ron Jackson, the Executive Director of the Texas Youth Council and my boss for five years, reviewed portions of the manuscript and provided many helpful suggestions. Jack O'Connell, of the state of Washington's Law and Justice Planning Office, provided the most critical, and yet the most helpful, review of the book's content.

My deepest gratitude, however, goes to my wife Laurie, who, between coordinating all technical aspects of the manuscript's preparation and running a complex twentieth-century household, shared the excitement, the drudgery, the anticipation, and the hard work related with this experience.

# Introduction

## The Tragedy of the Present Juvenile Justice System

Mark is on the run. He cautiously peers around the store's corner onto the dark street. His tattered brown jeans and white T-shirt are all that protect him from the cold North wind. The tennis shoes on the bottom of his long legs are damp and muddy. His brown eyes scan the street furtively in the hope of recognizing the car of a friend. Mark reaches down and fingers the switchblade in his pocket. He looks around the corner into the lighted store and waits.

Mark first began getting in trouble when he was eight years old, when he would steal money from his mother's purse. She tried to discipline him as best she could, but most of the time she was alone because her husband had to travel a lot on his job. One Sunday afternoon, when Mark was ten, the minister of their church and the Sunday school director came by to visit. They informed Mark's mother that her son had stolen the Sunday school collection money. Mark, hiding behind the corner of the living room, listened intently. When his mother saw him, he grinned sheepishly at her and darted back into his room. At first, the church officials said they would not let Mark come to Sunday school anymore. But Mark's mother said she would get help for her son at the local child guidance center.

At the first meeting with the social worker, Mark's parents were told that it was their fault that their son was in trouble, that he felt rejected by them and was stealing just to get their attention. Mark's father blew up at the social worker and walked out. His mother, on the verge of tears, remained. Upon the social worker's advice, the parents reluctantly became more lenient with Mark and took him on fun outings even when his behavior did not warrant such rewards. For three weeks, everyone thought that Mark was doing better. Then on Friday night, when Mark's father got in from a week on the road, there was a police car with its light flashing in front of his house. Mark and a boy two years older had broken into a neighbor's house, stolen everything of value, and then proceeded to tear the house apart.

The neighbor was furious. Not only would the house have to be repainted and recarpeted, but the jewelry that had been stolen had been handed down for four generations. The police turned Mark over to the juvenile probation authorities, where he was found guilty by the local juvenile judge. When Mark's parents asked him why, at first he gave them his usual grin. After repeated confrontation, he began to cry, saying he didn't know why. The older boy was sent to the state training school, while Mark was placed on probation for one year. It was only six weeks later, however, that Mark was caught burglarizing a local grocery store at midnight, when his parents had been sure he was in bed asleep.

The juvenile probation officer, who had used individual counseling with Mark, decided that what he needed was a different home placement. He was held in the detention center for six weeks. Mark, who now was almost twelve years old, was placed in a home with a truck driver and his wife. They were very friendly to Mark, and he was beginning to do better in school. The husband drank a lot, however; and one night when he was dead drunk and out, his wife made sexual advances to Mark and seduced him. The next night, when a similar situation began to develop, Mark ran away and hitchhiked to a city 100 miles away. The truck driver and his wife did not report Mark's leaving for six days; they "thought sure he would come back any day."

Even though the police put out a statewide pickup notice on Mark, it was six months before he was found, and then it was only because a night watchman caught him and another boy burglarizing a tool shop. Mark was returned to his home community, where he was found guilty of burglary again. The town and his family were getting somewhat fed up with Mark and his behavior. But the local juvenile judge rejected commitment to the state training school. In a private talk with the judge, Mark, unlike other boys, had not tried to deceive or "con" the judge. Instead, he admitted everything, but seemed confused and worried about his own behavior. Mark was only twelve, and the judge thought the community should do better for the youngster. This time he was placed in a group home that had recently been organized. He attended school in the day and participated in a confrontive form of group therapy at night. Mark did well in school during the day, but always seemed upset or withdrawn after the group therapy sessions at night. Then one night, during a session in which the group was especially critical of his best friend, he picked up a chair and attacked the boys.

This time the judge had no choice. Mark was committed to the state training school for an indefinite period of time. When Mark arrived, he took one look at the place and decided this was one place he wanted to get out of as quickly as possible. He talked to the boys in his dormitory and found out that if you smiled and spoke to all the staff, did not fight, and really acted like the program was helping you, you could get out in five to six months. So Mark did as the boys suggested. Between classes and activities he greeted all the staff. During group counseling he confessed to all the bad things he had done and promised that he would never do them again. He told the vocational counselor that if he could start learning a trade, it would help him stay out of trouble when he got out of the school.

Mark was then placed in an auto mechanics class, where, though he was interested, he could not understand what was going on. Rather than admitting that and perhaps being kept at the training school longer, Mark hung around the teacher, smiled and looked interested, and ran errands for him. At the five-month point, Mark's case was brought up at the progress review meeting. The caseworker detailed Mark's progress in individual and group counseling. The auto mechanics teacher reported that he had Mark with him most of the school day and he was a model student. When asked how Mark did on the tests, the teacher replied that he did not believe in tests. But through his observations, he knew Mark was doing well. The dormitory supervisor stated that the boy had not been in any trouble in the residence hall. Only the recreation supervisor voiced any concern that Mark was holding back and not really showing his true self. The caseworker, with her master's degree, countered by explaining that according to the psychiatrist, Mark had gone through an adolescent adjustment reaction and that was the cause of the former delinquency. The committee voted 3 to 1 in approval of Mark's release.

When the family heard that Mark was coming home, they were initially shocked that he could have improved so fast. With somewhat disbelieving and subdued pleasure they agreed to have him return home. They were informed that through a recent federal grant, Mark would receive more intensive parole supervision than that given most youth on parole. When Mark arrived home, the family greeted and hugged him, glad that he was home and hoping that what the training school staff had said was true. Mark just sheepishly grinned and settled back into his home.

Things went along well for Mark, because it was still summer and all Mark had to do was lay around the house, watch TV, and hang around with his friends. When school started, his parole officer made sure that he was placed in a slower, special education classroom. The first week was fine because the teacher, who was a young attractive woman, tried to build positive attitudes about school by providing games and entertainment. It was during the second week, when school really started, that Mark began arguing with his teacher and the other students. Then one day he did not show up at school or at home. He had run away again. His parents were frustrated and felt the situation was hopeless. Not only did they not have their son, but every time they looked for help, they met only disappointment and failure.

It is at this point, a few weeks later, that we find Mark hiding around the corner of the all-night grocery store. Mark is scared. He doesn't know how he got where he is. He knows only that he is tired and hungry and has to get some money. He could call his parents, but he knows they will just call the cops. He shivers as the cold wind blows across his shirt. The people with whom he had last slept kicked him out because he didn't have any money for food. He doesn't want to rob the store. He walks back toward the alley. But he knows he has to get some money, just a little money; he will ask the old man nicely.

He walks into the store and slowly goes up and down the aisles looking at different items, nervously glancing toward the cash register. The store is empty. The old shopkeeper begins to stare at Mark. Now he is really scared. He has to make a move. Now! He walks hurriedly up to the shopkeeper, pulls out his knife, and demands the money. The shopkeeper looks attentive, but does not seem afraid. He tells Mark to put the knife down and walk out. Mark only gets more agitated and shakes the knife at the old man. The shopkeeper opens the cash register and hands Mark the dollar bills. Mark quickly turns to leave. The shopkeeper quietly and efficiently pulls out a gun and tells Mark to stop. Mark sees the gun and reaches frantically for the door. The gun fires! Mark feels the hot seering pain go through his back into his heart. As he slumps to the floor in his last gasps of breath, he looks up at the old shopkeeper with tears in his eyes—and then he falls over, dead.

## Purpose of this Book

All the elements in the history of Mark are true. Throughout the United States, other Marks, and Susans and Juans and Bills, are caught up in the same destructive cycle. This book has been written in part to explain why our juvenile justice system, on the whole, fails in its task of truly helping Mark and the others like him. Why, with so many diverse opportunities, do we still seem to fail? This question, and other related questions, will be answered in the following chapters.

The question may arise, why, in a book that is presenting a review of studies that demonstrate what has been effective with delinquent youth, should programs that have failed be discussed. First, it must be understood that *not everything works*. In fact, most methods with delinquents have not worked. Those approaches must be clearly detailed and explained so that we can finally stop using them. Second, in outlining the ingredients of effective programs, it is useful to contrast those programs with other ones that lack effectiveness.

However, the foremost purpose of this book is positive. Successful methods and approaches are highlighted and discussed in detail. The effective ingredients of successful programs are teased out for close inspection and then combined with similar ingredients from other programs. The goal of the book is to improve the rehabilitation efforts in isolated juvenile justice programs as well as in the system as a whole.

The fact that rehabilitation is the stated goal of the juvenile justice system was reasserted in a national survey of juvenile legal codes conducted by the National Assessment of Juvenile Corrections Project (Levin and Sarri, 1974). Compared with the adult system, where punishment, retribution, and protection of society are also emphasized as purposes, the juvenile justice system is clear in its authorized mission—*to rehabilitate*. This book will discuss where rehabilitation has worked and where it has failed.

## Methods Used in this Study

The first step in this research was to find any written article or report that deals with the rehabilitation of juvenile delinquents. All relevant journals, abstracts, and newsletters were reviewed. In addition, state and local agencies were contacted for copies of their recent research reports. The cooperation and support of these agencies in sharing data and results were extremely gratifying.

The first review was performed to identify those evaluation studies which met the criterion of utilizing either a randomly assigned control group or a matched control group. Use of such control groups greatly ensures that any improvement in the specially treated group is the result of the treatment approach and not the result of other causes. Figure I-1 presents the total number of 829 studies by the year in which they were initially reviewed. The criterion for inclusion in the next level of review was measurement of program effectiveness in terms of behavior. Only about 170 of the studies met both criteria. The other studies, those which did not meet both criteria, will not be referred to beyond this point.

The remaining studies, those which did meet the criteria of appropriate control groups and behavior as the measure of effectiveness, were then divided by the rehabilitations methods used, for example, individual counseling, casework, and so on. Each study was then described in terms of the youth in the program, the setting used, the program content, and the results. You will find many direct quotations from the original research when programs and treatments are described. The purpose in so doing is to obtain, as much as possible, the author's own description of what exactly was tried with the delinquent youth in the study.

To assist you in better understanding the review of research section of each chapter, the following list of terms is presented. Having a clear knowledge of these terms will allow you to understand the descriptions of the experimental studies and their results more easily.

## Definitions

**Experimental group.** The group of youth in a study who receive the experimental program or special treatment.

**Treatment group.** Another way of referring to the experimental group. Still refers to the group of youth who will receive the rehabilitation methods under study.

**Control group.** The group of youth who are specifically restricted from participation in the experimental treatment program but who otherwise are treated the same. Their performance is compared against those youth in the experimental group.

**Subjects.** The youths whose progress or lack of progress will be measured in the study. Includes both control and experimental group youth unless otherwise specified.

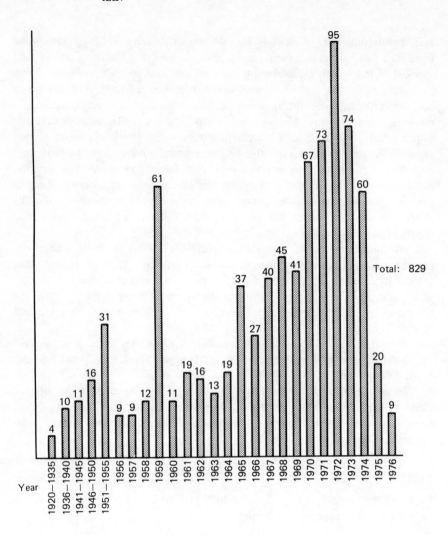

**Figure I-1.** Number of Juvenile Justice Studies Reviewed, by Year of Publication

**Randomly assigned control and treatment groups.** When participation by the youth in either the treatment program or the control group is determined in an unbiased situation through methods such as pulling a number from a hat or from a table of random numbers. The assumption can then be made that any differences in the performances of the two groups are due to the effects of the experimental treatment program.

**Matched treatment and control groups.** Groups of youth who are chosen because they are almost identical to each other in the critical areas of age, race, sex, and past history of delinquency. It is assumed that because the youth in the two types of groups are very similar in the important areas of their background characteristics that any differences in the behavior of the two groups are a result of the experimental treatment program.

**Statistically significant difference.** When the results comparing the treatment group's and the control group's performance are so far apart that the reported difference could only have occurred five or less times out of 100 by chance. Because of the low probability of occurring by chance, the difference is a result of some factor associated with the experiment. If matched or randomly assigned control groups were selected, the difference can be attributed to the effects of the experimental program. The statistically significant difference can either be positive or negative.

**Not statistically significant.** When any reported difference between the treatment and control groups is so small that it could have occurred by chance. Because the results of the control group are similar to the treatment groups, it is concluded that the treatment group was not effective, and the approach is not supported.

**Positive results.** When there is a statistically significant difference in favor of the treatment group having a better performance than the control group. Such results are beneficial to the youth in the treatment group and the approach utilized is supported.

**Negative results.** When there is either a statistically significant difference in which the treatment group does worse, or when the results are not statistically significant. In either case the treatment has not made a favorable impact upon the experimental group.

**Recidivism rate.** The proportion of youth who are returned to custody as a result of delinquent behavior compared with the total number of youth released within the same period of time. Recidivism can involve a youth being rearrested, reassigned to probation, or recommitted to an institution.

**Works.** A program *works* if it either reduces negative, delinquent behavior or increases socially functional behavior to a statistically significant degree. For a program to really be effective it should have documented results of success in more than one location or setting.

**Rehabilitation.** That activity or set of programs provided for delinquent youth that have as their result the increase in socially accepted behavior and the decrease in unlawful behavior.

It should be noted that the preceding definitions are presented in the context of the following discussions, even though they may have applicability to other discussions of research.

## Organization of the Book

This book is divided into two parts. The first part is concerned with treatment interventions and rehabilitation approaches that have been tried in a variety of both institutional and community settings. For example, individual counseling has been used by probation officers, parole officers, caseworkers in group homes, and others. The second part reports studies involving systemwide interventions or studies whose results have systemwide implications. Chapters in this part are concerned with diversion, probation, institutions, community residential care, and parole. At the conclusion of both parts is a summary chapter that defines what an ideal program or ideal system would look like based upon the conclusions of the preceding chapters.

Each chapter has two major sections, the review of the literature and the conclusions. The review of the literature discusses in chronological order all the relevant studies that were obtained concerning the particular topic under question. The youth involved, the program tried, and the reported results are presented for each study. In the conclusions section of every chapter, an outline table of the main elements of the programs and their results are summarized along with the number of youth in the study. Follow-up results are separated from the results reported while the program was in progress. Follow-up results are the most critical, since they reveal the long-term and lasting effects of the treatment approach.

The conclusions of each chapter present a summary of the findings presented. From that summary, specific predictions and recommendations are made concerning the use of that program or system. The purpose of the predictions and recommendations is to guide future policy and program planning in the juvenile justice system.

Further, general predictions and recommendations are also made at the close of each chapter. These statements are attempts to apply the knowledge gained in each chapter to a broader range of circumstances. The general predictions and recommendations as such are more tentative and will require further research validation. Finally, each chapter's references are listed at the end.

# Reference

Levin, Mark M., and Rosemary C. Sarri. *Juvenile Delinquency: A Comparative Analysis of Legal Codes in the United States.* Ann Arbor: University of Michigan, National Assessment of Juvenile Corrections, 1974.

**Part I:**
**Program Interventions**
**as Treatment**

# 1 Casework

## Review of the Research

From the 1930s to the present, social work has been viewed as an important treatment approach to combat juvenile delinquency. Today, with almost every program, whether in the community or in an institution, it is understood that social work and social workers will be a main part of the program. Even though Fischer (1973) raised questions with his review of casework approaches, casework continues to retain its dominance.

The following review documents the results of 10 studies involving thousands of delinquent youth and utilizing social work and casework interventions. One of the earliest studies involved an evaluation of the casework "study-and-make-recommendations method." The court records of two matched groups of 1000 boys were examined by Healy, Bronner, and Shimberg (1935). One group participated in a child guidance program that emphasized casework as the main program component. The other group received no treatment. The percentages of recidivists were similar for the two groups. The conclusion was that the "study-and-make-recommendations method" of delinquency prevention was "useless."

Glueck and Glueck (1934) examined the records of the 1000 boys referred to the child guidance program five years after their participation. Unfortunately no control group was utilized. However, the findings are are reported because of their consistency with the other studies reported in this chapter. The results indicated that 88 percent of the youth continued their misconduct, while 70 percent were convicted of a serious offense. It can be concluded that the program was not successful. The main program ingredients—casework, diagnosis and recommendations, tutoring, and utilization of foster homes—were not sufficient to prevent further delinquency.

Seventeen years later, a friendship casework program with 325 boys was evaluated by Powers and Witmer (1951). Boys were referred to the program by judges as "difficult boys" who needed help. A matched group of 325 boys served as a control group. *Friendship casework* was described as follows:

The bulk of our work will be accomplished through the personal intimacy of our workers with the individual boy and with his family. To make him understand himself and the world that he lives in, so that he can find satisfaction in his life without harming himself or others, will be the chief effort of our workers (Powers and Witmer, 1951, p. 94).

3

The program lasted for over seven years, and the overall results were negative. The police and court records for the two groups were identical. The project did not result in any reductions in the frequency, seriousness, or number of police and court appearances.

However, the program did succeed with some youth. The authors attempted to analyze the factors accounting for those positive effects:

The individual case analyses presented in the preceding chapters suggest that the significant factors can be isolated and that good results are likely to occur only when the factors are present in favorable combination. These factors appear to be: (1) the emotional maladjustment in the home and in the boy is not too extreme; (2) the boy and usually, his parents desire help with the problem; (3) the counselors' services are consistently and skillfully related to the source of the difficulty (Powers and Witmer, 1951, p. 564).

Two of the factors, the degree of maladjustment and the desire for help, are usually not under the control of the rehabilitation worker. However, the third ingredient, that of relating the rehabilitation services to the specific problem of youth, can be influenced. The principle of helping that this factor suggests is: As the relationship between the solution and the problem is made more specific, the probability of successful intervention is increased. The contribution of treatment specificity will be discussed throughout this book. With this point in mind, the overall negative results of friendship casework must not be overlooked.

Miller (1962) reported the results of a delinquency prevention program that emphasized street corner and family casework. The program also gave some attention to community organization for the purpose of delinquency reduction. The effects of the program upon 205 subjects distributed across seven street gangs were compared to a control group of 112 youth. The casework service agents interacted with the treatment group on an average of three to four times a week. Casework services were provided on a group as well as individual basis. The major result of the program was that there was *no* significant impact made by the casework project on repeat court appearances of the youth. The findings do not support the use of street corner and family casework to reduce delinquent behavior.

A predelinquency program in Washington, D.C., was reported upon by Tait and Hodges (1962). There were 111 youth in the experimental group, compared with 68 control youth. The average age was between seven and nine years of age. The program consisted of social casework, home interviews, "diagnosis with recommendations," and psychiatric services. However, in the authors' words, "The heart of the program was social casework, and other services rendered were for the most part ancillary" (p. 61). After one year of follow-up, there was *no* significant difference between treated and untreated youth in terms of court and police referral. This program, with its emphasis on casework, was not effective enough to obtain significantly better results than an untreated control group.

A random sample of girls with potential problems entering a vocational high school in New York City were assigned to an experimental group or a control group (Meyer, Borgatta, and Jones, 1965). There were 189 girls in the experimental group and 192 girls in the control group. The treatment program emphasized casework and group therapy. The results of the four-year program were: no significant difference in school attendance; no significant difference in completion of high school; no significant difference in school conduct or grades; and no significant difference in delinquency, as measured by girls referred to court. The authors concluded,

On these tests no strong indications of effect are found and the conclusion must be stated in the negative when it is asked whether social work intervention with potential problem high school girls was in this instance effective" (Meyer, Borgatta, and Jones, 1965, p. 180).

Potentially delinquent boys, identified as such in the first grade, were assigned to a treatment or control group as part of a 10-year study of casework and family counseling (Craig and Furst, 1965). Twenty-nine boys served as experimental subjects, and 29 comparable boys served as a control group. Over a five-year period the treatment group received "psychiatric and reaching out social work" as well as child guidance therapy. Diagnosis and referral, as well as direct services, were offered as treatment services. A 10-year follow-up, beginning at initial contact when the child was in the first grade, revealed that there were no significant differences in the number or rate of delinquency between the experimental and control groups. The authors concluded that this approach gave no hope for reducing delinquent behavior in children identified as potential problem children. Such a conclusion is, indeed, warranted.

The use of the casework approach for delinquent boys in England was evaluated by Smith, Farrant, and Marchant (1972). Fifty-four boys from a suburb of Manchester were matched with a control group of 74 boys of similar background. The treatment consisted of casework, which involved assisting the youth with social development, referring him to other agencies, helping with employment problems, and working with the family. The other main component of the treatment was organized recreation. In fact, the only part of the program that was systematic was the soccer team. Volunteers were utilized, but they received no training.

At the 12-month follow-up, the results of the program were examined. There were two indicators of no success and one indicator of effectiveness. There was no significant difference in the reconviction rate, which was 50 percent for the treatment group and 62 percent for the control group. And no significant difference was apparent in the seriousness of the offenses. However, the one behavioral result that was positive for the treatment group was the number of court appearances. Obviously, this study does not provide support for the casework approach, since two of the three main criteria were negative. The following study utilized casework in a police delinquency reduction project.

A diagnostic and referral system was set up by the Seattle Police Department to reduce delinquency (LaFollette, 1973). A group of randomly selected first offenders, age 16 or younger, were referred to the project. The treatment consisted of diagnosis and social agency referral by well-trained social workers. The two groups of youth were followed-up for 6 to 18 months. The results of the project were negative. There was no significant difference between the treatment and the control group in the number or seriousness of offenses. The conclusion is that even a diagnosis-and-referral system, utilizing highly trained social workers with the close cooperation of the police department, did not make a difference in subsequent delinquency.

Another casework program, the Chicago Youth Development project was a six-year project to reduce delinquency in a target area (Gold and Mattick, 1974). The subjects of the study were inner-city boys between 10 and 19 years of age. Two inner-city areas were chosen, one to serve as the target area and one for the control area. For comparison of the arrest statistics, 970 experimental and 571 control youth were used. Overall, however, thousands of boys, hundreds of girls, and thousands of adults came in contact with the project.

The treatment project utilized street worker casework, a boys club, and community organization to reduce delinquency. The report of the study describes competent people, many who had the skill of empathy. The approaches utilized varied over the years. However, the results indicate that the project made *no* significant difference upon delinquency. There was also no significant difference in the drop-out rate, the employment rate for the youths, or the appropriateness of their activities. In reading the voluminous report of the study, one is impressed with the dedication of the workers in the project. But one is also impressed with the unsystematic nature of the programs that were utilized. The conclusion: No matter how competent or dedicated the staff, they must have an effective program and it must be systematically implemented.

In Seattle, a series of studies were implemented to determine the effectiveness of an intensive casework and group treatment program (Berleman, Seaberg, and Steinburn, 1972). Fifty-two boys were placed in the treatment group, while 50 boys were placed in the control group. The ages of both groups ranged from 12 to 14 years. The treatment consisted of intensive casework and social services over a one- to two-year period. The boys also participated in 2½ hours of group counseling per week, and they were seen at home or at school for crisis intervention counseling.

At the 18-month follow-up point, the school discipline and police records were found to be significantly *worse* for the treatment group compared with the control group. There was also no significant difference in commitment to the training schools. The authors concluded,

To have this effort fail and to have this failure so well documented that few rationalizations can be made to mitigate the outcome inevitably raises the question of whether such intervention efforts should continue (Berleman, Seabert, and Steinburg, 1972, p. 344).

These authors had the benefit of the early studies reviewed in this section. It was their intention to combat what they perceived as a weakness in those studies, through increasing the quantity of contacts and the duration of caseworker contacts. The problem is that their more intensive approach not only achieved the same lack of success as the earlier studies, but, in fact, the results were worse. One conclusion is that while some casework makes no difference in delinquency reduction, a great deal of casework makes things worse.

## Conclusions

Ten studies utilizing appropriately selected control groups have been presented. In each, casework was the dominant program ingredient in the treatment of delinquency. In those studies, casework was utilized with almost 3000 youths. The results were conclusively negative (see table 1-1). Casework was *not effective* in the rehabilitation of delinquent youth.

**Specific Prediction**: Youth service bureaus, diversion programs, probation departments, institutional programs, and parole programs that place a strong reliance on casework as a program component will fail.

**Specific Recommendation**: Casework should be discontinued as a program for delinquency prevention or for the rehabilitation of delinquent youth.

Before we completely bury casework, we should examine why it fails as a treatment approach. Casework basically involves three ingredients: diagnosis, recommendations, and direct services. Clearly, diagnosis and recommendations are not enough to help anyone if the recommendations are never implemented or if they are implemented poorly. A program that utilizes only diagnosis and recommendations is doomed to failure from the start.

The third ingredient, direct services, also does not seem to be empirically effective. Any direct service approach is always dependent upon the availability of the provider of services. When the program ends for a particular youth, his access to direct services ends. Providing direct services can, at best, only be effective as long as the service provider is around. Whether social, medical, or educational services are provided, direct service approaches require follow-up to determine if the individual is functioning adequately on his or her own.

**Table 1-1**
**Casework Summary**

| Researchers | Number of Youths | | Treatment Approach | Results |
|---|---|---|---|---|
| | Experimental | Control | | |
| Healy, Bronner, and Shimberg (1935) | 1000 | 1000 | Casework study and recommendations | No significant difference in recidivism |
| Powers and Witmer (1951) | 325 | 325 | Friendship casework | a. No significant difference in police records<br>b. No significant difference in court records |
| Miller (1962) | 205 | 112 | a. Family casework<br>b. Detached group work | No significant difference in court appearances |
| Tait and Hodges (1962) | 111 | 68 | Social casework | a. No significant difference in court referral<br>b. No significant difference in police referral |
| Meyer, Borgatta, and Jones (1965) | 189 | 192 | a. Casework<br>b. Group counseling | No significant difference in court referrals |
| Craig and Furst (1965) | 29 | 29 | a. Casework<br>b. Family counseling | a. No significant difference in number of delinquency referrals<br>b. No significant difference in rate of delinquency referrals |
| Berleman, Seaberg, and Steinburn (1972) | 52 | 50 | a. Casework<br>b. Group counseling<br>c. Family counseling | a. School discipline problems greater<br>b. Police referral greater for treatment group |
| Smith, Farrant, and Marchant (1972) | 54 | 74 | a. Casework<br>b. Family casework<br>c. Recreation | a. No significant difference in reconviction rate<br>b. No significant difference in seriousness of offenses<br>c. Significantly less court appearances for experimental |
| La Follette (1973) | Not specified (NS) | Not specified (NS) | Diagnosis and referral | a. No significant difference in offenses<br>b. No significant difference in seriousness of offenses |

**Table 1-1.** (cont.)

| Researchers | Number of Youths | | Treatment Approach | Results |
|---|---|---|---|---|
| | Experimental | Control | | |
| Gold and Mattick (1974) | 970 | 571 | a. Streetworker caseworker <br> b. Boys club <br> c. Community organization | a. No significant difference in delinquency <br> b. No significant difference in drop-outs <br> c. No significant difference in employment <br> d. No significant difference in the boys activities |

**General Prediction:** Programs that emphasize diagnosis and recommendations only will fail. Programs that provide direct services will fail, unless there is follow-up that gives the individual the skills to work out his or her own problems.

**General Recommendations:** Diagnosis and recommendations should be an initial component of any program. This is often referred to as a needs assessment. Such a needs assessment can help make a program relevant to the participants. No program should just involve direct services. There should be a transition or follow-up component that ensures that the individual can provide the service for himself.

Succeeding chapters will come back to the problem of the ineffectiveness of direct services and offer some alternative approaches.

## References

Berleman, W.C. J.R. Seaberg, and T. Steinburn. Delinquency prevention of the Seattle Atlantic Street Center—A final evaluation. *Social Service Review* 46 (1972): 323-346.

Craig, M.M., and P.W. Furst. What happens after treatment? A study of potentially delinquent boys. *Social Service Review* 39 (1965):165-171.

Fischer, J. Is Casework effective? A review. *Social Work* 18 (1973):5-21.

Glueck, S., and E. Glueck. *One Thousand Juvenile Delinquents, Their Treatment by Court and Clinic.* Cambridge, Mass.: Harvard Univ. Press, 1934.

Gold, M., and H.W. Mattick. *Experiment in the Streets: The Chicago Youth Development Project.* Springfield, Va.: National Technical Information Service, 1974.

Healy, W., A.F. Bronner, and M.E. Shimberg. The close of another chapter in criminology. *Mental Hygiene* 19 (1935):208-222.

LaFollette, J.G. Social agency referral evaluation: January 1972-June 1973. Seattle (Wash.) Police Department, Seattle, 1973.

Meyer, H.J., E.F. Borgatta, and W.C. Jones. *Girls at Vocational High: An Experiment in Social Work Intervention.* New York: Sage, 1965.

Miller, W.B. The impact of a "total community" delinquency control project. *Social Problems* 9 (1962):168-191.

Powers, E., and H. Witmer. *An Experiment in the Prevention of Delinquency: The Cambridge-Somerville Youth Study.* New York: Columbia Univ. Press, 1951.

Smith, C.S., M.R. Farrant, and H.J. Marchant. *The Wincroft Youth Project.* London: Tavistock, 1972.

Tait, C.D., Jr., and E.F. Hodges, Jr. *Delinquents, Their Families and The Community.* Springfield, Ill.: Thomas, 1962.

# 2 Behavior Modification

## Review of the Research

In the last 10 years, behavior modification has become a widely used treatment approach in juvenile corrections. However, much of the research reported has not involved matched control groups or randomly assigned control groups. This review will discuss those studies of behavior modification which did utilize such control procedures. Fourteen studies will be presented in chronological order.

One of the most frequently cited studies of behavior modification is reported by Schwitzgebel and Kolb (1964). They involved 20 delinquent boys in a nine-month project, ostensibly for the purpose of paying them to talk into a tape recorder about their life experiences. The boys came to their appointments on an individual basis two to three times a week. In the beginning they were rewarded for attendance in addition to the $1.00 an hour salary. The interviews were continued until the youth were positively involved with new jobs.

The measured result of the program was that attendance became more prompt. After three years, follow-up data were gathered that showed significantly fewer arrests and less months incarcerated, when compared to a matched control group. However, there was no significant difference in the recidivism, as measured by those youths who went on to prison or the reformatory.

In analyzing the results, the authors attribute the partial success to the fact that individualized rewards were utilized. The amount of money was different for each youth. Food, soft drinks, and cigarettes were also used as reinforcements. The youths were given bonus rewards for exploring their feelings during the taped interviews and trying to plan solutions that would have beneficial consequences. Schwitzgebel and Kolb (1964) attributed the behavioral change of the subjects to the fact that the experimenters were empathetic, direct, and unorthodox in their relationships with the youths. A general conclusion that can be made is that behavior modification procedures that include the establishment of a positive relationship between the adult and the youth are more apt to succeed.

R. Schwitzgebel (1967) investigated the effects of behavior modification upon interview behavior and other behavior of 21 delinquent boys. A matched control group of 14 other delinquent boys was used. The 21 experimental subjects were divided into two groups: one group received rewards for positive statements about other people and for promptness; the other group was treated with "inattention and mild verbal disagreement" when they made negative

11

statements about people during the interview. The control group, the third group, received no differential consequences. Rewards for group one consisted of verbal praise, cigarettes, candy bars, and cash bonuses. Reinforcement occurred on a variable ratio schedule, which meant that the youths were not rewarded each time they were prompt or made positive statements. The youths also did not know which time they would be rewarded.

The results of the experiment were that prompt attendance and positive verbal statements were significantly increased as a result of the favorable rewards. The attempt to punish negative verbalizations did not result in a decrease in that type of statement. In terms of the positive interaction effects of the experimenter, the author said,

It should be noted that by the twentieth interview the attention of the E and participation in the project seemed to become very important reinforcers for most Ss. Arrival became more prompt in both groups and this tended to wash out earlier group differences presumably caused by differential treatment (Schwitzgebel, 1967, p. 141).

Not only did the attention of the adult become part of the reinforcement process, but participation in the project itself became reinforcing toward the end. An implication of this observation is that with people and activities that have the potential to be reinforcing, it is mainly *at the beginning* that external rewards are the most useful with delinquent youth. External reinforcement is useful to begin desired behavior. Another aspect of Schwitzgebel's (1967) study was the investigation of whether or not reinforcement of positive verbal statements would transfer to other behavior outside the interview setting. Actions in six situations at a restaurant were utilized to test whether the positive behavior would generalize. The behavior did *not* generalize in four out of six of the situations. The conclusion of this phase of the research is that reinforcement of one set of positive behaviors does not automatically transfer behaviors. Behavior of delinquent youth can be changed, but only when it is specifically defined and specifically reinforced.

In an institutional treatment program for delinquent youth in Washington State, behavior modification was utilized in an academic setting by Tyler and Brown (1968). A total of 15 court-committed boys between 13 and 15 years of age were the subjects. In the first phase, nine youths were in the treatment group and six were in the randomly assigned control group. For the final phase, the two groups' roles were reversed. The behavior that the study wanted to change was the daily test scores of the youths covering the preceding night's television news broadcast.

One group of subjects was rewarded on a straight salary basis, regardless of their daily test score. The other group's reinforcement was contingent upon their scores; the higher the score, the more money. The results of the study were that both groups got significantly higher scores when they were rewarded on a contingent basis. The authors also pointed out that two teachers involved in the study positively influenced behavior in other areas by planning exciting lessons. The main conclusion of the study is that specific behavior can be changed to a greater degree when rewards are made contingent upon how well the subjects perform the desired action. A secondary observation is that once more the personalities of the adults were positive aspects of the reinforcement process.

The next study to be discussed was conducted with 32 delinquent boys by Bednar, Zelhart, Greathouse, and Weinberg (1970). A behavior modification program was developed for youths in a public school class that provided programmed reading instruction. The boys were randomly assigned to either the treatment group or the control group. The focused behavior for change was reading achievement test scores. Attention, cooperation, and persistence during class were also reinforced.

The reinforcement procedure was divided into two phases. During the first phase, 10-cent rewards were administered on a diminishing schedule for increased attention, cooperation, and persistence during class. The second phase involved paying the youths up to 50 cents per reading achievement test for increased reading competence. In addition, bonus rewards of 25 cents were provided for those boys whose achievement scores were higher than the previous week. This phase lasted for 18 weeks. The results were that the reading achievement of the treatment group was significantly higher than the control group. The reading competence of the rewarded group increased, while the control group reading competence decreased. It is noteworthy that a regular reading program resulted in a decrease in reading achievement for the control group of delinquent youth. This fact documents the current ineffectiveness of school programs in teaching delinquents.

A final result of the study by Bednar *et al.* was that the general classroom behavior of the experimental group improved, while that of the control group did not. Rewarding general positive behavior at the beginning of the new program was effective. However, it was not necessary to continue those reinforcements. Behavior was not a problem from then on because the activity in which the youths were involved consumed their energy and attention. A conclusion is: Get the youth involved in constructive activities where they are rewarded for their achievements and they will have no time or energy for delinquency. The other finding is that external reinforcements are most necessary at the beginning of a new program. This conclusion was anticipated by Bolea and Romig (1966) in a program for high school drop-outs where concrete rewards were planned only during the first phase.

Wiltz (1970) studied the effects of teaching the families of six deviant boys the principles of behavior modification. Six other boys and their families were matched on a variety of factors to provide a control group. The treatment involved the parents meeting with a therapist once a week. The therapist "taught them how to control their conduct disordered children through principles of social learning." The families of the control group received no such training.

The behavior that was the focus of change was negative commands, disapproval, humiliation, noncompliance, negativism, yelling, negative physical contact, teasing, and destructive behavior. After five weeks of treatment, there was no significant difference in the negative behavior of the treatment group. The approach of teaching parents the principles of behavior modification did not result in a decrease in their deviant children's negative behavior. By trying to change a multitude of behaviors over a short time, this project violated the principle of specificity, and the results were negative. Another potential weakness was that the project only trained the parents in the *principles* of behavior change rather than the actual *skills*. It is a big assumption that teaching parents principles will translate into systematically implemented programs for their children.

Behavior modification with delinquent girls was investigated by Pavlott (1971). During an eight-week summer program in an open institutional setting, a token reinforcement system was established. Thirty girls were randomly assigned to the experimental group and 30 were assigned to the control group. Tokens were awarded to the experimental subjects, identified by a red ribbon worn on the left shoulder. The tokens could be cashed in for candy, ice cream, books, jewelry, cigarettes, clothes, and other items attractive to the girls. The behavior that was rewarded was socially acceptable behavior. Five of the teachers and four cottage mothers turned in daily incident reports summarizing negative behavior across 27 variables.

The results of the program were in the expected direction. There were significantly fewer negative incidents observed for the treatment group on 19 of the 27 variables measured. The girls in the treatment group also received more positive reports and less negative ones than the control group. Socially desirable behavior was increased through the use of token reinforcements. The author also observed that "differences were even greater for variables which were more behaviorally definable than for those which were of necessity more vague." This observation suggests the following treatment principle: The more specific and concrete you can be in the definition of the' behavior you want to change, the greater the possibility a reinforcement program will help succeed in changing the behavior.

The following study is reviewed even though matching with a control group only occurred on one variable—age. I present it here because it involved a whole institution changing over to a behavior modification system. Ferdun *et al.* (1972) discussed the results of this program at the Fred C. Nelles School, a training school for delinquent boys in Southern California. The 452 youth who participated in the program were compared with 329 youth from the Paso Robles School, boys of comparable age at a training school north of Los Angeles.

All line staff and program staff were trained in behavior modification principles and techniques. The Nelles system was developed to create and maintain a contingency managed program for all levels of the institution's program. The academic school staff were trained in writing educational contracts. The results indicate that the program had a positive impact on the students while they were at the school. The 12-month parole violation rate was 49 percent, a decrease from the 60 percent rate of three years earlier. However, the comparable rate of the comparison school was 42 percent, a decrease from an earlier 61 percent rate. The authors conclude:

Evaluating the evidence presented, it does not appear that the Nelles System has been responsible for any of the decline in the Nelles violation rate (Ferdun *et al.*, 1972, p. 36).

The conclusion is that behavior modification can affect the institutional behavior of delinquents, but the results *do not generalize* to improved functioning back in the community.

The very specific behavior of prompt appointment attendance was subjected to behavior modification procedures by Hanson (1972). Thirty-three delinquent males between 17 and 26 years of age were identified as nonprompt attenders. The different contingencies were presented in counterbalanced order in a 3 X 3 special Latin square design from which the best approach was identified for the 22 experimental subjects. This best contingency was then implemented for the subjects. The three contingencies utilized in the study were:

1. "Therapist approval for prompt attendance," positive contingency (14 Ss.)
2. "Therapist disapproval for tardiness," negative contingency (6 Ss.)
3. "Therapist disregard of appointment attendance," neutral contingency (2 Ss.)

In addition, there were 11 delinquents in the control group. The approval or disapproval was voiced shortly after the arrival of each youth.

The results of the study indicated that the control subjects and the neutral contingency group did not improve in appointment attendance. Both the negative and positive contingency groups significantly improved promptness compared with the control groups. The positive contingency subjects reduced the average magnitude of tardiness from 13.88 to 1.78 minutes per session. There was no difference between the positive contingency and the negative contingency. Verbal approval or disapproval was successfully utilized to increase prompt attendance. An implication for staff working with delinquents is that they can successfully change certain specific behavior by using praise or criticism when two conditions are followed: (1) the behavior praised or disapproved of is very simple and specific, and (2) the praise or criticism occurs immediately after the behavior. The study by Hanson (1972) demonstrates how specificity in definition of target behavior results in change.

Lupton (1972) reported a study of behavior management training that was not specific, and, as can be guessed, the results were not fruitful. The setting for the study was a wooded park where a day camp program was conducted. One or two youths who had school behavior problems were placed in each counselor's group. The counselors were matched and placed into two groups, control and treatment. The counselors in the treatment group received training in: "descriptions and characteristics of behavior problem children, behavior modification procedures and techniques, counselor-camper interaction, and problem solving techniques." The counselors in the control group received no such training. Through the course of the study, trained observers recorded the number and duration of behavior problems. At the end of the project, counselors rated themselves, and the campers rated their counselor, the program, and the other youths.

The results of the study suggest that there were no significant differences between the counselors trained in behavior management and those not so trained. There was no change in the number and duration of behavior problems exhibited by the problem youth. This study could be characterized as totally lacking in specificity. Neither specific target behaviors nor specific intervention techniques were identified or utilized. The best prediction when specificity is omitted in a behavior modification program is that it will fail.

FitzGerald (1974) studied the effects of different reinforcements upon delinquent youths who were on probation and under a court order to pay fines. The treatment agent was a probation officer in Utah. Twenty males, 14 to 17 years of age were randomly selected from a pool of 86 first-time probationers. The 20 subjects were then randomly assigned to one of four groups. Group I was the control group, which had a contingency contract to work for $1.50/hour that applied to the court fine, with no other inducements. The other three groups also worked at the same rate with individualized contingency contracts, but with the following extra rewards:

Group II: Time on probation would be shortened at the rate of one-half day for every 15 minutes work time.

Group III: They could earn points that could be applied to a weekly activity chosen by them.

Group IV: A combination of II and III, they could earn time off and weekly activities.

The activities that the youths chose were attending professional basketball games, professional hockey games, and the movies.

The author described the contingency contracting process that was utilized as follows:

For all subjects, a contingency contract stating exactly what was agreed upon, what the subject would do and what the experimenter would do, was signed and witnessed after thorough discussion and understanding was acknowledged (FitzGerald, 1974, p. 244).

The work times for the four groups over the three-month period were the following:

Control Group (I): 6 hours and 45 minutes

Time-Off Group (II): 50 hours and 30 minutes

Activity Group (III): 127 hours and 45 minutes

Activity and Time-Off Group (IV): 187 hours and 30 minutes

The activity group and the time-off/activity group did significantly more work than the first two groups. The time-off group in turn did better than the control group. The main conclusion was that weekly activities as reinforcers result in significant part-time work performance. FitzGerald observed that one reason reduced time-off probation was not an effective reinforcer was its distant payoff. Also, because probation may not be an aversive experience, time off from it may not be a motivating force. Clearly, weekly activities that are fun are a more positive stimulus. The implication is that for behavior to be modified, you need to know what is a positive reward from the frame of reference of the youths.

The effects of different behavior modification contingencies upon school attendance was studied by Fo and O'Donnell (1974) in Hawaii. Boys and girls aged 11 to 17 were referred to the project because of behavior and academic problems. The 26 youth were randomly assigned to four treatment groups:

1. Relationship that was always positive: 5 youth
2. Social approval contingent upon youth's appropriate behavior: 7 youth
3. Social and material reinforcement both contingent upon the youth's performance: 7 youth
4. Control group: 7 youth

The treatment agents—"buddies"—were part-time employees of the project who were trained in relationship and behavior modification techniques. The buddies were paid up to $144 a month, contingent upon their performance as good treatment agents. Each buddy worked with three youths individually and as a group. They went camping, surfing, fishing, to rock concerts, and did arts and crafts or just "rapped" together. The project extended over three six-week periods: baseline, an initial intervention period, and a second intervention period.

The behavior that was the focus of change was school attendance. The baseline period was used to observe frequency of school attendance for the four groups prior to any intervention. During the first intervention, the following treatment conditions were followed. There were three unique treatment groups.

1. Relationship treatment group—where the buddies provided an unconditional positive and warm relationship.
2. Social approval—where the buddies provided a positive relationship, contingent upon the youth's school attendance.
3. Social and material reinforcement treatment group—where the buddies provided a positive relationship and the $10 allowance, contingent upon positive school attendance.

The control group did not receive any treatment. During the second intervention, all three treatment groups received condition 3, social and material reinforcement.

There was a significant increase in school attendance in the groups where social approval and social and material reinforcement were contingent upon performance. The same two groups had significantly better school attendance than the relationship group and the control group. There was no significant difference between the two contingency groups' social approval versus social and material reinforcement, during intervention 1 or 2. The conclusion is that with the target behavior, school attendance, social approval is just as effective as social approval and material reinforcement when both are provided *contingent* upon the youth's behavior. It may be remembered that all groups received material reinforcement, but only treatment group 3 received any reward contingent upon school attendance. However, the authors suggest that the youth in the social approval only group may have seen the $10 per month as, in fact, contingent, even though it was not intended that way.

Another aspect of the study was that during the second intervention, the relationship group (noncontingent) received social and material reinforcement only when their performance warranted it (contingent). As a result, their school attendance significantly increased. The conclusions are clear. Noncontingent reinforcement is no more effective than no reward. Relationship therapy alone does not bring about behavior change. A positive relationship with the youths was necessary, but not sufficient to bring about behavior changes. Reinforcement contingent upon the performance of the target behavior, school attendance, was a sufficient condition when combined with a positive relationship.

Fo and O'Donnell (1974) also presented the results of a smaller study conducted to see if contingent social and material rewards could effect school grades. Four youth received contingent social or social and material rewards. Six youth received only the positive relationship. The time period was the same 18 weeks, with the same three interventions, as above. This time, however, there was no significant difference between the relationship group (noncontingent) and the contingent groups. The relationship groups' grades also did not improve when contingent social and material reinforcements were added.

The problem may have been that achieving good school grades requires the utilization of a complex set of behaviors that the youths just did not know. The youths may have wanted to achieve good grades and may have tried, but the goal required skills they did not have. To change a target behavior pertaining to school grades would have required teaching the youths study skills and other skills, even social skills, that would help them to get along better in school. Interestingly, the entire group of ten youths all maintained a D average prior to and following the study. The question arises, of what use is rewarding school attendance when the youths go to school and continue to do poorly?

Fo and O'Donnell (1975) attempted to extend the buddy approach of contingent social and material reinforcement to prevent youth from committing major offenses over a year's time. The authors present their rationale:

... delinquency is successfully treated upon demonstration that participation in a program results in fewer arrests and convictions than no such participation. Although delinquent acts were not directly targeted for intervention in the Buddy System, the implicit assumption was that these acts would be indirectly modified (Fo and O'Donnell, 1975, p. 253).

The authors have articulated the crucial objective. However, their assumption that it could be reached "indirectly" was proved faulty. Over the treatment year, 19.7 percent, or 52 of the treatment youths, committed major offenses, while only 15.2 percent or 27 control youths, committed similar offenses. Overall, the treatment was not effective.

The two groups were then subdivided according to whether they had committed a major or minor offense during the year preceding the study. The 264 treatment youths and the 178 randomly selected control group youths had all committed some type of delinquent offense, but only 48 treatment subjects and 25 control subjects had committed major offenses. Of the two groups, the treatment group that had committed prior major offenses committed significantly fewer further major offenses (37.5 percent) than the control group (64 percent). However, the treatment group mild offenders did significantly worse than the control group upon the commission of major offenses. This differential effect needs further investigation. However, the main conclusion is that overall, the positive relationship and the contingent reinforcement buddy program did not make a difference in the reduction of major crimes.

Jesness, Allison, McCormick, Wedge, and Young (1975) evaluated the effects of behavior modification contingency contracting upon youths on probation in California. Two hundred and fifty four male and female youths were randomly assigned to participate in the Cooperative Behavior Demonstration Project. Another 158 youths were in the control group. The probation caseworkers and their supervisors were given several days of training in contingency contracting and other behavior modification techniques. They were then required to develop contingency contracts for the problem behaviors of the treatment youths on their caseloads. Contingency contracting involved written agreements with the youths, where they would receive certain rewards for improved behavior.

The short-range results were favorable. Fifty-nine percent of the experimental group's target behaviors were eliminated while only 43 percent of the control group's target behaviors were eliminated. The results were significantly different. At the six month follow-up, however, there were no significant differences between the two groups in terms of number and severity of offenses. The conclusion is that contingency contracting can effect problem behaviors, but does not necessarily reduce delinquency.

The Jesness et al. (1975) study had some further results. The quality of the behavioral contracts was evaluated. It was found that the more operationally defined the contracts, the greater the reduction in problem behavior. There were less positive benefits with the more general and vague contracts. In analyzing the data, it was discovered that some probation officers obtained significantly better results than others. After reviewing the data on the probation caseworkers' personalities and attitudes, the authors concluded, "These data indicate that it was not the caseworker's personality or attitude toward behavioral methods per se, but the fact that he did or did not do adequate contingency contracting with a particular client that made the greatest difference" (Jesness et al., 1975, p. 21).

This result supports the principle of specificity with regard to staff effects upon treatment—if you want to know what the staff effects will be in terms of youth outcome as a result of a specific approach, measure the staff directly on the specific skills needed to effectively implement the approach. An implication is that staff effectiveness is related to the quality of skills they have in the specific job area where good performance is needed. In this study, the quality of the skill was the degree to which staff could operationally define problems and provide salient reinforcers.

## Conclusions

We have just reviewed 14 studies involving almost 2000 delinquent youths in programs from all across the United States. What have we learned? Behavior modification is certainly no panacea for juvenile delinquency. Behavior modification did work to change certain behaviors, such as school attendance, test scores, promptness, and classroom behavior. However, it did not affect something as global as delinquency or arrest rate (see table 2-1).

The more the youths can be involved in the process of behavior modification, the more apt the results are to be positive. For example, contingency contracting involves sitting down with a particular subject and discussing back and forth the different elements in the contract. In any treatment approach, it is acknowledged that you should have the support and involvement of the client.

However, many times advocates of behavior modification are accused of nothing less than brainwashing. Informing the subject of the behavior that needs to be changed defuses the charge of covert brainwashing. In the above review, the following projects informed the youth of target behavior, and each achieved positive results: Schwitzgebel (1967), Tyler and Brown (1968), Hanson (1972), FitzGerald (1974), Fo and O'Donnell (1974) and Jesness *et al.* (1975). The implications for juvenile corrections are especially crucial: If youths are rewarded or punished, they should know the concrete behavior on the part that caused the negative or positive consequences.

Differential reinforcement and contingency contracting can be utilized to change unacceptable behavior to specific alternatives that are fairly concrete and doable by the youths. This conclusion is optimistic. The implication is also present that if the more complex behaviors, such as getting and holding a job, can be broken down into concrete behaviors, then differential reinforcement and contingency contracting can be beneficially utilized to teach those behaviors.

**Specific Prediction:** Behavior modification will work only when the behavior to be changed is specific and behaviorally simple.

**Specific Recommendation:** Behavior modification should not be offered as a treatment modality for juvenile delinquency reduction. For certain elementary behaviors, differential reinforcement and contingency contracting should be utilized to help motivate the youths to change. Complex behaviors should be broken down into behaviorally doable steps and differentially reinforced.

It may be remembered from the Jesness *et al.* (1975) study that the more concrete and specific the behavioral contracts were, the more the goal was reached and the behavior of the youths positively affected. This result, along with specific conclusions of this chapter, suggest the following general prediction and recommendation.

**General Prediction:** Programs in human services that are abstract and general in terms of their goals and objectives will fail.

**General Recommendation:** Program goals and objectives should be stated in as simple and behaviorally observable terms as possible.

Not only do behavioral goals allow you to measure obtainment of the goal, but they facilitate communication concerning program objectives and methods. The biggest problem in most organizations is staff communication, and anything that can help overcome that hurdle is of use. The central focus and theme of a program can be more easily upheld, or even modified, if it is stated in simple, behavioral terms.

**Table 2-1**
**Behavior Modification Summary**

| Researchers | Number of Youths | | Intervention | Results | Follow-up Results |
|---|---|---|---|---|---|
| | Experimental | Control | | | |
| Schwitzgebel and Kolb (1964) | 20 | 20 | a. Paid hourly wage for interviews b. Paid bonuses for self-direction c. Rewarded attendance with food and cokes | Improved prompt attendance | After 3 years a. Fewer arrests b. Less months incarcerated c. No significant difference in recidivism |
| Schwitzgebel (1967) | 21 | 14 | a. Rewards for positive verbal statements and promptness b. Inattention and mild disagreement for negative statements | a. Prompt arrival b. More positive statements in interview c. No decrease in negative statements d. No transfer to improved social behaviors at restaurant | No |
| Tyler and Brown (1968) | 9 | 6 | Differential reinforcement based upon improved current events test scores | Increased number correct on current events test | No |
| Bednar et al. (1970) | 16 | 16 | a. Attention, cooperation, and persistence in a reading program was rewarded b. Higher reading achievement test scores were rewarded with money | a. Reading achievement scores increased b. General classroom behavior improved | No |
| Wiltz (1970) | 6 | 6 | Training parents in behavior modification | No significant difference in observed deviant behavior | No |
| Pavlott (1971) | 30 | 30 | Token reinforcements for socially acceptable behavior | Fewer negative incidents recorded | No |
| Ferdun et al. (1972) | 452 | 329 | a. Trained staff in behavior modification b. Instituted a contingency management system | Effective institutional program operation | No significant difference in parole violation rate |

**Table 2-1.** (cont.)

| Researchers | Number of Youths | | Intervention | Results | Follow-up Results |
|---|---|---|---|---|---|
| | Experimental | Control | | | |
| Hanson (1972) | 22 | 11 | a. Verbal approval for prompt attendance b. Verbal disapproval for late attendance | Increase in prompt appointment attendance | No |
| Lupton (1972) | NS | NS | Trained counselors in behavior modification | No decrease or difference in behavior problems | No |
| FitzGerald (1974) | 15 | 5 | Weekly activities as reinforcement for working off probation fines | Increased work performance | No |
| Fo and O'Donnell (1974) | 19 | 7 | Contingent social and material rewards | Increased school attendance | No |
| Fo and O'Donnell (1974) | 4 | 6 | Contingent social and material rewards | No difference in school grades | No |
| Fo and O'Donnell (1975) | 264 | 178 | Contingent social and material rewards | Treatment group did not commit less major offenses | Treatment group did not commit less major offenses |
| Jesness et al. (1975) | 254 | 158 | Training probation officers in contingency contracting | Negative behaviors remitted | No significant difference in offenses No significant difference in severity of offense |

### References

Bednar, R.L., P.F. Zelhart, L. Greathouse, and W. Weinberg. Operant conditioning principles in the treatment of learning and behavior problems with delinquent boys. *Journal of Counseling Psychology* 17 (1970):492-497.

Bolea, A., and D. Romig. Effective motivation for high school drop outs. Unpublished manuscript. Lincoln: University of Nebraska, 1966.

Ferdun, G.S., M.P. Webb, H.R. Lockard, and J. Mahan. *Compensatory Education 1971-72.* Sacramento: California Youth Authority, 1972.

FitzGerald, T.J. Contingency contracting with juvenile offenders. *Criminology: An Interdisciplinary Journal* 12 (1974):241-248.

Fo, W., and C. O'Donnell. The buddy system: Relationship and contingency conditions in a community intervention program for youth with nonprofessionals as behavior change agents. *Journal of Consulting and Clinical Psychology* 42 (1974):163-168.

24

Fo, W., and C. O'Donnell. The buddy system: Effect of community intervention on delinquent offenses. *Behavior Therapy* 6 (1975):522-524.

Hanson, G. Behavior modification of appointment attendance among youthful delinquents. *Dissertation Abstracts International* 32 (1972):6648.

Jesness, C., T. Allison, P. McCormick, R. Wedge, and M. Young. Cooperative Behavior Demonstration Project. Sacramento: California Youth Authority, 1975.

Lupton, F.D. The effects of a behavior management training program on counselor performance in regular day camps which include children with behavior problems. Doctoral dissertation. University of Illinois at Urbana-Champaign, 1972.

Pavlott, J. The effects of reinforcement procedures on negative behaviors in delinquent girls. Pittsburgh, University of Pittsburgh, 1971.

Schwitzgebel, R., and D.A. Kolb. Inducing behavior change in adolescent delinquents. *Behavior Research Therapy* 1 (1964): 297-304.

Schwitzgebel, R. Short-term operant conditioning of adolescent offenders on socially relevant variables. *Journal of Abnormal Psychology* 72 (1967): 134-142.

Tyler, V., and G. Brown. Token reinforcement of academic performance with institutionalized delinquent boys. *Journal of Educational Psychology* 59 (1968):164-168.

Wiltz, N. Modification of behaviors of deviant boys through parent participation in a group technique. *Dissertation Abstracts International* 30 (1970): 4786-4787.

# 3 Academic Education

## Review of the Research

Thomas Jefferson felt that the hope for the future of the American democracy depended on the educational level of its citizens. Correctional administrators have shared this view, especially with regard to the rehabilitation of juvenile delinquents. Sixteen studies will be discussed here that have used education as a method for helping delinquents.

Bowman (1959) studied the effects of an innovative school program upon youths having school problems. Seventeen delinquent youths, 4 girls and 13 boys, were combined with 60 male and female ninth graders who were doing poorly in school. Most of the youths had discipline problems in school. All were in the lower-lower socioeconomic status on Warner's Index. For evaluation purposes, the students were divided randomly into three groups.

One of the groups was a control group; here the students continued in their regular program. The other two groups were placed in special classes. The teachers were selected because of their interest in and sympathy with youths having trouble in school. The goals of the program were to make the school pleasant; to help the students learn basic reading, writing, and arithmetic skills; to provide success experiences; and to teach practical skills. The method was to move slowly and not push the subjects to compete with each other. The first three morning hours of each day consisted of arithmetic, English skills, discussions, and films. The fourth and fifth hours were made up of study hall, discussion groups, hand work, and special projects. The last hour was used for regular classes elsewhere in the school, like home economics and physical education.

The program results indicate that the youth in the special program had a 1/3 decrease in their delinquency rate, while the control group's rate increased by 300 percent over the two years. There was also a significant difference in school attendance and success in later job experiences for the treatment group. There was, however, no significant difference in improvement in academic skills for the experimental group. Also, there was no significant difference for the two groups in their drop-out rate from school. When offered a chance to return to the regular school program, subjects declined in favor of remaining in the special classes.

This program affected the delinquency of the youths, but did not accomplish more academically than a regular school program. The first implication is that academic skills are not critical to a reduction in delinquency if the youths stay in a nontraditional, special program. Understanding adults and a program directed toward general success and practical skills did impact delinquent behavior favorably. Just keeping youth in school can reduce delinquency, because school occupies a large part of the day that otherwise would be used to get into trouble. Another explanation for the success of the treatment group is that those youths who dropped out had better job success because the practical skills they learned in the program were more relevant to success in the world of work than traditional school subjects.

Jacobson and McGee (1965) reported their studies evaluating the effects of an innovative educational approach upon delinquent boys committed to the Federal Youth Center in Englewood, Colorado. There were 24 boys randomly assigned to the treatment group, and 26 boys placed in the control group. They averaged 19 years of age. All youths participated in the regular institutional program, the difference being that the treatment group attended a special "reeducation" program with understanding teachers. The program consisted of daily one-and-one-half-hour discussion groups in which the direction of the group was controlled by the youths. Films, pamphlets, and topics of interest and concern were the focus. A problem-solving approach was utilized to help the youths with some of their concerns.

The results were *not* favorable. There was no significant difference in academic achievement between the two groups. In fact, the experimental group had significantly more disciplinary reports than the control group. At follow-up, two years later, there were no significant differences between the two groups in community adjustment or in reincarceration rate. What was envisioned as a positive experience for the youths—namely, a nonstructured educational program that emphasized personal interests and problems—resulted in poorer performance while the boys were at the Youth Center.

The authors, Jacobson and McGee (1965), reported more favorable results for those youth who participated in the reeducation project and who took three or more regular academic courses. The failure rate of 17 experimental-group youth and 8 control-group youth was compared. The experimental group had a significantly less parole failure rate, 41 percent compared to 75 percent. The conclusion is that the reeducation program alone did not make a significant difference. However, when it was followed by a traditional academic approach, the youths were more successful in the community. The conclusion is that the effectiveness of a counseling-type group discussion approach lies in its ability to prepare youths to use traditional educational courses to learn what they need. At best, nonsystematic, youth-centered discussion groups help the youths explore what their needs are, but do not provide the skills to meet those needs. In some way, the traditional academic courses delivered those skills to the treatment group in the preceding study.

Behavior modification was utilized by Tyler and Brown (1968) to improve the results of a current events course for delinquent youths in an institution in Washington State. A total of 15 court-committed boys between 13 and 15 years of age participated in the study. In the first phase, nine youths were in the treatment group and six were in the control group. Placement in the two groups was by random assignment. For the second and final phase of the study, the two groups' roles were reversed. The youths' daily test scores covering the preceding night's television news broadcast were the focus of the differential reinforcement.

One group of subjects was rewarded on a straight salary basis regardless of their daily test score. The other group's reinforcement was contingent upon their scores: the higher the score, the more m oney. The results of the study were that both groups got significantly higher scores when they were rewarded on a contingent basis. The authors also pointed out that the two teachers involved in the study positively influenced behavior by planning exciting lessons with other subjects. The conclusion is that test scores can be improved for delinquent youths when they are provided with teachers who plan exciting lessons and provide a differential reinforcement system. However, nothing global, such as a reduction in arrests or delinquency, occurred.

Meichenbaum, Bowers, and Ross (1969) reported the results of the manipulation of teacher expectancies upon institutionalized delinquent girls. Six girls in the treatment group were matched with eight girls in the control group. The treatment involved telling the girls' four teachers that the six girls had been identified as "late bloomers" based upon the results of observations and test scores. In fact, there was no such test, and the instructions to the teachers were contrived to manipulate their expectancies. The results were only partially supportive. There were no significant differences in the teachers' levels of attention or amounts of interaction during the two-week treatment phase.

The treatment group did significantly better on objective tests, but not on subjective tests. The treatment group did receive higher ratings in classroom behavior. The period of time, two weeks, was too short and the number of observations were too few to ensure that lasting changes did occur. The effectiveness of this approach is questionable since positive changes were observed only on two out of four of the criteria. The next study, which was similar, had totally negative results.

Knill (1970) researched the effects of the manipulation of teacher expectancies for male reformatory inmates. The goal was to observe the effect of telling a teacher that a particular student had untapped potential on the student's self-concept, attitude toward others, and behavior outside the classroom. There were 38 experimental subjects and 90 control subjects. They were all male inmates at a training school and were randomly assigned to participation in either of the two groups. All subjects were given a battery of tests that included the test of general ability, a semantic differential, and the Minnesota Multiphasic Personality Inventory (MMPI). The teachers were then given a list of experimental subjects who had been randomly selected and "were told that according to the test results these men had shown a 'high potential for intellectual gains.' " It was expected that such instructions would cause the teachers to treat the youths more positively, and that such experiences would result in positive changes in the youths.

There were no significant differences between the control group and the experimental group on any of the variables under study. The variables included the test of general ability, the semantic differential, the MMPI, and reports on work, discipline, and school performance. The measures were made at the end of three months. We can conclude that simply manipulating the teacher's expectancy of performance does not result in attitude or behavior change in delinquent youths. Manipulation of teacher expectancy is a nonspecific treatment approach that does not focus on identifying a youth's deficiencies and remediating them. This study supports the view that nonspecific approaches do not result in substantial changes in delinquent youths.

A behavior modification program was developed for delinquent boys in a public school programmed reading instruction class by Bednar, Zelhart, Greathouse, and Weinberg, 1970. The 32 boys were randomly assigned to either the treatment group or the control group. The target behavior was reading achievement test scores and cooperative classroom behavior. The reinforcement procedure was divided into two phases. During the first phase 10-cent rewards were administered on a diminishing schedule for increased attention, cooperation, and persistence during class.

The second phase involved paying the youths up to 50 cents per reading achievement test for increased reading competence. In addition, bonus rewards of 25 cents were provided to those boys whose achievement scores were higher than the previous week. This phase lasted for 18 weeks. The results were that the reading achievement of the treatment group was significantly higher than the control group. The reading competence of the rewarded group *increased*, while the control group reading competence *decreased*. The fact that the control group's reading ability decreased documents the current ineffectiveness of public school programs in teaching delinquents.

An additional result of the Bednar *et al.* study was that the general classroom behavior of the experimental group improved, while that of the control group did not. Reading achievement and classroom behavior were successfully improved with delinquent youths utilizing money as a reward. We can not generalize from this study and state that all teaching content can be effectively taught to delinquents when accompanied by rewards, because programmed instruction, which is very sequential and systematic, was used to do the actual teaching. It can be concluded that where learning curricula for delinquent youths are systematic and sequential, and when rewards are provided for appropriate behavior and educational performance, the youths will make significant educational gains.

Halstead (1970) reported research designed to improve the reading ability of delinquent youths who were below average in their intellectual functioning. The subjects in the experimental group were 12 children who were failing in school, retarded in their reading ability, and who had a perceptual disturbance. The control group was made of seven children with similar IQ scores, 89.4 average. The experimental group average IQ score was 84.9, not significantly different. The similar control group was formed after the experimental group's intelligence was assessed.

The treatment involved an individualized educational program that was designed around the youths' intake diagnoses. The other main components of the program that lasted over a year were: behavior modification, patterning exercises, a responsive environment, and multiple sensory stimulation. To summarize from Halstead (1970):

The program consisted of two phases: (1) Patterning exercises to reduce perceptual distortion and take advantage of vicarious functioning; (2) Multiple sensory stimulation utilizing an animated typewriter. Operant conditioning, token reward and immediate feedback were used to enhance and motivate learning (Halstead, 1970, p. 60).

The experimental group gained 1.8 years in reading ability. The control group gained only 0.24 years over the same time period, one year. The experimental group's higher gain was statistically significant and over 700 percent better.

The delinquent youths who were below average in intelligence were taught a significant amount through a systematic and comprehensive program. Since Romig (1974) has reported that 63 percent of the youths committed to the Texas Youth Council were in the same below average, though not retarded, range of intelligence, the above program is needed in a multitude of training schools. The ingredients of the program were:

1. Intake diagnosis
2. Individualized programs based upon the diagnosis (specificity)
3. Positive emotional support from teachers
4. Multisensory stimuli
5. Various delivery techniques
6. Rewards to the students for learning

Since it has already been documented that when even only one or two of the above program ingredients are used the youth successfully learn, it is very logical that a *comprehensive* program that combines all the elements will achieve outstanding results.

The next study, conducted by Reckless and Dinitz (1972), was designed to see if teachers who were trained to be role models and "significant others" for potentially delinquent boys could effectively intervene. The study involved 632 experimental subjects and 462 control subjects randomly assigned to their respective group. The boys were identified by their principals and sixth grade teachers based on the ratings of the likelihood of their becoming delinquents. The treatment, which was thought to be "preventive medicine," involved special classes throughout the experimental youths' seventh grade public school program.

The theory behind the approach of the project was that the inner-city boy at the threshold of adolescence needed to internalize models of behavior and perceptions of self that could build up some inner self-control, which in turn could withstand the "happenstances" of his family, neighborhood and companions (Reckless and Dinitz, 1972, p. 157).

The project had a two-pronged approach: provide positive role models and use the role models to lead discussions on relevant topics.

The role-model lesson plans that were developed for this program were organized around five themes: the world of work, the world of school, the world of government, the world of the family, and getting along with others (Reckless and Dinitz, 1972, p. 156).

The discussions were designed to involve the youth as much as possible. The teachers were trained to provide a "significant other" relationship with the boys. Discipline in the classroom was based upon methods that the group agreed to; accordingly, youth were not sent to the principal's office for discipline.

The results of the special program were negative during the seventh grade and three years later. There were no significant differences in the drop-out rate, attendance, grades, and school achievement tests of the two groups. There were no significant differences three years later in terms of the police contact rates. The experimental group's rate of police contact was 37.7 percent, while that of the control group was 36.4 percent. No significant difference was noted in the school drop-out rate, which was around 20 percent for both groups. The two main program elements—teachers providing positive relationships and group discussions—did not make a difference in subsequent delinquency of seventh grade boys who were identified as potential delinquents. Just as Jacobson and McGee's (1965) similar program failed with institutionalized delinquent boys, so did this program. A positive relationship of staff with the boys is not a sufficient condition to bring about rehabilitation. The boys must learn something beyond how to discuss relevant issues in the classroom. They need to learn how to deal with those relevant issues outside the classroom, and *how* implies skills.

Raffaele (1972) investigated the effects of educational contracts upon reading achievement. Forty institutionalized delinquent youths were subjects in the study. All subjects were male. The boys were randomly assigned to eight groups, with five boys per group. Four groups were assigned to the contract treatment condition and four groups were assigned to noncontract control condition. Two of each of the contract and control groups were assigned to one of two instructors. The contract groups negotiated the following relevant aspects of improving one's reading ability: the specific skills that would need to be learned, the kinds of materials that would be used, the level or grade of difficulty the materials would be at, and the length of time to be utilized by each student with the materials. A planned reading program was set up for the noncontract group without the negotiations. Two instructors were utilized, one, a doctoral student with 10 years of teaching experience, the other, master's degree student with one year of teaching experience.

Tests of both silent and oral reading ability were utilized to measure the improvement in reading. There were no significant differences in results between the two approaches. The contract method made a difference on one subscale of the oral reading test, while the noncontract method students scored higher on one subscale of the silent reading test. Regardless of method, students who had the more experienced teacher scored higher on both tests than those who had the less experienced teacher.

The conclusion is that the contract method, which consists of student involvement in curriculum planning and implementation, did not significantly improve reading ability. The reason it did not succeed is that the significant ingredient of differential reinforcement was not utilized. Contracts are effective when rewards are presented for improved performance, as has been documented by Tyler and Brown (1968) and Bednar et al. (1970). The fact that one instructor's students did better regardless of method supports the proposition that programs succeed or fail differentially, based upon the effectiveness of the staff member (Carkhuff, 1971) and the "quantity and quality of [staff] skills."

The effectiveness of Glasser-type discussion groups and paired-learning approaches with delinquent youths were studied by Scheaf (1972). From an initially tested population of 192 students, 60 delinquent boys who were classified as disabled readers were divided into two treatment groups and one control group. The boys were students at a newly opened but "traditionally oriented state institution" for first-time offenders. Each of the three groups consisted of 20 youths who were randomly assigned.

The program for all three groups was eight and one-half weeks long. Treatment group I read in pairs for 30 to 45 minutes per day from library books. Learning to read was left up to the students, though they were rewarded for reading in pairs with candy and praise. Treatment group II had the same program as group I, with the addition of Glasser-type discussions that lasted approximately 45 minutes four days a week. The classroom meetings have been described by Glasser in *Schools Without Failure*. They are meetings "in which the teacher leads a whole class in a nonjudgemental discussion about what is important and relevant to them." The control group participated in one hour of unstructured recreation four days a week.

There was no significant gain in reading achievement for the students in either treatment group. The two treatment approaches had no effect upon reading achievement.

The diagnosis for the students was somewhat specific—low reading ability. The expected treatment gain was specific—an increase in reading achievement scores. However, both treatment conditions, to read with a partner and to discuss relevant topics in a group, were nonspecific. The negative results are predictable. This approach contrasts with Halstead's (1970) multisensory stimulation, patterning exercises, behavior modification, and responsive adult environments. A further conclusion is that while Glasser's goal in *Schools Without Failure* is laudatory, his method of large group discussions about relevant subjects as the means is questionable. In fact, the students in the eight-and-one-half-week treatment program did not learn to read better, and in that respect, they continued to fail.

One program (Lewis, 1973) was designed to test whether the introduction of a humanities program would positively affect the rehabilitation of young criminal offenders. Young male inmates who could perform at the high school level were selected for participation in the program. Many of the inmates came from broken homes and had poor relationships with their fathers, but tended to accept middle-class values anyway. A matching procedure was utilized, in which two groups of 59 control subjects were matched with the 59 experimental treatment subjects.

An experimental education program was conducted during the academic year 1968-1969 at a state correctional facility for offenders 15 to 21 years old. The program consisted of teaching the youths humanities in the evening. There were four increasingly difficult stages in the program. As a result, the program had some positive effects on the inmates while they were still in custody. However, in a 33-month follow-up, there was no evidence that the program had a significant effect on post-prison behavior. Thirty percent of the students who were in the special course were returned to prison.

The conclusion was that a program exposing inmates to a humanities course did not result in an improvement in their rehabilitation. A dydactic teaching approach does not result in behavior change. This result is consistent with Glaser's (1974) observation on prison education: it does not make a difference in itself. The contribution of educational programs is only significant when the individual achieves a diploma or certificate that improves his or her employment opportunities. The result is also consistent with the results of other studies in this chapter in which discussion groups were held on topics related to a humanities course. In each case the results were negative.

At the O.H. Close School, a facility of the California Youth Authority, an evaluation was done on the effects of a ward aide program upon youths' subsequent parole performances (Ferdun, 1974). Eighty youths who were achieving well in school and had "stable personalities" were matched with 53 control-group youth. The 80 treatment youth provided tutoring in the classroom and participated in recreational activities with younger wards who needed assistance. It was thought that having the additional responsibility would positively affect a youth's later behavior.

The results were mixed. The youths participating as ward aides did attend school more than the control group. However, after 9 to 12 months on parole, there was no significant difference in the recidivism rates of the two groups. The program probably did affect the youths' abilities to cope more successfully with school, just by their utilization as tutors. The study does not describe any special training that the ward aides went through. However, training in how to be good tutors could easily transfer to learning skills in school. Another conclusion is that just attending public school does not necessarily prevent further delinquency.

The effects of different behavior modification contingencies upon school attendance was studied by Fo and O'Donnell (1974) in Hawaii. Twenty-six preadolescent boys and girls were randomly assigned to four groups. The treatment agents—"buddies"—were part-time employees of the project who were trained in relationship and behavior modification techniques. The behavior that was the focus of change in the first study was school attendance.

The results were that there was a significant increase in school attendance in the groups in which social approval and social and material reinforcement were contingent upon performance. These two groups had significantly better school attendance than the relationship group and the control group. During the second intervention, the relationship group (noncontingent) received social and material reinforcement only when their performance warranted it (contingent). School attendance then significantly increased. School attendance of predelinquent youth can be positively increased when rewards are provided for attendance.

Fo and O'Donnell (1974) tested these conditions on a more complex set of behaviors—improvement in school grades. Four youths received social or social and material rewards contingent on improvement, while six youths received only the positive relationship. The time period in this study was 18 weeks. However, this time there were no significant differences between the two relationship groups in improvement of school grades. Obtaining improved school grades requires a whole set of complex skills (study skills, learning to learn, and classroom survival skills) that were probably not known to the youths. Behavior modification alone cannot result in better performance of skills that are not known. However, behavior modification techniques, when combined with quality teaching programs, will probably result in increased achievement in more complex problem areas.

An intensive graduate equivalency diploma (G.E.D.) program in a juvenile court setting was evaluated by Odell (1974). Sixty boys with an average age of

16 years participated in the study. All were under the supervision of juvenile court caseworkers and were from a lower-class background. There were two control groups. Group I received no special help except the traditional casework program. Group II was a treatment control where the boys and their parents participated in intensive group and individual counseling. There were two experimental groups that received the same treatment, except that boys in group III had the additional help of follow-up job and school placement. The program in the two treatment groups consisted of the following:

. . . high interest subject matter, programmed learning, and a tutorial system in which each youth proceeds at his own pace. Tutors were area college students and community volunteers (Odell, 1974, p. 313).

There were 15 boys randomly assigned to each group. Participation in the program lasted three months.

The results were favorable. At three-, six-, and nine-month follow-up points, the two G.E.D. groups had a significantly higher degree of participation in school or work and were making significantly higher weekly salaries than the two control groups. The recidivism was significantly higher for the casework and counseling groups than for the education groups. The positive conclusion is that a special G.E.D. program can significantly affect a youth's rehabilitation. This result is consistent with the already-noted conclusion of Glaser (1974): Education has an impact when it results in the achievement of a diploma or certificate by the inmate. The probable explanation for this is obvious.

The program ingredients of high-interest material, programmed instruction, individualized tutoring, positive relationships with the tutors, and the presence of a concrete goal (the G.E.D.) account for the success of the project. One program ingredient that was present but not noticed by Odell was the concrete goal. In many educational programs there is an absence of concrete goals. The establishment of a learning goal that is specific and observable will positively affect learning. This conclusion has been given additional support through Gagne's (1975) study. In a paired-associate learning experiment, delinquent youth who verbally established their level of aspiration or learning goal did significantly better.

Before leaving the Odell Study, it should be noted that casework, individual counseling, and group counseling did not result in significantly positive outcomes.

## Conclusions

Can education rehabilitate juvenile delinquents? Yes, under certain conditions. Education, in and of itself, is not necessarily effective because it has been programmed differently in various settings. Certain approaches consistently achieved negative results, while other methods consistently achieved favorable results. To better understand what did work and what the successful ingredients were, several tables have been compiled.

A summary of the results of the various educational programs is presented in table 3-1. As can be observed, understanding teachers teaching basic academic skills were effective. The second main approach that was successful was the utilization of differential reinforcement and rewards. Three ingredients did not make a difference. The manipulation of teacher expectancies, which is not a treatment, did not work. Behavior modification was not effective in improving student's grades, the reason for this being that behavior modification is only effective in increasing behavior that is clearly doable on the part of the youth and within his or her behavioral repertoire. The third unsuccessful ingredient was understanding teachers providing problem-solving-type discussion groups. Not only can we dismiss the type of discussion group presented in Glasser's *Schools Without Failure* because it failed in one study that tested it out, but we can reject it because two additional studies, trying something similar, also achieved negative results.

For a better understanding of what worked and what possibly can be repeated, table 3-2 presents a list of those program ingredients present in studies

**Table 3-1**
**Educational Programs Summary**

A. *What Worked:*
  1. Understanding teachers combined with 3 R's and practical skills
  2. Understanding teachers combined with discussion group and academic skills
  3. Differential reinforcement
  4. Rewarding positive classroom behavior and learning
  5. Positive emotional support combined with individualized program
  6. Contingent social and material rewards
  7. Special G.E.D. program
B. *What Did Not Work:*
  1. Understanding teachers combined with discussion groups
  2. Manipulation of teacher expectancies
  3. Understanding teachers combined with role-model discussion groups
  4. Contract teaching without differential reinforcement
  5. Rewards for reading in pairs
  6. Glasser-type discussion groups
  7. Participation in a humanities course
  8. Participation as student aides
  9. Contingent social and material rewards in improving school grades

**Table 3-2**
**Program Ingredients Present in Those Studies Where the Youths Learned**

1. Special classes
2. Understanding teachers
3. Emphasis upon practical skills
4. Reading, writing, and arithmetic
5. Individualized pacing
6. Discussion group combined with academic skills
7. Differential reinforcement
8. Exciting lessons
9. Rewarding attention, cooperation, and persistence in class
10. Rewarding reading achievement
11. Individualized diagnosis
12. Individualized program
13. Behavior modification
14. Positive emotional support
15. Variety of delivery techniques
16. Multisensory teaching
17. Contingent social rewards
18. Contingent material rewards
19. High-interest material
20. Programmed learning
21. Individualized instruction
22. Specific learning goal

that achieved favorable results. As can be seen, many of the program elements are present more than once, and some components are very similar to others, with the only difference being a semantic one. Because of these factors, the list was reduced to that presented in table 3-3. The composite list has those unique program ingredients which, when combined, could support each other and maximize learning.

**Specific Prediction**: Classroom education that includes at least four of the composite program ingredients will succeed. A positive emotional relationship provided by the teacher will in and of itself not be sufficient.

**Specific Recommendation**: To maximize classroom learning, all the composite program elements should be included.

We now know what will significantly increase classroom learning for delinquent youths. The issue becomes, does classroom learning result in the

**Table 3-3**
**Composite Program Ingredients for Effective Correctional Education**

1. Understanding teacher
2. Individualized diagnosis
3. Specific learning goal
4. Individualized program
5. Basic academic skills
6. Multisensory teaching
7. High-interest material
8. Sequential material
9. Rewarding attention and persistence, initially
10. Differential reinforcement of learning performance

prevention of subsequent delinquency and the achievement of a favorable community adjustment? Does learning traditional academic subjects result in reduced delinquency? Unfortunately, the answer is no. Webb (1971) reported that the achievement of large gains in reading ability by 987 academically deficient California Youth Authority wards did not result in reduced recidivism. There is nothing magic about reading that helps a person live and work more effectively.

**General Prediction:** Rehabilitation programs that focus only upon the teaching of academic skills will fail to reduce recidivism.

**General Recommendations:** The quality of correctional education programs should be upgraded by utilizing the composite program ingredients.

The cumulative effects of the combined elements from the successful programs should prove beneficial. Carkhuff and Berenson (1976) recommend that teaching methods are the preferred mode of behavioral science treatment. The content of their teaching programs flow from the diagnosed and unique needs of the target population. The delivery of help for behavior change utilizes a systematic process that is similar to the composite program ingredients. Table 3-4 tallies this chapter's studies and results.

## References

Bednar, R.L., P.F. Zelhart, L. Greathouse, and S. Weinberg. Operant conditioning principles in the treatment of learning and behavior problems with delinquent boys. *Journal of Counseling Psychology* 17 (1970):492-497.

**Table 3-4**
**Academic Education Summary**

| Researchers | Number of Youths | | Type of Program | Results | Follow-up Results |
|---|---|---|---|---|---|
| | *Experimental* | *Control* | | | |
| Bowman (1959) | 11 | 6 | a. Special class b. Understanding teachers c. Emphasize practical skills d. Reading, writing, and arithmetic | a. Experimental group had better school attendance b. Experimental group had less delinquency rate c. No significant difference in academic skills d. No significant difference in dropouts | No |
| Jacobson and McGee (1965) | 24 | 26 | a. Reeducation program where teachers were friends b. Daily discussion group about problems | a. No significant difference in academic achievement b. Experimental had more disciplinary reports | a. No significant difference in reincarceration rate after 2 years b. No significant difference in community adjustment |
| Jacobson and McGee (1965) | 17 | 8 | a. Reeducation program with discussion group b. Regular academic courses | | Experimental group had significantly less failure on release |
| Tyler and Brown (1968) | 9 | 6 | Differential reinforcement based upon improved current events test scores | Increased numbers of correct answers on tests | No |
| Meichenbaum, Bowers, and Ross (1969) | 6 | 8 | Manipulation of teacher expectancies during a 2 week period | a. No significant difference in teacher attention or interactions b. No significant difference on subjective test scores c. Ratings of appropriate behavior were higher d. Higher scores on objective tests | No |
| Knill (1970) | 38 | 90 | Manipulation of teacher expectancies over a three month period | a. No significant difference in test scores b. No significant difference in school, work and discipline reports | No |

**Table 3-4.** (cont.)

| Researchers | Number of Youths | | Type of Program | Results | Follow-up Results |
|---|---|---|---|---|---|
| | *Experimental* | *Control* | | | |
| Bednar *et al.* (1970) | 16 | 16 | Rewarding positive classroom behavior and reading achievement test scores | *a.* Reading achievement score significantly increased *b.* General classroom behavior increased | No |
| Halstead (1970) | 12 | 7 | *a.* Individualized educational program built around intake diagnosis *b.* Positive emotional support *c.* Variety of educational delivery techniques *d.* Behavior modification | Higher reading achievement gain | No |
| Reckless and Dinitz (1972) | 632 | 462 | *a.* Special classes with role-model lesson plans *b.* Teachers trained to be "significant others" to boys | *a.* No significant difference in school grades *b.* No significant difference in school achievement | *a.* No significant difference in police contact *b.* No significant difference in dropout rate |
| Raffaele (1972) | 20 | 20 | Contract teaching without differential reinforcement | No significant difference in reading improvement | No |
| Scheaf (1972) | 40 | 20 | *a.* Rewards for reading in pairs *b.* Glasser-type group discussions | No significant difference in gains in reading achievement | No |
| Lewis (1973) | 59 | 59 | Participation in a humanities course | Improved institutional behavior | No significant difference at 33 month follow-up in recidivism |
| Ferdun (1974) | 80 | 53 | Participation as student aides for younger wards | | *a.* No significant difference in recidivism *b.* Experimental group attended school better |
| Fo and O'Donnell (1974) | 19 | 7 | Contingent social and material rewards | Increased school attendance | No |
| Fo and O'Donnell (1974) | 4 | 6 | Contingent social and material rewards | No difference in school grades | No |

**Table 3-4.** (cont.)

| Researchers | Number of Youths | | Type of Program | Results | Follow-up Results |
|---|---|---|---|---|---|
| | Experimental | Control | | | |
| Odell (1974) | 30 | 30 | a. High-interest subject matter<br>b. Programmed learning<br>c. Tutorial system<br>d. G.E.D. | a. Better participation in school or work<br>b. Higher mean weekly income | Lower recidivism rate |

Bowman, P.H. Effects of a revised school program on potential delinquents. *The Annals of the American Academy of Political and Social Science* 322 (1959):53-61.

Carkhuff, R.R. Training as a preferred mode of treatment. *Journal of Counseling Psychology* 18 (1971):123-131.

Carkhuff, R.R., and B.G. Berenson. *Teaching as Treatment.* Amherst, Mass.: Human Resource Development Press, 1976.

Ferdun, G.S. Educational research. In *A Review of Accumulated Research in the California Youth Authority*, Keith Griffiths, ed. Sacramento: California Youth Authority, 1974.

Fo, W., and C. O'Donnell. The buddy system: Relationship and contingency conditions in a community intervention program for youth with nonprofessionals as behavior change agents. *Journal of Consulting and Clinical Psychology* 42 (1974):163-168.

Gagne, E.E. Effects of immediacy of feedback and level of aspiration statements on learning tasks for different youngsters. *Journal of Abnormal Child Psychology* 3 (1975):53-60.

Glaser, D. Remedies for the key deficiency in criminal justice evaluation research. *Journal of Research in Crime and Delinquency* 11 (1974): 144-154.

Glasser, W. *Schools Without Failure.* New York: Harper and Row, 1969.

Halstead, L. A new approach to teaching retarded children to read. *Corrective Psychiatry and Journal of Social Therapy* 16 (1970):59-62.

Jacobson, F., and E. McGee. Englewood Project: Re-education: A Radial correction of incarcerated delinquents. Unpublished research. Englewood, Colorado, 1965.

Knill, F. The manipulation of teacher expectancies: The effect on intellectual performance, self-concept, interpersonal relationships, and the institutional behavior of students. *Dissertation Abstracts International* 30 (1970): 5239-5240.

Lewis, M.V. *Prison Education and Rehabilitation: Illusion or Reality? A Case Study of an Experimental Program.* University Park, Pennsylvania: Institute for Research on Human Resources, 1973.

Meichenbaum, D.H., K.S. Bowers, and R.R. Ross. A behavioral analysis of teacher expectancy effect. *Journal of Personality and Social Psychology* 13 (1969):306-316.

Odell, B.N. Accelerating entry into the opportunity structure: A sociologically based treatment for delinquent youth. *Sociology and Social Research* 16, 1974, 312-317.

Raffaele, J.A. An investigation into the effects of student contracts upon the attitudes and achievement of reading of institutionalized adjudicated juvenile delinquents. Doctoral dissertation. University of Pittsburgh, 1972.

Reckless, W.E., and S. Dinitz. *Prevention of Juvenile Delinquency—An Experiment*. Columbus, Ohio: Ohio State Univ. Press, 1972.

Romig, D. A study of intelligence test scores of delinquent youth in the Texas Youth Council. Research Report No. 1. Austin: Texas Youth Council, 1974.

Scheaf, W.A. The effects of paired-learning and Glasser-type discussions on two determinants of academic achievement, and on reading achievement of male delinquents. *Dissertation Abstracts International* 33 (1972):482-483.

Tyler, V., and G. Brown. Token reinforcement of academic performance with institutionalized delinquent boys. *Journal of Educational Psychology* 59 (1968):164-168.

Webb, M. Reading and recidivism. Educational Research Series Report No. 6. California Youth Authority, 1971.

# 4

## Vocational and Work Programs

### Review of the Research

"If a youth has a job, he will not become delinquent" has been an accepted principle regarding crime and delinquency. The accuracy of this principle will now be examined in the 12 studies concerning the effectiveness of vocational and work programs upon delinquent youths presented in this chapter.

Hackler (1966) discussed the impact of an experimental work program upon delinquency in Seattle, Washington. There was a random assignment of 200 boys between 13 and 15 years of age to one of five groups:

Group 1: The boys had part-time jobs with a supervisor who was informal and who tried to communicate that he thought the boys were normal rather than deviant.

Group 2: The youths worked with a supervisor who was more formal and who set rigid limits on the behavior of the boys.

Group 3: The boys worked on various jobs on their own and had assistance from a special employment agency.

Group 4: A Hawthorne control group, the youths participated in a teaching-machine learning program.

Group 5: These boys made up the control group and were not even told about the research study.

The results were negative.

There were no significant differences among any of the treatment groups and the control group upon arrest rate and the official delinquency rate. The author concluded disappointedly,

The control group seemed to show more change in a favorable direction than the four experimental groups. The differences are not large but they show, clearly and painfully, that the action program had no impact on the boys (Hackler, 1966, p. 160).

We can conclude that having employment, regardless of the type of supervision, does not make a significant difference in a youth's delinquent behavior. Just as

43

understanding teachers did not make a significant difference on a youth's delinquency, a work supervisor who tried to provide an emotionally positive relationship also made no favorable difference. Although the youths may have experienced positive relationships, they were unable to learn any skills from them that aided success in the community.

The effects of a vocational approach to rehabilitation were studied by Zivan (1966). Boys who had been in trouble were divided into two groups in a residential program in New York: those receiving the special vocational training and those who did not. The boys were randomly assigned to groups and averaged 16 years of age. Vocational guidance was given to each youth in the treatment group in the following sequence: assessment counseling, developmental counseling, and preplacement counseling. Counseling occurred on an individual and group basis. In addition, they attended an occupational orientation class that consisted of role playing, presentations via audiovisual aids, field trips, and talks by workers from various occupations. The youths participated in institutional work programs in which they performed various chores. The program had a follow-up component through which a boy received supportive aftercare and job placement aid.

The results were negative. While the youths were in the program, there were no differences between the treatment group and the control group in behavioral ratings of institutional conformity. At 6- and 12-month follow-up, there were no significant differences in community behavior ratings, in participation in work or school, or in job wages. Also, no significant differences were seen in recidivism in favor of the treatment. According to Zivan, a main problem was that a number of the boys had to return to public school because of their young age and in turn experienced considerable difficulty. Preparing youths for work when they will return to public school is the opposite of specificity in appropriate treatment. Naturally it failed. One main criticism of employers was that the boys lacked skilled training, which further points up the fact that you do not place youths in situations for which they have not been trained. It is documented later that group and individual counseling, which were the main ingredients in the Zivan program, are ineffective. The other unsuccessful components were an occupational information class, job placement help, and participation in an institutional work program.

Molof (1967) reported an extensive outcome evaluation on the effects of a forestry camp work program. There was a random assignment of 251 boys to the camp program and 218 to the regular institutional program. The forestry camp program involved working 40 hours a week under staff from the Forestry Service. The work assignments included rather strenuous forestry and conservation work, as well as fire fighting. The length of stay in the program averaged six to seven months. The program involved small groups, working in close contact with staff. The results of the analysis of the recidivism rates revealed no significant difference between the work program and the control program. After

15 months of follow-up, the recidivism rate for the forestry camp was 39 percent, while that for the control group was 35 percent. The work program did not make a significant impact upon recidivism.

While the three previous studies were negative in their findings, a study by Sullivan and Mandell (1967) achieved more satisfactory results. The participants were 264 male youths between 16 and 21 years of age. All subjects were institutionalized in a city jail; they were randomly assigned to the treatment and control conditions. The treatment consisted of training them in the use of computer and data processing equipment and providing a special remedial reading program. The youths were in the program for two months. Control group boys participated in the regular jail routine.

The results of the program were that the trained youths had a significantly lower recidivism rate and had better jobs. There was no significant difference in unemployment. However, boys who had the training were in a higher percentage of white-collar jobs, were on jobs that provided on-the-job training, had jobs with companies using data processing, and were in jobs where upward mobility was present and possible. One reason for the favorable results is that the vocational program emphasized training for an industry—data processing—which has a high demand for qualified workers. The boys did get jobs in companies that had data processing activities. The main positive ingredient about their jobs compared with those of the control group was the presence of the possibility of upward promotions. Because the youths in the control group were employed the same amount as the treatment group, we see that once more there is nothing inherent in employment that prevents delinquency. However, when employment provides a strong hope for movement up a career ladder, then such employment can make a difference.

Kovacs (1967) evaluated the effects of an intensive vocational training program upon youths who were on parole. The program took place in the community, and 126 young males were placed either in the treatment group or the matched control group. The boys were between 17 and 21 years of age. The program typically lasted from 1½ months to 2 months. The program elements were compensatory education, stressing job placement and vocational training; prevocational training, utilizing films and field trips; and programmed instruction. In addition, the program emphasized socialization through group discussions and role playing, as well as through visits to art galleries and plays. Group counseling was also provided by paraprofessionals. The control group was on regular parole throughout.

The results were negative. At 3- and 12-month follow-up points, there was no significant difference between the two groups in their recidivism. There were also no significant differences in the rating scales measuring employment and school behavior. Given the quantity of different program elements that were tried, one would be totally surprised by the disappointing results. However, when the program elements are examined individually, we find those which have been documented as being unsuccessful: group discussions, group counseling, occupational orientation, and job placement. It only strengthens the case that some of the traditional program elements of vocational and prevocational training are not effective when put to the test of follow-up results.

A comprehensive vocational counseling program was developed and followed up by Shore and Massimo (1969). The subjects in the study were 20 boys between 15 and 17 years of age who were randomly placed into two groups. The control group received no treatment and was not contacted during the 10-month program. The boys all had histories of delinquent activity. They were referred to the program at the point of suspension or upon dropping out of public school. The goal of the program was to help them obtain, maintain, and advance on a job that was mutually and systematically selected. Job selection was based upon interest ability, and goals. Counseling was provided prior to and after employment to focus on the youth's problems and expectations with regard to work. The therapist, from the point of view of action therapy, helped the youths find jobs and provided transportation for court appearances, shopping, and pleasure trips. The counselor also assisted in helping the youths handle their newly earned incomes. Remedial education was individualized and initiated when the youths wanted help in upgrading their skills on the job.

The results were positive and in support of the treatment program. The treatment group made significant academic gains in reading, vocabulary, and arithmetic. They also showed significant improvement in perception of interpersonal relations, as measured by the Thematic Apperception Test. After five years, the treatment group had significantly fewer arrests than the control group. They additionally experienced fewer job turnovers and had significantly higher salaries. The therapist presented a significantly different program from any the youths had previously experienced, as evidenced by flexibility, action, lack of compulsory activities, and no contact with traditional helping agencies, including the school system. The image of this program was completely different than the images of all the traditional programs in which the youths had experienced failure.

Another unique and effective ingredient of the program was its emphasis upon problem solving and remedial education as an aid after the youths had obtained jobs. Most vocational programs end at vocational placement; this one just got started at that point. The extra help and tutoring enabled the youths to develop career skills. Seven of the treated youths went on to obtain additional vocational-technical training. The authors observed that the youths in the control group,

... because of limited skills, were gainfully employed over long periods but in unskilled jobs and showed involvement in many legal difficulties. Therefore, employment by itself does not seem to serve as a deterrent to crime if this employment has no meaning, no status, and no opportunities for learning and personal growth (Shore and Massimo, 1969, p. 773).

The implication is, of course, that when an individual finds meaning, status, and the opportunity for learning and advancement in a job, negative behaviors such as delinquency decrease. Jobs and job placement do *not* necessarily make a significant difference. However, jobs that have value to the individual and provide an opportunity for advancement can help reduce crime and delinquency. The goal is to utilize career decision-making skills that help the youths relate their values to potential jobs. The second goal is to initiate career ladder training that teaches the individual how to advance on a job.

Robin (1969) reported the negative effects of a work program designed to reduce delinquency. The experimental group, composed of 50 teenage boys, received jobs that paid at least the minimum wage, while 54 control-group boys did not participate. Random assignment was utilized. The treatment group received counseling that focused on keeping the youths involved in school as well as in employment. The results were that there were no significant differences in charges for serious offenses between the two groups during the program. At follow-up, the treatment group did not have a better delinquency record than the control group. The study reinforces the conclusion that there is nothing inherent in having a job that prevents a youth's delinquency.

The responsibility for the vocational program for delinquent youths in many states has been assigned in recent years to the state rehabilitation commission. This shift in assignment is, in part, a result of the passage of Public Law 89-333, the Amendments to the Vocational Rehabilitation Act, in 1965, which allowed public offenders to be eligible for vocational rehabilitation services provided by federal funds. In Massachusetts, Goldberg and Johnson (1972) evaluated the effectiveness of vocational rehabilitation services with delinquent youths. Two treatment groups were comprised of 13 experimental-control pairs. The study involved older teenaged boys from Framingham and Cambridge. It was expected that the program would decrease delinquent behavior while increasing social and work adjustment for delinquent boys remaining in the community.

The comprehensive vocational rehabilitation program included casework services, diagnosis, referral, vocational training, and job placement. There were no significant differences between the treatment group and the control group on pre-post measures of adjustment. There were also no significant differences in the recidivism rates for the two groups. The conclusion is that vocational rehabilitation programs are not necessarily effective with delinquent youths.

Job placement as a treatment activity was extensively evaluated by Ferdun and Lockard (1973). A job placement program was set up for youths who were on their way out a training school that had provided vocational training. Job placement services were provided by a special job placement staff for youths living within a 150-mile radius of the training school. There were two treatment groups and one control group. One of the treatment groups was provided job placement services directly (137 youths). The youths in the other treatment group were referred to other agencies who provided job placement services (135 youths). Assignment of the 141 control-group youths and all the treatment youths was on a random basis.

At the three month follow-up point, data were collected on the youths' job performance in the community. No significant difference existed between the three groups in the amount of time employed. Nor did any difference exist among the three groups with regard to the proportion of youths who obtained employment in jobs related to the one they were trained in. Considering the large number of youths involved in the study, it can be concluded that job placement as a rehabilitation service is not effective.

In a secondary data analysis, it was discovered that even within the short period of time, three months, only a small number of youths (14.5 percent) were employed in jobs for which training had been provided to them prior to their release. Forty percent of the youths were unemployed, in spite of vocational training and special job placement services. This fact is especially remarkable when one reviews the list of over 27 different job training areas that were taught. The conclusion is that traditional vocational education programs in a training school are irrelevant in terms of preparing delinquent youths for employment.

FitzGerald (1974) studied the effects of different methods of reinforcement upon the work behavior of delinquent youths. The teenagers were on probation and under an obligation to work off part of their probation fine. The treatment agent was a probation officer in Utah. Twenty males, 14 to 17 years of age were randomly selected from a pool of 86 first-time probationers. The 20 subjects were then randomly assigned to one of four groups. Group I was the control group, which had a contingency contract to work for $1.50/hour to be applied to the court fine and no other inducements. The other three groups also worked at the same rate with individualized contingency contracts, but with the following extra rewards:

Group II: Their time on probation would be shortened at the rate of one-half day for every 15 minutes work time.

Group III: They could earn points that could be applied to a weekly activity they had chosen.

Group IV: A combination of groups II and III, they could earn time off and weekly activities.

The activities chosen by the youths were attendance at professional basketball games and the movies.

The results indicated that contingency contracting did not result in outstanding work achievement. The activity group and the time-off/activity group did significantly more work than the first two groups. The time-off group in turn did better than the control group. The main conclusion is that weekly activities as reinforcers result in significant part-time work performance. There was, however, no evidence of a reduction in delinquency.

An intensive G.E.D. program to provide a school equivalency diploma in a juvenile court setting was evaluated by Odell (1974). Sixty boys with an average age of approximately 16 years participated in the study. All were under the supervision of juvenile court caseworkers and were from a lower-class background. There were two control groups. Group I received no special help except the traditional casework program. Group II was a treatment control where the boys and their parents participated in intensive group and individual counseling. There were two experimental groups that were the same, except that boys in group III had the additional help of follow-up job and school placement. The high-interest program utilized programmed learning to help the youths obtain their G.E.D. high school equivalency diploma. There were 15 boys randomly assigned to each group. Participation in the program lasted three months.

The results were favorable. At three-, six-, and nine-month follow-up points, the two G.E.D. groups had a significantly higher degree of participation in school or work and were making significantly higher weekly salaries than the two control groups (see table 4-1). The recidivism was significantly higher for the casework and counseling groups than for the education groups. The positive conclusion is that a special G.E.D. program can significantly affect a youth's rehabilitation. This result is consistent with the already-noted conclusion of Glaser (1974): Education has an impact when it results in the achievement of a diploma or certificate by the inmate. The probable explanation for this is obvious, and this conclusion is supported by the mean weekly income comparisons that can be observed in table 4-1. The youth receiving the G.E.D. and job follow-up help not only had a higher starting salary, but, over the three-month period, their salary increased significantly. The salary increase over time shows that the youths were given help in job advancement skills. Job advancement moved the youths into a career-ladder frame of reference. Such a frame of reference appears to be a strong motivating force to improve and not recidivate.

The link to reduced recidivism suggested by this study is as shown in figure

**Table 4-1**
**Mean Weekly Income for Those Working**

| Time Period | I. Control | II. Group and Individual Counseling | III. G.E.D. and Follow-Up Help | IV. G.E.D. |
|---|---|---|---|---|
| 3 months | $22.50 | $34.20 | $56.90 | $42.30 |
| 6 months | $34.20 | $36.70 | $65.10 | $48.70 |
| 9 months | $35.60 | $43.40 | $86.00 | $60.90 |

Adapted from Odell, 1974, p. 315.

4-1. The additional element provided by this program, and crucial to its success, was educational tutoring, which was a support program to the primary program of getting a job. As a result, better jobs were obtained and held, with the subsequent reduction in recidivism. The other point that must be stressed is that the youths received help after job placement. Treatment did not just end at placement, as with so many of the other programs reviewed in this chapter.

The Chicago Youth Development project was a six-year project to reduce delinquency in a target area (Gold and Mattick, 1974). The subjects of the study were inner-city boys between 10 and 19 years of age. Two inner-city areas were chosen; one to serve as the target area and one for the control area. For comparison of arrest statistics, 970 experimental and 571 control youth were used.

The treatment project utilized street worker casework, a boys club, and community organization to reduce delinquency. The report of the study describes competent people, many who had the skill of empathy. The approaches utilized varied over the years. One of the main tasks of the caseworkers was job placement. The results indicated that the project made no significant difference in the drop-out rate and the youths' employment behaviors. With regard to job placement, the authors noticed that it was easier to find the jobs than to keep the youths placed in them. There was a 70 percent drop-out rate after only a few weeks. The boys gave various reasons for quitting, such as the job was too far away, the pay was too low, they didn't like the job, or they had trouble with their supervisors. Job placement, itself, was not all that difficult or impossible, but we see once again that placement did not prevent job drop-out and subsequent delinquency. The reasons given for job failure can be summarized into three broad problems: (1) interpersonal problems; (2) salary prob-

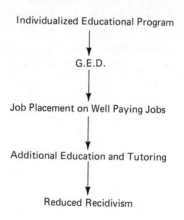

Individualized Educational Program

↓

G.E.D.

↓

Job Placement on Well Paying Jobs

↓

Additional Education and Tutoring

↓

Reduced Recidivism

**Figure 4-1.** The Link to Reduced Recidivism Suggested by Odell (1974)

lems; and (3) job satisfaction problems. Interpersonal problems are related to the lack of social skills in which most delinquents are deficient. Salary problems exist because of the low level of job entry skills and a lack of a G.E.D. or high school diploma, which a preceding study found to be crucial.

The final problem, job satisfaction, is related to being placed on jobs that are not liked and that require behavior on the part of youths that they did not like (for example, traveling too far to work). Lack of job satisfaction is tied to inadequate career decision-making skills. Such career decision making involves the systematic identification of values and abilities. As was demonstrated by Shore and Massimo (1969), systematic job selection results in a positive effect. It should also be noted that after job placement when the youths started experiencing so many problems, there was no follow-up program for help; and as has been discussed in this chapter, the presence of follow-up programs generally results in a greater degree of success.

## Conclusions

After reviewing 12 studies involving over 3300 youths, the following points can realistically be concluded concerning vocational approaches to the rehabilitation of juvenile delinquency. Job placement, vocational training, occupational orientation, field trips, and work programs do not positively affect juvenile delinquency. Just as it was observed that school attendance did not reduce delinquency, it can be similarly concluded that job placement and attendance does not reduce criminal behavior. It was additionally demonstrated that the so-called comprehensive vocational programs, including state department vocational rehabilitation programs, which are only a composite of the above ineffective approaches plus casework, do *not* work either. The hope that somehow an additive effect of inadequate programs would compensate for their inadequacy did not materialize.

Some programs did work. What were their ingredients? The key factor that overlapped in all the successful programs was that the youths were provided job opportunities where either advancement was possible or they were given supportive educational skills and diplomas that made advancement likely. Advancement and the possibility of improvement are necessary conditions for the success of vocational rehabilitation. Willis (1975) demonstrated success with adult inmates through his blue-collar college, where he provided inmates with the learning skills necessary to move from working in menial jobs to becoming supervisors on such jobs. For example, one element of the college program involved giving the inmates sufficient skills to set up their own business and compete against their former supervisors if they were blocked by them in any way.

Job advancement skills, support educational programs, a career-ladder frame of reference, or skills for starting new and competing businesses all work to involve youths or inmates positively in careers. It is not simply vocational training or a job that counts; it is giving the individual a job where he or she can have hope for advancement. The American Dream is not that you go out and become a millionaire on the first job you get, but that the possibility is always there for the future. The American Dream offers the idea that tomorrow will be better and brighter than today. A job that offers advancement entices youths with the American Dream. They remain motivated because they have hope for personal advancement. Programs are needed for delinquent youths that give them skills to advance, thus fostering a more positive outlook for the future.

What is required of rehabilitation staff is to teach the youths the intermediate steps needed to reach the goals they want. The youths can see their employers' big cars or big offices and want them, but not know how to go through the steps of a career ladder to reach that goal. They do not understand the steps and the programs that their bosses had to go through to get where they are. It is up to the rehabilitation worker to help these youths systematically develop their long-range goals and then help them develop plans of the steps required to reach those goals. Only in this way can these youths put that first menial jobs into perspective.

The effective programs that were reviewed in this chapter had the additional and important elements of follow-up help, problem solving, and systematic job selection. The importance of follow-up help in any rehabilitation program is that it can facilitate the transfer of the effectiveness of the helping program from the delivery setting to the real world. Chapter 2 demonstrated how differential reinforcement can motivate youths to repeat those skills which they can do. The problem is, of course, that job advancement requires complex skills these youths probably lack.

It is necessary for the rehabilitation worker to provide programs that ensure that youths receive those skills needed. The skills may be vocational, educational, or one that helps in interpersonal adjustment. Differential reinforcement would be used to reward the youths for using their skills and succeeding.

Problem solving and systematic job selection were also found to be effective. However, what would be even more favorable would be to teach those skills directly. In that way, problem solving and career decision making would be in the youths' behavior repertoires where they could be used at any time. The ability of the youths to help themselves is consistent with the adolescent developmental drive to be independent. When they have problems they are reluctant to share with someone else, they can solve the problems because they have the skills themselves.

**Negative Specific Prediction**: Vocational training, work programs, and job placement are not effective in and of themselves to rehabilitate juvenile delinquents.

**Positive Specific Prediction**: Teaching job advancement skills, providing support learning skills, providing educational programs that culminate in G.E.D. or diploma, furnishing follow-up help, and involving the youths in systematic career decision making will result in decreased delinquent behavior.

The specific recommendation flows from the positive prediction. Simply, the recommendation is to develop career programs that utilize the above ingredients.

**Specific Recommendation**: Vocational programs for delinquents should include the following program components:

1. Educational programs that support career goals
2. Systematic career decision making
3. Job advancement skills
4. Career advancement plans
5. Follow-up help after job placement

In the above review of the literature, it has been shown that when only one of the key program components was provided, positive results occurred. It seems clear that if all ingredients are incorporated, the results will be much more favorable.

The general prediction and recommendation for this chapter are further implications drawn from the theory concerning job advancement and its beneficial reduction of delinquency. See table 4-2 for the chapter studies and results.

**General Prediction**: Any rehabilitation program that holds out concrete hope for improvement to the client and has a relatively detailed plan for delivering on that hope has a greater likelihood of success than programs that neglect these two areas.

**General Recommendation**: Rehabilitation programs should be developed around a plan that shows the individuals specifically how they will improve and systematically move toward their highest goals.

### References

Ferdun, G., and H. Lockard. Jobs related to training: Final Report. Educational Research Series Report No. 12. California Youth Authority, 1973.

FitzGerald, T.J. Contingency contracting with juvenile offenders. *Criminology: An Interdisciplinary Journal* 12 (1974):241-248.

**Table 4-2**
**Vocational and Work Programs Summary**

| Researchers | Number of Youths | | Type of Program | Results | Follow-up Results |
|---|---|---|---|---|---|
| | *Experimental* | *Control* | | | |
| Hackler (1966) | 160 | 40 | Participation in a work project | *a.* No significant difference in personality and attitude tests *b.* No significant difference in arrest rate *c.* No significant difference in official delinquency rate | No |
| Zivan (1966) | 77 | | *a.* Vocational counseling *b.* Occupational orientation class *c.* Institutional work program *d.* Job placement | No significant difference in institutional behavior ratings | *a.* No significant difference in recidivism after 12 months *b.* No significant difference in follow-up behavior ratings *c.* No significant difference in measures of vocational adjustment |
| Molof (1967) | 251 | 218 | *a.* Forestry camp work program *b.* Small staff-to-student ratio | | No significant difference in recidivism after 15 months |
| Sullivan and Mandell (1967) | 264 | | *a.* Vocational training in data processing *b.* Remedial reading program | | *a.* Lower recidivism rate for treatment group *b.* Better jobs for treatment group *c.* No significant difference in unemployment rate |
| Kovacs (1967) | 126 | | *a.* Vocational training *b.* Programmed instruction *c.* Job placement *d.* Prevocational training *e.* Group discussions *f.* Field trips *g.* Group counseling | | *a.* No significant difference in recidivism rate at 12 months *b.* No significant difference in employment and school behavior at 3 months |

**Table 4-2.** (cont.)

| Researchers | Number of Youths | | Type of Program | Results | Follow-up Results |
|---|---|---|---|---|---|
| | Experimental | Control | | | |
| Shore and Massimo (1969) | 10 | 10 | a. Job placement b. Preemployment counseling c. Systematic job selection d. Problem solving of job problems e. Remedial education for advancement | a. Significant educational achievement b. Greater improvement in perception of interpersonal relations | a. Significantly less arrests at 5 years b. Significantly higher salary c. Significantly fewer job turnovers |
| Robin (1969) | 50 | 54 | a. Participation in a work program b. Counseling | No significant difference in serious offenses | No significant difference in delinquency record one year later |
| Goldberg and Johnson (1972) | 13 | 13 | Comprehensive vocational rehabilitation program a. Casework b. Referral c. Vocational training d. Job placement | | a. No significant difference in vocational adjustment b. No significant difference in recidivism |
| Ferdun and Lockard (1973) | 272 | 141 | a. Job placement b. Referral to an agency that provided job placement | | a. No significant difference in time employed at 3 months b. No significant difference in number of youths who obtained employment related to training c. A low percentage of youths were in jobs for which they had received training |
| FitzGerald (1974) | 15 | 5 | Weekly activities as reinforcement for working off probation fines | Increased work performance | No |
| Odell (1974) | 30 | 30 | a. Job placement b. G.E.D. c. High-interest subject matter d. Programmed learning e. Tutorial system | a. Better participation in school or work b. Higher mean weekly income | Lower recidivism rate |

**Table 4-2.** (cont.)

| Researchers | Number of Youths | | Type of Program | Results | Follow-up Results |
| --- | --- | --- | --- | --- | --- |
| | Experimental | Control | | | |
| Gold and Mattick (1974) | 970 | 571 | a. Job placement<br>b. Streetworker caseworker | | No significant difference in delinquency drop outs and boys' activities |

Glaser, D. Remedies for the key deficiency in criminal justice evaluation research. *Journal of Research in Crime and Delinquency* 11 (1974): 144-154.

Gold, M., and H.W. Mattick. *Experiment in the Streets: The Chicago Youth Development Project. Final Report.* Ann Arbor Institute for Social Research, Michigan University, 1974.

Goldberg, R.T., and B.C. Johnson. *Vocational and Social Rehabilitation of Juvenile Delinquents.* Massachusetts Rehabilitation Commission, 1972.

Hackler, J.C. Boys, blisters, and behavior: The impact of a work program in an urban central area. *Journal of Research in Crime and Delinquency* 3 (1966):155-164.

Kovacs, F.W. *Evaluation and Final Report of the New Start Demonstration Project.* Denver: Colorado Department of Employment, 1967.

Molof, M.J. Forestry camp study: Comparison of recidivism rates of camp-eligible boys randomly assigned to camp and to institutional programs. Research Report No. 53. California Youth Authority, 1967.

Odell, B.N. Accelerating entry into the opportunity structure: A sociologically based treatment for delinquent youth. *Sociology and Social Research*, April 1974.

Robin, Gerald H. Anti-poverty programs and delinquency. *Journal of Criminal Law, Criminology and Police Science* 60 (1969):323-331.

Shore, M., and J. Massimo. Five years later: A follow-up study of comprehensive vocationally oriented psychotherapy; *American Journal of Orthopsychiatry* 39 (1969):769-773.

Sullivan, C., and W. Mandell. *Restoration of Youth through Training.* Staten Island, N.Y.: Wakoff Research Center, 1967.

Willis, D. *The Blue Collar College: A Study of How Low Income Jobs Can be Developed as Stepping Stones to Higher Income Jobs for the Ex-offender.* Pontiac, Illinois: Pontiac Correctional Center, 1975.

Zivan, M. Youth in trouble: A vocational approach. *Final Report of a Research and Demonstration Project, May 31, 1961-August 31, 1966.* Dobbs Ferry, N.Y.: Children's Village, 1966.

# 5     Group Counseling

## Review of the Research

The most frequently used methods for the rehabilitation of juvenile delinquents involve group counseling, group therapy, and group discussions. It is commonly felt throughout the United States that group counseling greatly enhances the rehabilitation of juvenile delinquents. The group counseling thrust has been heavy; and partly because of this, numerous studies have been conducted to prove or disprove the theory of its benefits.

Gersten (1951) performed one of the earliest evaluations of group counseling and juvenile delinquency. The study involved 44 male inmates from the New York State Training School for Boys. The boys, who were between 13 and 16 years of age, were matched and placed into two equal groups. The institutional program was the same for the two groups, except that the control group did not participate in group counseling. The counseling boys were divided into three small groups.

The type of boys dealt with, being of below average intelligence, do not verbalize so readily and are also inclined to be active. Therefore, to make them feel more at ease and less self-conscious in their discussions, handicrafts were introduced beginning with the sixth session (Gersten, 1951, p. 312).

After the sixth session, the handicraft activity was continued because of an increase in group interaction. Since there were a total of 20 sessions, we conclude that the dominant method for 15 sessions was the activity group.

To provoke discussion, the leader introduced different topics by reading articles or suggesting role playing. The most positive technique was reading stories to the boys about famous people from underprivileged backgrounds and asking the boys to identify the traits that caused the prominent individuals to succeed. The therapist adopted the role of another group member and tried to provide a warm relationship toward the boys. The results were positive. The boys in the counseling groups achieved six times the amount of educational progress as the control group. This measured difference on educational achievement tests, plus the boys' increase in intelligence test scores, was statistically significant. The positive results may have been due to the warm relationship between the boys and the group leader, and by the change in group format from just talking to activities and talking. No significant differences were observed in general institutional behavior, as measured by the Haggerty-Olsen-Wickman

57

general institutional behavior, as measured by the Haggerty-Olsen-Wickman ratings.

The effects of group counseling with mentally defective delinquents were measured by Yonge and O'Conner (1954). They randomly assigned seven youths to each of two workshop groups. The treatment group received group counseling twice a week, while the control group remained in the workshop. A group discussion format was utilized along with the following guidelines:

A non-directive approach was used, with the therapist assuming a permissive though not a passive attitude. The principles employed were essentially those laid down by Foulkes for analytical groups—(a) weaning the group from being led, (b) refraining from set topics, programmes, or systematic discussions, (c) keeping his own personality in the background (Yonge and O'Conner, 1954, p. 948).

The results showed a significant decrease in negative behavior while the youths worked in the workshop. They became significantly more diligent with their work than the control group. One goal of the group counseling was to allow youths to ventilate their negative ideas. With program time, samples of the discussions indicated that the youths did express their negative thoughts. The counseling resulted in positive workshop behavior while the experiment was being conducted. There was no follow-up to see if the behavior reduced delinquency in the institution or upon release.

Mann (1955) utilized a group therapy approach in an institutional program in New York for mentally defective delinquents. Eleven youths were randomly assigned to the experimental group, and 11 youths were assigned to a treatment control group that participated in an academic skills class. The experimental group participated in group therapy for 12 weeks. The therapist and his approach were described as follows:

At times he listens as the group discharges its hostility. At other times he asks questions in order to stimulate further thinking and discussion. Sometimes he clarifies doubts and confusions and may offer points of information which are pertinent to the immediate discussion (Mann, 1955, p. 61).

There were no significant differences in the two variables under study. There were no significant differences in intelligence test score gains nor in the personality test scores between the two groups.

Group counseling was provided in a public school setting with predelinquent youth who were behavior problems by Caplan (1957). The boys were in junior high school and were 12 to 15 years of age. There were 17 boys assigned to the treatment group and matched with 17 boys in the control group. The group counseling approach was based upon the nondirective therapy techniques of Carl Rogers. The following summarizes the author's approach:

Group counseling emphasizes a permissive relationship in which an individual can evaluate himself and his opportunities, can choose courses of action, and can accept responsibility for those choices (Caplan, 1957), p. 124).

The results were mixed in success. The youths in the treatment group experienced more significant gains in a positive self-concept than the control group. There was a significant decrease in negative citizenship grades for the group counseling group. However, the treatment made no difference in the youths' academic performance. Group counseling improved the youths' views of themselves and their classroom conduct, but did not affect the more complex behavior required to improve academic performance.

The effects of group counseling upon reading achievement in male delinquents participating in a juvenile court clinic was investigated by Roman (1957). There were three groups of seven male youths each. One group received group counseling only, another received educational classes in remedial reading, while the third group participated in both group counseling and remedial reading. The treatment for all three groups was for seven months, with one meeting a week. The group counseling approach utilized was the interview type. The reading achievement scores of all three groups improved, but there was no significant difference in the improvements. The group counseling did not make a significant difference in the youths' gains in reading achievement.

Snyder and Sechrest (1959) evaluated the effects of group therapy upon mentally defective juvenile delinquents. There were 16 youths in the treatment group. Twenty-nine youths were divided between a "placebo" control and a regular control group, 16 and 13 youths respectively. The group approach centered around discussions of predetermined topics. "The sessions were planned, the role of the therapist was directive, the climate permissive and the material concrete" (Snyder and Sechrest, 1959, p. 120). The results were only partially successful. There was a significant increase in positive behavior reports in the treatment group. However, there was no significant difference in the groups' negative behavior reports and in the number of court appearances.

The research staff of the department of corrections of New York City (1960) evaluated a group therapy program involving newly incarcerated offenders. One hundred and twenty youths averaging 17 years of age were divided into two experimental comparable groups. The treatment group participated in the regular institutional program, with the exception of additional twice-a-week group therapy sessions. The control group remained active in the regular institutional program. The group therapy was provided by psychologists and lasted for six months. At the end of the treatment period, it was found that no significant difference existed between the two groups in their institutional rule violation rate. In other words, group therapy did not positively impact institutional behavior in this study.

Friedland (1960) evaluated the effectiveness of group counseling with delinquent youths who were institutional runaways. Thirty-six youths who were runaways from a relatively open treatment facility were assigned to the counseling group or the control group. The treatment program consisted of weekly group counseling sessions for 20 weeks. The control group participated in the regular institutional program. The results of group counseling upon the runaway behavior of the boys was unfavorable. During the 20-week program, in addition to the lack of effect upon runaway behavior, there was no significant difference between the counseling group and the control group on institutional adjustment, as measured by the Haggerty-Olson-Wickman ratings. Where several of the first studies reviewed in this chapter achieved favorable results from group counseling, there have now been three consecutive evaluations where no significant impact was made on the youths.

Group counseling was tried with 16- to 18-year-old male youths on parole and supervised by the California Youth Authority (O'Brien, 1961). Thirty-two youths were placed either in the control group or the treatment group. For seven months the treatment group received weekly group therapy. The group therapy was based upon psychoanalytic methods. The youths in the control group received regular parole supervision. The results of the personality test, the California Psychological Inventory, were in the opposite of the desired direction. The control group improved, while the experimental group deteriorated. After a seven-month follow-up period, the recidivism rate comparison indicated no significant difference. The negative results of this study are critical because they were obtained on follow-up after the counseling was discontinued.

Feder (1962) observed the effects of group counseling upon delinquent youths who spent eight weeks in the New Jersey Diagnostic Center. Eighty youths were randomly assigned to two control groups and two experimental groups. All the subjects were 14 to 17 years old and had been newly admitted to the diagnostic center. The treatment involved the boys in twice-a-week discussion group counseling for eight weeks. The control group received no exposure to therapy. There were some positive changes in the personality test variables. However, all the behavioral indices were *negative*. No significant difference existed in the ward adjustments of the youths. There were no significant differences in the frequency with which the control groups or the experimental groups were sick or in the number of discipline reports. Based upon this study, the effectiveness of group counseling in promoting institutional adjustment is questioned. There were no transfers of what occurred in group counseling to the youths' behavior, even during the time they were participating in the treatment.

O'Brien (1963) investigated a special approach to group counseling with delinquent youths who were on parole or probation. All the youths were attending public high school. There was a random assignment of boys to either the experimental or the control group. The boys were generally from the lower socioeconomic population and were judged severe in their delinquency. The treatment was unique in that prior to beginning the group therapy, the youths participated in 18 hours of didactic pretherapy training. This training involved teaching the youths facts and concepts, through lectures, films, and field trips, that would facilitate the development of group therapy. The importance of significant interpersonal relationships was also covered in the pretherapy phase.

The second phase of the treatment involved 82 hours of group psychotherapy that emphasized the utilization of transference and ego support. The control group participated in the regular public school program. The results were favorable. During the treatment significantly fewer members of the group therapy youth dropped out of school, and significantly fewer had to be returned to confinement. Perhaps the lower drop-out rate was due to the half-day group counseling that was probably more interesting than the normal public school curriculum. The inclusion of pretherapy training may have assisted in making the group therapy approach more successful.

Adams and Hopkinson (1964) achieved mixed results using group counseling with juvenile delinquent boys on probation. Ninety-six boys were appropriately placed in either a control group or experimental group. The treatment group attended weekly group counseling in small groups of six boys each. The control group participated in regular probation, which consisted of approximately one contact per month. At the end of the six-month treatment period, the results of the two groups were compared. There were significantly fewer contacts between the group counseling boys and the police. However, there was no significant difference in the rate of incarceration. Even with the more intensive probation contact through group counseling, the results were not more than partially favorable.

Craft, Stephenson, and Granger (1965) investigated the effects of group psychotheraphy upon juvenile delinquents in a mental hospital setting. Two groups of 25 youths each were randomly assigned to either the treatment group or the control group. Each group resided on a different ward of a psychiatric hospital in England. The youth were 13 through 25 years of age. The treatment group received group psychotherapy two to three times a week "to discuss their own problems." They also participated in a self-government council that met a couple of times a week. Both groups had a work and reward program.

The control group received a more authoritarian, disciplinary approach, with some individual treatment. The youths varied in the amount of time they were hospitalized, from 3 to 18 months, as well as in treatment. The follow-up comparisons were made after 14 months. The boys in the group counseling program did significantly worse in terms of the number of offenses committed since discharge. There was no significant difference in the number of youths holding various jobs; in both groups the majority were employed. In this study, group counseling was not only found to be ineffective, but, in fact, *worse* in terms of the subsequent offenses upon follow-up.

Two separate studies by Seckel (1965) will now be reviewed. The first study involved an investigation into the effectiveness of group counseling and/or community meetings for institutionalized delinquent youths. The subjects in the study were male youths committed to the California Youth Authority. There were 295 subjects randomly assigned to one of four treatment conditions. Group I had only small group counseling once a week. Group II had community-living unit meetings four times a week, while group III had both small group counseling and the community-living unit meetings. Group IV was the control group and had neither of the treatments. The youth in all four groups participated in a similar institutional routine.

The within-program measures of effectiveness were favorable, while the follow-up observations were negative. There was a significant change in attitude scores and a significantly smaller number of disciplinary reports for the treatment groups. However, at 15- and 30-month follow-up points, no significant difference existed between the treatment groups and the control group in parole revocation rate. All the failure rates were high (70 percent at 30 months). There was also no difference among the three treatment groups upon parole failure rate. The results suggest that neither group counseling or community meetings help a youth when he returns to his community. However, both group counseling and community meetings favorably affect a youth's institutional adjustment. But, there is no cumulative or qualitative effect. Just meeting in a group, any group, where the youths can blow off steam, helps them manage their acting out behavior at the time. Since the once-a-week meeting did as well as the four- and five-times-a-week meetings, one meeting a week to discuss problems and ventilate would seem sufficient to affect institutional behavior. However, it must be stressed that neither the group counseling nor the group meetings had any carry-over effects in terms of the youths' behavior in the community.

The second study by Seckel (1965) involved older California Youth Authority wards, who were approximately 19 years of age. There were 96 boys randomly assigned to each of the two groups. The treatment group received small group counseling once a week. The control group and the experimental group (except for time spent in counseling) participated in the regular institutional program. The parole violation rates of both groups revealed no significant differences on follow-up at 15 and 30 months. Group counseling made no significant difference in the youths' community adjustments. Since some studies have investigated differential effects of group counseling upon youth because of their age, race, or extent of delinquency, Seckel examined those factors. No significant effects were found to result from the youths' background characteristics. The group counseling was equally ineffective with youths of different age, race, and delinquency histories.

Approximately half the studies dealing directly with group counseling as treatment have been reviewed. To summarize briefly what has been found, it can be seen that 4 of the 15 studies presented had positive results. These studies were by Gersten in 1951, Yonge and O'Connor in 1954, Caplan in 1957, and O'Brien in 1963. Two of the studies reported negative results. These were by

O'Brien in 1961 and Craft, Stephenson, and Granger in 1965. The nine studies left in the first half of this chapter made no significant difference in the behaviors of the subjects involved. Numerically, it can be seen that 73 percent of the studies made no significant difference, or made negative contributions, to the youths' behaviors. Now it will be of interest to delve into the remaining studies and discover the final percentage of negative or neutral results of group counseling as treatment.

Since the majority of studies to this point have demonstrated the nonsuccess of group counseling, the next study (Persons, 1966) is unique in its favorable results. Forty-one pairs of boys at an Ohio training school were prematched on a multitude of variables and then randomly assigned to either a treatment group or a control group. The treatment group participated in twice-a-week group therapy and once-a-week individual therapy for 20 weeks. The group therapy had a teaching orientation that tried to "encourage in each boy the development of warm interpersonal relationships" (Persons, 1966, p. 388). The therapist not only tried to teach the boys about how their past behavior was self-defeating, but used his approval or criticism to differentially reinforce their behavior, as appropriate. Role playing was used both by therapist and the boys. In the last three weeks of the program, the focus was on the difficulties the boys would face in returning to their communities. While the treatment group experienced the above activities, the control group participated in the regular institutional program.

The results were that the treatment group boys improved on all the personality tests significantly greater than the control group. They also had less disciplinary reports and received significantly more freedom passes. Academically, their performance was better than the control group. In a report of the follow-up results, Persons (1967) reported that the boys that were in the treatment program did significantly better. After 9½ months, they had less recidivism and less parole violations than the control group. There was, however, no significant difference in the number of offenses committed by both groups.

To better understand why this group therapy program succeeded where so many others failed, let's examine the ingredients of Person's program:

1. Group therapy with teaching focus
2. Individual therapy
3. Therapist initially supportive then gradually more conditional in praise
4. Therapist used verbal praise and criticism to shape behavior
5. Therapist focused on the youth's past and present self-defeating behavior
6. Role-playing used by therapist and group
7. Significant focus upon community adjustment
8. Attention given to helping the youth develop interpersonal skills.

As can be seen, Persons' program was more specific and comprehensive than the programs that failed. Further, Persons also emphasized behavior modification and teaching, which have achieved favorable results in other programs. Even though follow-up help was not provided, follow-up performance of the youths was attended to through the phase of therapy that focused upon community adjustment.

Truax, Wargo, and Silber (1966) studied the effects of group therapy with therapists who offered high levels of empathy and nonpossessive warmth. Most of the previous evaluations of group therapy involved boys. The present study utilized institutionalized delinquent girls in Kentucky. Forty girls were randomly assigned to the treatment group, while 30 girls in like fashion were assigned to the control group. The group therapy was held twice a week for three months in groups of 10 youths each. The unique elements in the treatment were the high levels of empathy and nonpossessive warmth provided by the therapists.

Accurate empathy is defined . . . as the therapist's communication of his moment-to-moment understanding of the patient's feelings, experiences, and perceptions from the patient's personal vantage point; at relatively high levels the therapist verbalizes feelings or experiences which are present but not in the patient's current field of awareness (Truax, Wargo, and Silber, 1966, p. 267).

The therapist was conditional only to the extent of encouraging the youths to discuss personally relevant issues. The control group participated in the regular institutional program. The results were favorable for the treatment group in terms of less time institutionalized during one-year follow-up. There were both positive and negative results on the psychometric measures. The conclusion is that group therapy with therapists who are empathetic and nonpossessively warm may have some positive effects with delinquent girls.

Leckerman (1967) provided group counseling and group counseling preparation to institutionalized delinquent youths in Florida. There was a random assignment of 28 boys to one of three treatment groups or the one control group. The counseling-only group met for eight one-hour sessions over a period of three weeks. The counseling-preparation-only group listened to a tape recording of excerpts from a group counseling program three times over three weeks. The combined counseling preparation and counseling group listened to the preparation tape prior to their first three group counseling sessions.

The group counseling was described as group-centered and was "oriented toward enabling the clients to clarify their self-concepts and to practice new methods of adjustment in a relatively secure setting" (Leckerman, 1967, p. 12). The results were negative, since none of the three treatment groups experienced a significant change in the number of misconduct reports that they received. Not only do the results once again question the effectiveness of group counseling as a treatment approach with delinquent youth, they also question the effectiveness of counseling preparation.

Group therapy with institutionalized girls in New Zealand was reported by

Taylor (1967). Twenty-two delinquent girls were randomly assigned to the treatment group and the control group. The group therapy was held once a week for approximately 40 weeks. The therapist utilized a psychoanalytic approach:

A psychoanalytic orientation in group psychotherapy helped to encourage (1) the development of transference relationships, (2) the expression of emotional conflict, and (3) the growth of ego strength (Taylor, 1967, p. 172).

The control group participated in the routine institutional program. There were positive changes on the personality test for both groups after 40 weeks. There was, however, no significant difference in time of release. The follow-up measurement revealed no significant difference between the treatment and the control groups in the reconviction rate after six and one-half months of follow-up.

Herman (1968) evaluated the effectiveness of psychodrama with institutionalized delinquent boys in New York. Twenty-four boys were randomly selected from a group of 100 boys to participate in the treatment. There were four groups of six boys each who met once a week for two hours over a 10-week period. Participation was voluntary. Before each group session the boys were allowed to play 15 minutes of basketball. The group sessions involved the discussion and reenactment of experiences from the past.

After the first meeting the sessions began to deal with events and scenes from the past more often than from the immediate time dimension. However, anybody who came to a meeting anxious to release feelings accruing from current stress was permitted to do so (Herman, 1968, p. 212).

The boys were supportive of each other's experiences. The results were somewhat favorable. There were significantly more youths on the campus honor roll and fewer rule infractions from the treatment group than from the control group. There was no significant difference in the length of stay of the two groups. The positive results may have been more the result of the action nature of therapy, psychodrama, and basketball, than of the group counseling aspects.

A combination of studies were conducted with male and female delinquents in Kentucky and Wisconsin institutions by Truax, Wargo, and Volksdorf (1970). The first aspect of the research that will be discussed is a continuation of an earlier study (Truax, Wargo, and Silber, 1966) that dealt with therapists who had high levels of empathy and nonpossessive warmth providing group therapy. In the earlier study, group counseling with such therapists proved superior to no group counseling. Using 80 delinquent youths randomly assigned to treatment and control conditions, it was found that group counseling with empathetic, warm, and genuine therapists made a significant difference compared to group counseling with nonempathetic therapists. The difference was observed in the youths' personality test score gains and, more importantly, in the reduced time of incarceration after a one-year follow-up.

The second variable that was investigated with the same population was vicarious therapy pretraining. Half the youth were exposed to a 30-minute tape recording prior to the first session. The tape was used to demonstrate what effective group therapy was actually like. The results indicated that providing such pretraining did not make a significant difference in one-year follow-up incarceration rates. A third variable was allowing the youth to meet in alternate sessions without the therapist present in addition to the regular therapy. Beginning after approximately the ninth session, these youth met without their therapist for group meetings once between each regular session. These results were negative. The youth receiving alternate sessions showed no significant difference in most of their personality measures and were not incarcerated significantly less. All the youths in the preceding studies were in group therapy twice a week for three months, except for the group with alternate sessions alone.

These studies question the use of alternate sessions without a therapist and the use of therapy pretraining to contribute to the effectiveness of group counseling in the rehabilitation of juvenile delinquents. The findings also gave additional support to the use of therapists who provide the therapeutic conditions of empathy, warmth, and genuineness. In analyzing the results, it was found that the genuineness and nonpossessive warmth were highly correlated with empathy ($r = .93$ and $.97$ respectively). Such high correlations would suggest that in fact the main therapeutic condition is empathy. Truax, Wargo, and Volksdorf hypothesized that those youths who were in groups that engaged in high levels of verbal self-exploration would do better. Not only did they not do better, but they did worse. They were institutionalized significantly more than youths who were in groups that did not engage in a deeper level of self-exploration. This result questions one of the alleged purposes of group therapy, to get participants to discuss emotionally relevant content.

Sowles and Gill (1970) compared the effectiveness of group counseling against individual counseling and against no counseling with institutionalized delinquent boys and girls. The youths averaged approximately 14½ years of age and were randomly assigned to one of the three groups. Each group had 15 boys and 5 girls. The subjects met either for the group or individual counseling twice a week for approximately five months.

Workers encouraged the delinquents to develop stable and acceptable relationships with peers and staff, to explore their experiences and feelings which may have contributed to the delinquent offenses and to cope with their feelings of frustration in more acceptable ways. (Sowles and Gill, 1970, p. 400).

The control group participated in the routine program.

No significant differences were seen between the counseling groups and the control group in the number of escapes, number of disciplinary reports, duration of incarceration, number of parole violations, and amount of reinstitutionalization after follow-up. The only positive change that was significant was in the psychometric attitude test scores. The results add to the weight of evidence *against* most types of group counseling's effectiveness.

Ohio youths on probation were evaluated on the effects of a discussion group program upon their subsequent arrest rates (Ostrom, Steele, Rosenblood, and Mirels, 1971). Nineteen delinquent youths were matched with 19 comparable youths in terms of a variety of background characteristics. The treatment youths met for seven two-hour sessions over a two-month period. Role playing was utilized to teach the consequences of their behavior to the youths. The group leaders praised responses that indicated the youths were adopting more internal loci of control, where they felt they had more control over the events in their lives. The group members were paid $2 each session. The control group participated in the regular probation program involving periodic supervision by the youths' probation officers. After eight months of follow-up, the treatment group did not perform significantly better in terms of their arrest rate. This result indicates not only negative effects for group discussions, but also that paying youths to participate in a program does not assist in rehabilitation.

Smith (1972) evaluated the effects of group counseling upon male delinquents on probation. Forty-two boys were randomly assigned to group counseling either from a trained counselor or a probation officer, while 21 youths were similarly assigned to the control group. The treatment groups met for 75 minutes each week for four months. The group counseling approach was "the common problems model, which attempts to deal with the real problems of group members." A nondirective, responsive stance was adopted by the group leaders, with the goal of developing a "supportive atmosphere." The youths in the control group remained in the regular probation supervision program.

The results were that neither group counseling with trained counselors nor group counseling with probation officers as leaders made any difference in the probation failure rate during the treatment or after the two-month follow-up. Aside from the once-again documented failure of group counseling, there is the additional implication that trained group counselors often do no better than paraprofessionals with juvenile delinquents.

Institutionalized delinquent girls at an Indiana girl's school participated in group counseling (Redfering, 1973). Eighteen girls were randomly assigned to the treatment group and 18 girls were assigned to the control group. The treatment girls participated in the group counseling, while the girls in the control group were active in the regular institutional program. There were more positive attitude test scores using a semantic differential test for the treatment group on some of the concepts only. After one year of follow-up, the girls receiving counseling had more releases from the institution than the control group. However, there was no significant difference in the recommitment rate and no significant difference in the number of youths employed or in school. Group counseling helped the girls adjust to the institution and earn release, but it did not result in any transfer in appropriate behavior to the community.

The final group counseling study to be reviewed in this chapter was by Andrews and Young (1974). Delinquent males in a Canadian prison were randomly assigned to a treatment group (24 youths), and to a control group (23 youths). The average age of the youths was 17.5 years. The group counseling utilized was a two-session orientation program over a three- to five-day period. Each session was one and one-half hours long. The sessions were structured with the leader providing information on the history of prisons and the local institutional rules. The group leader,

attempted to verbalize positive statements regarding the rules and officers, to positively reinforce (verbal and gestural approval) positive statements by residents, to ignore negative statements, and to outline in detail and encourage the residents to outline the immediate and longer-term reinforcement contingencies in effect for rule compliance and deviance (Andrews and Young, 1974, p. 9).

The results of five weeks of follow-up indicated that the short-term group counseling made no significant difference in the attitude measures, the staff behavior ratings, or the misconduct reports of older youth. The younger youth (16 to 17 years) who had the orientation counseling had less misconduct reports. In general, however, the overall results of the short-term group counseling were negative.

The last of the 28 studies has been presented. Only two of these studies had entirely positive results, (Persons, 1966; and Herman, 1968). The study by Truax, Wargo, and Volksdorf in 1970 resulted in favorable follow-up results at the one-year point. This leaves 10 of the preceding 13 studies showing results of no significant difference.

Viewing the chapter's studies as a whole, 21 percent of the group counseling studies resulted in positive behavior changes in the subjects involved. This leaves an astounding 79 percent that had no significant difference in behavior or that actually gave negative results. The next section of the chapter deals with the implications of these findings.

## Conclusions

To decide whether group counseling is effective in the rehabilitation of juvenile delinquents, 28 studies involving over 1800 youths have been reviewed. Table 5-1 is the summary chart of the studies that were reviewed in this chapter. The results of the majority of studies were that group counseling did not result in significant behavior changes. At best, group counseling allowed for the verbal ventilation of negative feelings of institutionalized delinquents. Such emotional catharses did at times positively affect the youths' immediate institutional adjustments. However, institutional behavior changes did not transfer outside the institution.

**Table 5-1**
**Group Counseling Summary**

| Researcher | Number of Youths | | Intervention | Results | Follow-up Results |
|---|---|---|---|---|---|
| | *Experimental* | *Control* | | | |
| Gersten (1951) | 22 | 22 | a. Discussion and activity group b. Role playing c. Therapist tried to establish warm relationship | a. Increased educational achievement and IQ b. No significant difference in measured behavior rating | No |
| Yonge and O'Connor (1954) | 7 | 7 | a. Group discussion b. Nondirective approach | a. Decrease in negative workshop behavior b. Increase in diligence in workshop | No |
| Mann (1955) | 11 | 11 | Group counseling | a. No significant difference in intelligence b. No significant difference in personality test scores | No |
| Caplan (1957) | 17 | 17 | Group counseling | a. Improved self-concept b. No significant difference in academic performance c. Decrease in negative citizenship grades | No |
| Roman (1957) | 14 | 7 | a. Group counseling b. Group counseling combined with remedial reading | No significant difference in reading achievement scores | No |
| Synder and Sechrest (1959) | 16 | 29 | Group therapy | a. Increase in positive behavior reports b. No significant difference in negative reports c. No significant difference in behavior court appearances | No |
| New York City (1960) | 120 | | Group therapy | a. No significant difference in rule violations in the institution | No |

**Table 5-1.** (cont.)

| Researcher | Number of Youths | | Intervention | Results | Follow-up Results |
|---|---|---|---|---|---|
| | Experimental | Control | | | |
| Friedland (1960) | 36 | | Group counseling | *a.* No significant improvement in runaway behavior *b.* No significant difference in institutional adjustment | No |
| O'Brien (1961) | 32 | | Psychoanalytically oriented group therapy | Treated group performed less satisfactorily on the personality test | No significant difference in parole revocation rate |
| Feder (1962) | 40 | 40 | Discussion group therapy | *a.* No significant difference in ward adjustment *b.* No significant difference in frequency of sick call *c.* No significant difference in discipline incidents | No |
| O'Brien (1963) | NS | | *a.* Didactic pre-therapy training *b.* Utilization of transference and ego support in group therapy | *a.* Significantly fewer drop-outs from public school *b.* Significantly fewer incarcerations | No |
| Adams (1964) | 96 | | Group counseling | *a.* No significant difference in incarceration rate *b.* Significantly fewer police contacts | No |
| Craft, Stephenson, and Granger (1965) | 25 | 25 | *a.* Group psychotherapy *b.* Self-government | | *a.* Significantly greater number of offenses *b.* No significant difference in jobs held |
| Seckel (1965) | 208 | 87 | *a.* Group counseling *b.* Community meetings | *a.* Significant attitude changes *b.* Significantly fewer disciplinary reports | *a.* No significant difference in parole revocation rate at 15 months *b.* No significant difference in parole revocation rate at 30 months |

**Table 5-1.** (cont.)

| Researcher | Number of Youths | | Intervention | Results | Follow-up Results |
|---|---|---|---|---|---|
| | Experimental | Control | | | |
| Seckel (1965) | 96 | 96 | Group counseling | | a. No significant difference in parole revocation rate at 15 months b. No significant difference in parole revocation rate at 30 months |
| Persons (1966) | 41 | 41 | a. Group therapy with teaching as focus b. Individual therapy c. Therapist used verbal differential reinforcement | a. Significantly better personality test scores b. Significantly better institutional behavior c. Improved academic functioning | a. Less recidivism b. Fewer parole violations c. No significant differences in offenses |
| Truax, Wargo, and Silber (1966) | 40 | 30 | Group therapy with therapists having high levels of empathy and nonpossessive warmth | Some changes on personality and attitude tests | Less time institutionalized at 1 year |
| Leckerman (1967) | 21 | 7 | a. Group counseling b. Group counseling preparation | No significant difference in number of misconduct reports | No |
| Taylor (1967) | 11 | 11 | Psychoanalytic group therapy | a. Mixed results on personality tests b. No significant difference in time of release | No significant difference in reconviction rate at 6½ months |
| Herman (1968) | 24 | 76 | Group counseling with psychodrama approach | a. Significantly more youth on honor roll b. Fewer rule infractions c, No significant difference in length of stay | No |
| Truax, Wargo, and Volksdorf (1970) | 40 | 40 | Group therapy with therapists offering high levels of empathy, nonpossessive warmth, and genuineness | Positive changes on some personality measures | Less time in institution at 1 year |
| Truax, Wargo, and Volksdorf (1970) | 40 | 40 | Vicarious therapy pretraining | No significant difference in most personality measures | No significant difference in time out of institution after 1 year |

**Table 5-1.** (cont.)

| Researcher | Number of Youths | | Intervention | Results | Follow-up Results |
|---|---|---|---|---|---|
| | Experimental | Control | | | |
| Truax, Wargo, and Volksdorf (1970) | 40 | 40 | Alternate sessions with therapist absent | No significant difference in most personality measures | No significant difference in time out of institution after 1 year |
| Sowles and Gill (1970) | 40 | 20 | Group counseling | a. Positive change in attitude test scores  b. No significant difference in escapes  c. No significant difference in disciplinary reports  d. No significant difference in duration of incarceration | After 10 years follow-up  a. No significant difference in parole violations  b. No significant difference in recidivism |
| Ostrom, Steele, Rosenblood, and Mirels (1971) | 19 | 19 | a. Small group discussions  b. Role playing | No | No significant difference in arrest statistics after 8 months |
| Smith (1972) | 42 | 21 | a. Group counseling by trained counselors  b. Group counseling by probation officers | No significant difference in probation failure rate | No significant difference in probation failure rate after 2 months |
| Redfering (1973) | 18 | 18 | Group counseling | More positive attitude test scores on some concepts | After 1 year follow-up  a. Significantly more girls released  b. No significant difference in recommitment  c. No significant difference in number of youths employed or in school |
| Andrews and Young (1974) | 24 | 23 | Group counseling | | After 5 weeks follow-up  a. No significant difference in attitude measures  b. No significant difference in staff behavior ratings  c. No significant difference in misconduct reports of older youths  d. Younger youths had fewer misconduct reports |

The Truax studies pointed out that the group leader's ability to provide empathetic responses had more to do with whether the group worked or did not work than did other variables. Youths who experienced group counseling with therapists offering high levels of empathy, nonpossessive warmth, and genuineness were able to spend more time out of the institution than the control group. Persons (1966) obtained significantly positive follow-up results with group therapy that had *teaching* as a focus of the group. The group leader also provided *differential reinforcement*, which has been documented in chapter 2 as being effective.

The positive results of 6 studies should not overshadow the generally neutral or negative effects of group counseling in 22 other studies. Group counseling failed to produce positive results with youths on probation, in institutions, or on parole.

**Specific Prediction**: Group counseling, in and of itself, as a program will fail to successfully rehabilitate the majority of delinquent youths.

**Specific Recommendation**: Group counseling should not be relied upon as a vehicle to rehabilitate.

The overall neutral or negative effects of group counseling are indeed discouraging. However, the results are consistent with a principle of rehabilitation that was articulated in chapter 1. Group counseling as a direct service fails because it is, at best, only effective as long as the youths are regularly attending the group counseling. This conclusion is supported by Ostrom *et al.* (1971), who observed that with youths receiving group counseling in the community, those who dropped out of the group significantly increased in their delinquency. Programs that provide direct services will fail unless there is follow-up that gives the individual the skills to work out his or her own problems. As far as group counseling is concerned, it is shaky reasoning to assume that it helps delinquents, even while the direct service is being provided. In fact, most of the studies examined here documented its ineffectiveness.

Why did it fail? First, the program staff took youths who possessed a variety of specific behavioral problems that could be summarized as negative behaviors that got them into trouble and lacked some positive behaviors that could help them succeed. They were, then, placed in a setting where the solution was to talk about their problems with other youths and an adult group leader. At best, all group counseling did was to get input from the youths as to what they thought their problems were. However, the input was then not utilized to make objective diagnoses. It was not utilized for the development of a program plan. Specific interventions, with reinforcement for the youths when they achieved progress, did not occur. There was no follow-up that provided the youths with help in transferring the learning from the group experience to their lives. There was only the youths talking and providing input.

Sometimes the leader provided general direction or advice to the group as a whole, based upon the input, but such general advice for a variety of specific problems *failed*. The specific problems of the youths can be viewed as targets that should have been the focus of the change agent. Group counseling as an intervention missed the target altogether. The implication is that any general, nonspecific approach will fail. The recommendation is that intervention that is most *specifically* and *directly* tied to the objectively diagnosed problem will succeed, and should therefore be utilized. This *principle of specificity* is one possible reason for the progress in medical science.

**General Prediction:** The more general and nonspecific a treatment intervention is, the more likely it will fail. Conversely, the more specific the treatment and the more directly tied to the individual's problem, the more likely success will be achieved.

**General Recommendation:** Rehabilitation of any population should be based upon specificity. There should be the acquisition of specific input, the development of a specific and objective diagnosis, the planning of a specific program, the provision of specific intervention, and the provision of the specific follow-up and transition applications back to the community.

Hopefully, if such a recommendation is followed, future generations of researchers will not have to go through the arduous task of wading through study after study of unfavorable results.

**References**

Adams, S., and C. Hopkinson. Evaluation of the Intensive Supervision Caseload Project. Research Report No. 12. Los Angeles County Probation Department, 1964.

Andrews, D.A., and J.G. Young. Short-term structured group counseling and prison adjustment. *Canadian Journal of Criminology and Corrections*, 14 (1974): 5-13.

Caplan, S. The effects of group counseling on junior high school boys' concepts of themselves in school. *Journal of Counseling Psychology* 4 (1957): 124-128.

Craft, M., G. Stephenson, and C. Granger. A controlled trial of authoritarian and self-governing regimes with adolescent psychopaths. *American Journal of Orthopsychiatry* 34 (1965):543-554.

Feder, B. Limited goals in short-term group psychotherapy with institutionalized delinquent adolescent boys. *International Journal of Group Psychotherapy* 12 (1962):503-507.

Friedland, D.M. *Group Counseling as a Factor in Reducing Runaway Behavior from an Open Treatment Institution for Delinquent and Pre-Delinquent Boys.* Unpublished Ph.D. dissertation. New York University, 1960.

Gersten, C. An experimental evaluation of group therapy with juvenile delinquents. *International Journal of Group Psychotherapy* (Nov. 1951):311-318.

Herman, L.A. An exploration of psychodrama. *Group Psychotherapy* 21 (1968):211-213.

Leckerman, L.A. The effects of counseling preparation on the outcome of group counseling with institutionalized juvenile delinquents. Ph.D. dissertation. Florida State University, 1967.

Mann, A. Group therapy-irradiation. *The Journal of Criminal Law, Criminology and Police Science* 46 (1955):50-65.

New York City. Department of Correction. *A Preliminary Evaluation of the Relationship between Group Psychotherapy and the Adjustment of Adolescent Inmates in a Short-Term Penal Institution.* Rikers Island Penitentiary, New York, 1960.

O'Brien, W.J. *Personality Assessment as a Measure of Change Resulting from Group Psychotherapy with Male Juvenile Delinquents.* California Youth Authority, 1961.

O'Brien, W.J. *An experimental use of modified group therapy in a public school setting with delinquent adolescent males.* Doctoral dissertation. University of California, Berkeley, 1963.

Ostrom, T.M., C.M. Steele, L.K. Rosenblood, and H.L. Mirels. Modification of delinquent behavior. *Journal of Applied Social Psychology* 1 (1971): 118-136.

Persons, R.W. Psychological and behavioral change in delinquents following psychotherapy. *Journal of Clinical Psychology* 22 (1966):337-340.

Persons, R.W. Relationship between psychotherapy with institutionalized boys and subsequent community adjustment. *Journal of Consulting Psychology* 31 (1967):137-141.

Redfering, D.L. Surability of effects of group counseling with institutionalized delinquent females. *Journal of Abnormal Psychology* 82 (1973):85-86.

Roman, M. *Reaching Delinquents through Reading.* Springfield, Ill.: Charles C. Thomas, 1957.

Seckel, J. Experiments in group counseling at two youth authority institutions. Research Report No. 46. California Youth Authority, 1965.

Smith, J.E. The effects of group counseling on the behavior of juvenile probationers. Ph.D. dissertation. Lehigh University, 1972.

Snyder, R., and L. Sechrest. An experimental study of directive group therapy with defective delinquent boys. *American Journal of Mental Deficiency* 64 (1959):117-123.

Sowles, R.C., and J.H. Gill. Institutional and community adjustment of delinquents following counseling. *Journal of Consulting and Clinical Psychology* 34 (1970):398-402.

Taylor, A.J.W. An evaluation of group psychotherapy in a girls' borstal. *International Journal of Group Psychotherapy* 17 (1967):168-177.

Truax, C.B., D.G. Wargo, and L.D. Silber. Effects of group psychotherapy with high adequate empathy and nonpossessive warmth upon female institution-alized delinquents. *Journal of Abnormal Psychology* 71 (1966):267-274.

Truax, C.B., D.G. Wargo, and F.R. Volksdorf. Antecedents to outcome in group counseling with institutionalized juvenile delinquents. *Journal of Abnormal Psychology* 76 (1970):235-242.

Yonge, K.A., and N. O'Conner. Measurable effects of group psychotherapy with defective delinquents. *British Journal of Psychiatry* 100 (1954):944-952.

# 6

# Individual Psychotherapy

## Review of the Research

Individual counseling and individual psychotherapy are dominant ingredients in many institutional and community-based programs. When they are not the dominant method of rehabilitation, they are, at least, provided for support. This chapter will review those studies which have researched the effectiveness of individual psychotherapy with delinquent youths.

Adams (1959) evaluated the results of individual psychotherapy with delinquent girls institutionalized in California. Ninety-four girls from 13 through 20 years of age were appropriately assigned to the treatment and control groups. The individual therapy was based upon a psychiatric approach. It was compared with girls in the regular institutional program and with girls who received a combination of individual and group therapy. The girls in the treatment groups received approximately 40 hours of therapy.

There was no significant difference in favor of the girls who received the therapy compared to the control group on their parole suspension rate. There was also no significant difference between those girls receiving individual therapy versus those receiving both group and individual therapy. In other words, neither the individual counseling nor the individual plus group counseling made an improvement in the girls' community adjustments. The research revealed that if the individual therapy were administered by a psychiatrist or a psychologist, the parole suspension rate was almost 2½ times *higher* than if it were provided by a case worker. The more extensively trained therapists did considerably worse in terms of facilitating the girls' subsequent community performances.

Rudolf (1960) investigated the effects of individual psychotherapy upon institutionalized delinquent males. There was a random assignment of 534 boys to either the treatment group or the control group. The boys were between 18 and 22 years of age. The treatment group received individual psychotherapy that was based upon the psychoanalytic model. The treatment lasted approximately six months. Other than the individual psychotherapy sessions, both groups participated in the regular institutional program. No significant difference was revealed in the institutional adjustment of the two groups. The individual psychotherapy did not make a difference in the youths' immediate institutional behavior.

The possibility that some delinquent youths might be more amenable to individual psychotherapy was studied by Adams (1961a). Upon entering the training school, the delinquent youths were clinically diagnosed as being amenable or not amenable to the proposed treatment. After the determination of the youths' amenableness to the individual interview therapy, they were randomly assigned to either the control group or the treatment group. Altogether there were four groups with 100 youths per group:

1. Treatment amenables
2. Treatment nonamenables
3. Control amenables
4. Control nonamenables

The boys in the study were approximately 20 years of age, and the length of treatment averaged nine months.

The individual therapy was found to result in a significant difference in parole performance in favor of the amenable youths who received the individual therapy. The nonamenable therapy youths did worse on parole, but the difference was not significantly greater than the comparable control group. The conclusion is that some youths who are diagnosed by a clinical staff to be open to individual psychotherapy can use the therapy to make a better adjustment while on parole.

In contrast to the previous study, a straightforward evaluation of individual psychotherapy by Adams (1961b) obtained negative results. Institutionalized male delinquents were provided with the therapy. The control group participated in the regular institutional program. There were 164 boys assigned to the two groups. The results showed no improvement in the youths' parole revocation rates or in their first parole suspension rates as a result of the individual treatment. The control group did as well on the two parole performance criteria. Once again individual psychotherapy, as a treatment modality, did not make a significant difference.

Meese (1961) conducted an experimental program for juvenile delinquent boys involving individual counseling and guidance conferences. Young delinquent boys were assigned to the treatment or control group. The boys in the experimental group received individual counseling once a week. After the treatment, both groups were tested on academic achievement and reading skill. The treatment group did significantly worse than the control group on both measures. This study, therefore, supports the principle of specificity by negative example. To improve academic achievement and reading, you do not provide a program as unrelated and nonspecific as individual counseling.

Individual interview therapy was utilized with delinquent boys institutionalized at the Preston School of Industry in Northern California (Guttman, 1963). There were 106 boys randomly assigned to the treatment group and 109 youths randomly assigned to the control group. The average age of all the boys was 17½ years. The treatment group received individual interview therapy based upon a psychiatric approach for one hour twice a week. The therapy was provided by a psychiatrist, psychiatric social workers, and psychologists. The control group participated in the routine institutional programs, as did the treatment group, when they were not at their individual therapy sessions.

The results were far from favorable. Not only did the treatment group not perform significantly better than the control group, they did *significantly worse* in their parole performance. The parole performance was evaluated after 15 months of follow-up. The treatment group did not do significantly better than the control group while in the institution. No significant difference existed in the number of placements to the disciplinary unit. There was no significant difference in the number of special incident reports filed against the two groups. Further, no improvement was seen in the number of youth rated "amenable" to the therapy. This study documents the ineffectiveness of individual psychiatric interviews as treatment.

Guttman (1963) reported the results of a similar evaluation of individual psychotherapy, this time with younger delinquents. The youths were approximately 15 years of age and were boys institutionalized at a Southern California training school. There was a random assignment of 62 boys to the treatment group and 61 boys to the control group. The boys in the treatment group received individual therapy that emphasized the formation of a "positive relationship" between the therapist and the youths. The therapy sessions were twice a week for approximately one hour over an eight-month period.

The results were negative. The within-treatment measures of institutional adjustment were very unfavorable. The treatment group was assigned a significantly greater number of times to the disciplinary unit. There was no improvement in the treatment group in the number of incident reports compared to the control group. After 15 months of follow-up, there was no significant difference in the parole performance of the two groups. Performance of the "amenable to treatment" youth did not improve either. The results are consistent with the previously discussed overall ineffectiveness of individual psychotherapy. The lack of positive results of "relationship psychotherapy" is consistent with the similar lack of results with "relationship teaching," as documented in chapter 3.

Individual psychotherapy was provided to institutionalized delinquent girls by Jurjevich (1968). There were 14 girls in the treatment group, matched with 14 girls in a control group. Therapy was provided on the average of 23 sessions per girl. The focus of treatment is described as follows.

The main method of achieving changes in the girls was considered to be helping them comply with the reasonable demands of training and discipline, and accept the stresses of their situation without overreacting (Jurjevich, 1968, p. 107).

The therapist was described as being "warm, respectful and when necessary, frank." The results were unfavorable. No significant change was seen on the behavior ratings of either the counselors or the girls' teachers. After two years of follow-up, no significant difference existed in the parole performance of the youths, as measured by the parole rating scales. The positive benefits of individual psychotherapy were once again absent.

Thomas (1968) utilized unique methods with an individual counseling program in a public school setting. The youths in the study were delinquency-prone adolescents. Twenty-five students each were randomly assigned to the control group and the treatment group. The delinquency proneness was based upon teacher-staff ratings of adjustment, school attendance, and the Jesness Inventory. Therefore, the diagnosed problems were school attendance and school conduct behavior. The treatment was to provide individual counseling that focused upon

1. Clarification of student goals
2. Methods of achieving goals
3. Selection of new behavioral responses to old problems
4. Evaluation of the effects of new responses upon old problems

The specific content of the problems or goals was decided upon by the youths. The treatment was provided weekly over the nine-month school year by the youths' social studies teacher.

The results were positive on eight of nine criteria. The treatment made a significant beneficial difference in the youths' grade point averages, school attendance and promptness, teacher ratings of adjustment, referrals to the dean, suspensions from school, number of withdrawals from school, and number of probation court referrals. However, no significant difference was seen in the number of police contacts by the two groups. Unfortunately, no follow-up assessment was reported. But the results are the most favorable of any study discussed in this chapter. This study utilized processes that were not present in the earlier programs. There was a systematic attempt to focus the students on goals and solutions to their problems. In addition, a feedback evaluation process was in use, since the students' counselor was also their teacher for one class. When in the role of the teacher, the counselor could provide classroom simulations for the students' solutions.

The study of Sowles and Gill (1970) involving group counseling was discussed earlier. The effects of individual counseling were also examined and will now be presented. Institutionalized delinquent boys and girls averaging 14½ years of age were randomly assigned to a control group and a treatment group. Each group had 15 boys and 5 girls. The youths in the treatment group met twice a week for individual counseling until each youth had received approximately 40 hours. The counseling process was described as follows:

Workers encouraged the delinquents to develop stable and acceptable relationships with peers and staff, to explore their experiences and feelings which may have contributed to the delinquent offenses, and to cope with their feelings of frustration in more acceptable ways (Sowles and Gill, 1970, p. 400).

The control group participated in the regular institutional program, as did the treatment group, except for the time those youths attended their therapy sessions.

The overall results of the study were negative: every behavioral index showed no significant improvement. No significant difference was seen between the treatment group and the control group in the number of escapes, the number of disciplinary reports, and the duration of incarceration. The treatment group did achieve a more positive change in their attitude test scores. After 10 years on follow-up, still no significant difference was apparent in favor of the treatment group in parole violations and in the amount of recidivism. The results were conclusively negative in terms of the influence of individual counseling upon the subsequent behavior of both male and female delinquents.

## Conclusions

The studies in the preceding review, wevaluating the effects of individual psychotherapy with juvenile delinquents, involved over 1640 youth. The summary of the 10 studies is presented in table 6-1. The results in eight of the studies were completely negative. In one of the remaining two, the results were negative except for those youths diagnosed as "amenable." The final study, conducted by Thomas (1968), departed significantly from the traditional content and processes of the other individual psychotherapy approaches. The results of that study were positive. Since the majority of studies obtained negative results, the following statements are justified.

**Specific Prediction:** The utilization of individual psychotherapy or counseling as treatment for juvenile delinquency will be unsuccessful.

**Specific Recommendation:** Individual counseling and psychotherapy, as it is now practiced and relied upon, should be discontinued.

Individual psychotherapy only serves, at best, to explicate the problem in terms of the youth's frame of reference. Such understanding is not an objective diagnosis and, as such, is probably inaccurate. The usefulness of gaining input from the youths is that their cooperation can be gained when the actual problem and solution are diagnosed and formulated.

After carefully examining the successful study by Thomas (1968), we find the following ingredients:

**Table 6-1**
**Individual Psychotherapy Summary**

| Researcher | Number of Youths | | Intervention | Results | Follow-up Results |
|---|---|---|---|---|---|
| | Experimental | Control | | | |
| Adams (1959) | 94 | | a. Individual psychotherapy b. Individual psychotherapy combined with group therapy | | No significant difference in parole suspension rate |
| Rudolf (1960) | 534 | | Individual psychotherapy | No significant difference in institutional adjustment | No |
| Adams (1961a) | 200 | 200 | a. Individual interview therapy with amenable youths b. Individual interview therapy with nonamenable youths | | a. Significantly better parole performance for amenable youths b. Worse, but not a significant difference in parole performance for nonamenable youths |
| Adams (1961b) | 164 | | Individual psychotherapy | | a. No significant difference in parole revocation rate b. No significant difference in first parole suspension rate |
| Meese (1961) | NS | | Individual counseling | Treatment group did worse on academic achievement | No |
| Guttman (1963) | 106 | 109 | Individual interview therapy | a. No significant difference in disciplinary unit placements b. No significant difference in special incident reports | a. The treatment group had worse parole performance after 15 months b. No significant difference of amenables |
| Guttman (1963) | 62 | 61 | Individual relationship psychotherapy | a. Greater number of more than once disciplinary unit placements b. No significant change in special incident reports | a. No significant difference in parole performance after 15 months b. No significant difference of amenables |

**Table 6-1.** (cont.)

| Researcher | Number of Youths | | Intervention | Results | Follow-up Results |
|---|---|---|---|---|---|
| | Experimental | Control | | | |
| Jurjevich (1968) | 14 | 14 | Individual psychotherapy | a. No significant change in behavior ratings of counselors<br>b. No significant change in behavior ratings of teachers | No significant difference in parole performance after 2 years |
| Thomas (1968) | 25 | 25 | a. Individual counseling<br>b. Goal setting<br>c. Goal achievement<br>d. Decisionmaking<br>e. Counselor feedback | a. Better grade point average<br>b. Better school attendance<br>c. Fewer suspensions from school<br>d. Fewer probation referrals<br>e. No significant difference in police contacts | No |
| Sowles and Gill (1970) | 20 | 20 | Individual counseling | a. No significant difference in escapes<br>b. No significant difference in disciplinary reports<br>c. No significant difference in duration of incarceration<br>d. Positive change in attitude test score | After 10 years follow-up<br>a. No significant difference in parole violations<br>b. No significant difference in recidivism |

1. *Talk with the youth.* This is where the counselor tries to understand the problem through the youth's own descriptions of his experiences.
2. *Set a behavioral goal.* This step occurs in the latter part of the counseling sessions. The counselor uses behavioral goals as a way to get the youth to try new solutions to his old problems.
3. *Practice new behavior in problem setting.* At this point the youth is able to try out the new behavior in the setting where his problem was identified. In this study, the setting was the classroom, where the youth's counselor was now his social studies teacher.
4. *Observe the results.* Because the counselor, now as the youth's teacher, is in

the classroom, he or she can observe the effects of the youth's attempts to try the new behavior.

5. *Evaluate and modify*. Now, back in the individual counseling session, the counselor and youth together can evaluate how well the new behavior works. They can discuss other ways to handle the same situation, and a new goal can be developed.

As can be seen, the Thomas program had considerably more steps than just talking with the youths.

An implication of this successful approach to the rehabilitation is that the counselor should be the person who can most directly observe the youths in the setting where their problems are occurring. If the problems are school problems, the counselor should be the teacher or teacher aide. In an institution, if the problems occur in the cottage or in the dorm, the counselor should be the houseparent. In those cases where the counselor can not be the staff supervisor, for example, at a place of employment, the counselor should observe the youths at least once between each counseling session. The preceding conclusions can be expanded to include any target population.

The other study obtaining positive results, Adams (1961*a*), found that youth specifically diagnosed as being amenable to counseling obtained positive benefits compared to their control group and compared to the nonamenable group. A possible conclusion is that individual counseling is beneficial for youths specifically disposed to such an approach. This finding lends support to the *principle of specificity* of treatment.

**General Prediction**: Rehabilitation programs that attempt to improve an individual's behavior will succeed if the following program elements are included:

1. Talk with and get input from the individual
2. Diagnose the problem and the problem setting
3. Set behavioral goal
4. Practice new behavior in the problem setting
5. Directly observe the results of the practice
6. Evaluate and modify the goal

**General Recommendation**: Staff members involved in the various phases of rehabilitation (teaching, recreation, vocational training, houseparenting, etc.) should provide the preceding program for each major problem that an individual has.

The preceding recommendation involves three organizational issues. First, only staff members who, in addition to being skilled in their specialty field, have the potential to implement the preceding behavior change program should be hired. Second, all staff members, including cooks, nurses, and maintenance and clerical staff, who would have occasion to help students or patients in a problem setting should be provided "counseling" training. They should be taught the specific skills identified above. The final issue is that the rehabilitation program schedule should be built with time for teachers, houseparents, etc. to work on the individual problems of their target population in the manner discussed above. For example, all teacher time is presently scheduled for group teaching or curriculum preparation. The revised schedule should allow time for the teacher to work with individual students. In this way, the problems that are causing a delinquent youth to fail in school—those which are independent of the subject matter—can be handled and hopefully resolved.

### References

Adams, S. Effectiveness of the Youth Authority Special Treatment Program: First interim report. Research Report No. 5. California Youth Authority, 1959.

Adams, S. Effectiveness of interview therapy with older youth authority wards: An interim evaluation of the PICO project. Research Report No. 20. California Youth Authority, 1961a.

Adams, S. Assessment of the psychiatric treatment program: Third interim report. Research Report No. 21. California Youth Authority, 1961b.

Guttman, E.S. Effects of short-term psychiatric treatment. Research Report No. 36. California Youth Authority, 1963.

Jurjevich, R.M. *No Water in My Cup: Experiences and a Controlled Study of Psychotherapy of Delinquent Girls.* New York: Libra, 1968.

Meese, B.G. An experimental program for juvenile delinquent boys. Unpublished Ph.D. dissertation. University of Maryland, 1961.

Rudolf, A. The effect of treatment on incarcerated young adult delinquents as measured by disciplinary history. Unpublished masters thesis. University of Southern California, 1960.

Sowles, R.C., and J.H. Gill. Institutional and community adjustment of delinquents following counseling. *Journal of Consulting and Clinical Psychology* 34 (1970):398-402.

Thomas, E.S. Effects of experimental school counseling of delinquency-prone adolescents. *Dissertation Abstracts* 28 (7-A), (1968):2572.

# 7

# Family Therapy

## Review of the Research

One of the most recently researched approaches to the rehabilitation of delinquent youths is family therapy. The dominant ingredient in the following programs was some type of involvement of the youth's family. The first program to be evaluated has been reported by Sacramento County (1973). The project was called the Sacramento 601 Diversion Project because of an emphasis on handling youths in need of supervision (truants and runaways) who fell under the legal provisions of Section 601 of the Welfare and Institutions Code. The project was designed to test whether the youths could be more effectively diverted by providing short-term family crisis counseling than by participation in traditional juvenile court intake procedures. There was a random assignment of 803 youths to the treatment group and 558 youths to the control group.

The treatment group participated in from one to five counseling sessions involving the youth and his or her family. As part of the program, the counselor dealt with the whole family at the point of arrest, the crisis. Specifically, the counselor attempted to help improve the communication processes used by the family to solve their problems.

The results of the project were favorable. There was a significant difference in the percentage of youths who went through family counseling and were diverted, 97 percent, compared with the control group, which diverted only 62.5 percent. A diverted youth did not have a petition filed against him, nor was he placed on informal probation. Members of the treatment group were placed in juvenile detention in significantly fewer instances than members of the control group. Manpower savings were calculated as a result of the project. It was found that there was a reduction in cost of seven-tenths of a position with the probation department. The beneficial results of this project can be attributed to the involvement of the youths' families at the crisis points and the subsequent attempts by the project staff to improve the communication patterns of the family.

Alexander and Parsons (1973) evaluated three different approaches to family treatment. The three approaches have been separated in table 7-1, even though they were a part of the same study and utilized the same 10 families as the control group. The families involved in the study were those of youths who had been referred to the Salt Lake City, Utah, probation department for such behavioral offenses as truancy and repeated running away from home. There was a random assignment of 86 families to the three treatment groups and the one control group. The age range of the 38 males and 48 female delinquents was from 13 to 16 years.

The first treatment intervention was a short-term behavior program. The purpose of the program was to improve the *communication patterns* of the delinquent youths and the members of their families.

In this process, therapists actively modeled, prompted, and reinforced in all family members: (a) clear communication of substance as well as feelings, and (b) clear presentation of "demands" and alternative solutions; all leading to (c) negotiation, with each family member receiving some privilege for each responsibility assumed, to the point of compromise (Alexander and Parsons, 1973, p. 220).

In addition to training the families in more satisfactory communication skills, the families were also taught the rudiments of contingency contracting. The therapists taught the families how to differentiate family rules from requests, and aided all family members in understanding the implications of each.

The second treatment program utilized a didactic group discussion of adolescent problems. The third treatment group received psychodynamic, insight-oriented family therapy. Throughout the duration of the study, the control group received no therapeutic attention or contact. The amount of time in treatment was six weeks for all groups. The second and third treatment approaches were originally provided as treatment control groups to counterbalance therapeutic attention.

The results were mixed for the communication skills program. The families in this group had higher favorable communication skills test scores than did the control group. They also had significantly less recidivism (better) for behavioral offenses (runaway, truance, etc.) than either the second or third treatment groups or the control group after 6 to 18 months of follow-up. There was no significant difference between the group discussions program and control group in recidivism (same). The psychodynamic, insight-oriented family program had significantly greater recidivism (worse) for behavioral offenses (73 percent) than the control group (50 percent). No significant difference was apparent between *any* of the treatment groups and the control groups in recidivism to the juvenile court for *criminal* offenses.

The results indicate that focusing upon family treatment per se does not facilitate improved family communication or improved behavior by the youths. Family treatment that *specifically* focuses upon improving the communication skills of the family members does result in improved communication and improved behavior. To test the importance of family communication skills as a causal factor in recidivism, all cases, regardless of treatment program, were

**Table 7-1**
**Family Therapy Summary**

| Researcher | Number of Youths | | Intervention | Results | Follow-up Results |
|---|---|---|---|---|---|
| | Experimental | Control | | | |
| Sacramento County (1973) | 803 | 558 | Family crisis counseling | a. Increased diversion<br>b. Decreased detention | |
| Alexander and Parsons (1973) | 46 | 10 | Family communication skills program | Improved communication as measured by posttest observation scores | a. Less recidivism for behavioral offenses<br>b. No significant difference in recidivism for criminal offenses |
| Alexander and Parsons (1973) | 19 | 10 | Family discussion group | | a. No significant difference in recidivism for behavioral offenses<br>b. No significant difference in recidivism for criminal offenses |
| Alexander and Parsons (1973) | 11 | 10 | Psychodynamic family therapy | | a. Greater recidivism for behavioral offenses<br>b. No significant difference in recidivism for criminal offenses |
| Parsons and Alexander (1973) | 20 | 20 | Family communication skills program | a. Improved communication as measured by observation<br>b. No significant change in paper-pencil measures of improved communication | No |
| San Diego County (1973) | NS | NS | a. Parent education<br>b. Focus on improving communication, discipline, and decision-making skills of parents<br>c. Lecture and group discussion | | a. No significant difference in re-arrest rate after 1 month<br>b. Significantly lower rearrest rate after 1 year |

**Table 7-1.** (cont.)

| Researcher | Number of Youths | | Intervention | Results | Follow-up Results |
|---|---|---|---|---|---|
| | Experimental | Control | | | |
| Stratton (1975) | 30 | 30 | a. Family crisis intervention counseling<br>b. Problem-solving approach | | After 6 months<br>a. Reduced re-arrests<br>b. Reduced use of probation services<br>c. Reduced days in detention<br>d. No significant difference in proportion of offenders detained |
| Miller (1962) | 205 | 112 | Family casework | | No significant difference in court appearances |
| Craig and Furst (1965) | 29 | 29 | a. Family counseling<br>b. Casework | | No significant difference in number and rate of delinquency referrals |
| Berleman, Seaberg, and Steinburn (1972) | 52 | 50 | a. Family counseling<br>b. Casework<br>c. Group counseling | | a. Greater school discipline problems<br>b. Increase police referral |
| Smith, Farrant, and Marchant (1972) | 54 | 74 | a. Family casework<br>b. Casework<br>c. Recreation | | a. No significant difference in reconviction rate<br>b. No significant difference in seriousness of offenses<br>c. Fewer court appearances |
| Wiltz (1970) | 6 | 6 | Training parents in behavior modification | No significant difference in observed deviant behavior | |

divided into success or recidivism groups. The communication observation scores were compared. As expected, the nonrecidivist families had better scores than the families of youths who recidivated. Because there was no significant difference in the rate of recidivism for criminal offenses, the conclusions on the benefits of family communication skills treatment are limited. It can only be concluded that family communication skills treatment can impact such behavioral offenses as truancy and running away.

Communication skills training was given further study by Parsons and Alexander (1973). They wanted to document that improved family communication was due to specific communication skills training. Forty male and female delinquents referred to the juvenile court for behavioral offenses were randomly assigned to one of four groups. There were two treatment groups, differing only in that one received pretesting and the other did not. There were two control groups. One was a treatment control, where the youth and their parents attended group discussions designed to control for experimenter attention. The two treatment groups participated in four weeks of two therapy sessions per week. The treatment consisted of discussion and practice on improving the family communication processes.

Following the four weeks of treatment, all four groups of families were posttested on their communication patterns. The results were positive on the four tests given to each group of families that assessed actual family interaction. The four tests measured the amount of verbal activity, the frequency of simultaneous speech, and the equal sharing of speech time. No significant difference was seen in two paper-and-pencil tests designed to measure mutual understanding of roles and behavioral expectations. There were no follow-up measures of impact upon subsequent delinquency. The conclusion is that focusing upon family communication patterns therapy can result in improved patterns of family interaction.

The next study to be reviewed involved a parent education project provided by the probation department of San Diego County (1973). Youths referred for truancy, running away, and/or incorrigible behavior were randomly assigned to a control group and a treatment group. The parents of the youths in the treatment group participated in a 10-week program of lectures and discussion groups. Each two-hour session involved an hour lecture on human growth and development followed by a one-hour discussion group.

The purpose of the parent education program was to improve the communication, discipline, and decision-making skills of parents. While the parents of the treatment group participated in this program, the youths and parents in the control group received no attention. After one month of follow-up, there was no significant difference in the rearrest rates of the two groups. However, after a year of follow-up, the treatment group rearrest rate had not changed, while the control group rate had increased significantly. Once again a program focusing on family communication skills achieved favorable results.

The final study to be discussed in this chapter was conducted by Stratton (1975), who evaluated the effectiveness of a family crisis intervention counseling program. The 30 youths randomly assigned to the program were chosen from those referred to the San Fernando, California, probation department for status or behavioral offenses. There was a random placement of 30 youths to a control group that received regular probation department services. The family crisis counseling was based upon the assumption that if the youths were separated from their families for treatment, that response would become the habitual response for future crises. A problem-solving approach that emphasized the following process was utilized:

a.   Intellectual understanding of the problem by the minor and the family
b.   Expression of feelings related to the arrest . . .
c.   Exploration of the coping mechanisms attempted before arrest by the minor and his family.
d.   Examination of why the coping mechanisms used before arrest were not working.
e.   Consideration of various alternatives . . . (Stratton, 1975, p. 10).

As can be seen, this process is somewhat systematic and involves the consideration of the emotional as well as intellectual aspects of the problem. The first family treatment session was provided within two hours of arrest. There was at least one follow-up session required. On the average, there were 2.5 sessions per family.

The results were generally favorable after six months of follow-up. The treatment group experienced significantly less rearrests, a reduced use of probation services, and a reduced number of days in detention than the control group. No significant difference was seen in the percentage of youths detained in the two groups. The unique aspects of the family counseling utilized were the immediate involvement of the family at arrest and the use of a systematic problem-solving approach. The assumption was that the use of a problem-solving approach with the family in a crisis situation would generalize and be used by the family in subsequent crises.

Before concluding this review of the literature on family counseling, five previously reviewed studies from earlier chapters must be mentioned. Four of the studies (Miller, 1962; Craig and Furst, 1965; Berleman, Seaberg, and Steinburn, 1972; and Smith, Farrant, and Marchant, 1972) involved family counseling or family casework. All four of the studies obtained negative results as far as the effectiveness of family counseling or family casework upon reducing subsequent delinquent behavior is concerned. The fifth study (Wiltz, 1970) involved training parents in behavior modification. The results of that study were also unfavorable in terms of reducing delinquent behavior. These last five studies were included because their findings constitute the groundwork for this chapter's conclusions.


## Conclusions

Over 2180 youths were involved in the 12 studies evaluated in this chapter. The general conclusion, which the last five studies and the Alexander and Parsons (1973) study support, is that family treatment does not reduce delinquent behavior. However, certain types of family treatment consistently achieved positive results. Specifically, when the family treatment focused upon improving the communication behavior toward a positive goal, significant decreases in delinquency occurred. In addition, crisis intervention counseling, especially when it was used to teach systematic problem solving, was successful. The San Diego County (1973) study, using parent education to focus on improving communication as well as discipline and decision-making skills of parents, achieved significantly reduced delinquency. To summarize these conclusions, the following points can be made:

1. Family counseling does not always work.
2. Teaching improved communication behavior does work.
3. Crisis intervention works when it is used to teach systematic problem solving.
4. Parent education works when it teaches parents disciplining and decision-making skills.

These conclusions lead to the following prediction and recommendation:

**Specific Prediction**: Family counseling will be effective when it focuses upon teaching parents communication, problem-solving, and disciplining skills.

**Specific Recommendation**: All treatment programs involving delinquent youths and their families should provide the family and the youth training in communication, problem-solving, and disciplining skills.

The specific recommendation includes delinquent youths who may be institutionalized but on their way back home. Family skills training may be all that is necessary to rehabilitate predelinquent and status offender youths, like those in the first seven studies. This conclusion can not be expanded for delinquents who have been involved in criminal behavior. There were no positive results for criminal offender delinquents who received family counseling.

Statements from other chapters have built a case for specificity of treatment. It appears that the majority of status offenders who are brought before the court for truancy, running away, and uncooperativeness with their parents need and will respond to treatment designed to improve family relationships. Running away and uncooperativeness with parents are clearly family problems. Truancy may be a family problem because the parents are not appropriately rewarding or punishing the youth for his or her school behavior. Truancy can also be a learning or school problem. Since family therapy significantly helped many of the status offenders, but not all, it was shown that for some youths, the family was not the problem.

The fact that the family may or may not be involved in the youth's delinquency leads to the following recommendation: In order to determine whether extended family treatment is needed, the family should be diagnosed in a live setting where their communication, discipline, and problem-solving behavior can be observed.

The conclusion cannot be made that the family is the root cause of all delinquency. Diagnosis is needed to discover the main problems of the youths, which may or may not involve the family. The need for adequate diagnosis leads to the following prediction.

**General Prediction**: Rehabilitation programs that do not attempt to objectively diagnose each delinquent youth's specific problems or skill deficiencies will fail.

In other words, shotgun approaches that attempt to provide one treatment for all the youths will not be as successful as those which try to individualize the programs. Individualization, in terms of going fast or slow, as is the case for slow learners, is not what is meant here. *Individualization* here means to diagnose and treat each youth for his specific and unique group of problems.

**General Recommendation**: At the beginning of a program for a given youth, he or she should be objectively diagnosed. Such diagnosis should take the form of ratings of the youth's live performance in various social, educational, and vocational settings.

Alexander and Parsons (1973) demonstrated that measured gains in certain skills correlated with improved functioning in the community. Therefore, such diagnostic tests can be used to decide when a youth can function in the community and does not need institutionalization for treatment. Through the findings in this chapter on the effectiveness and noneffectiveness of family counseling, we have been able to draw general conclusions on appropriate avenues for the successful rehabilitation of juvenile delinquents.

## References

Alexander, J.F., and B.V. Parsons. Short-term behavioral intervention with delinquent families: Impact on family process and recidivism. *Journal of Abnormal Psychology* 81 (1973):219-225.

Berleman, W.C., J.R. Seaberg, and T. Steinburn. Delinquency prevention experiment of the Seattle Atlantic Street Center—a final evaluation. *Social Service Review* 46 (1972):323-346.

Craig, M.M., and P.W. Furst. What happens after treatment? A study of potentially delinquent boys. *Social Service Review* 39 (1965):165-171.

Miller, W.B. The impact of a 'total community' delinquency control project. *Social Problems* 9 (1962):168-191.

Parsons, B.V., and J.F. Alexander. Short-term family intervention: A therapy outcome study. *Journal of Consulting and Clinical Psychology* 41 (1973):195-201.

Sacramento County. Preventing delinquency through diversion. In F. Berkowitz, *Evaluation of Crime Control Programs in California: A Review.* Sacramento: California Council on Criminal Justice, 1973.

San Diego County. Simplified analytical methods of behavioral systemization. In F. Berkowitz, *Evaluation of Crime Control Programs in California: A Review.* Sacramento: California Council on Criminal Justice, 1973.

Smith, C.L., M.R. Farrant, and H.J. Marchant. *Wincroft Youth Project: A Social Work Program in a Slum Area.* London: Barnes and Noble, 1972.

Stratton, J.G. Effects of crisis intervention counseling on predelinquent and misdemeanor juvenile offenders. *Juvenile Justice* 26 (1975):7-18.

Wiltz, N. Modification of behaviors of deviant boys through parent participation in a group technique. *Dissertation Abstracts International* 30 (1970): 4786-4787.

# 8

# Therapeutic Camping

## Introduction

One approach to the treatment of juvenile delinquents that has achieved considerable popularity is therapeutic camping. *Therapeutic camping*, or wilderness camping, attempts to change the delinquent youth's behavior by improving his self-concept through successful coping with the challenges of the wilderness.

Typically, the delinquent youth is placed in a group with 10 to 15 other delinquents of the same sex. The group has two or three adult leaders who live with the youths for the duration of the camping experience. In the shorter versions of therapeutic camping, the group goes camping in various wilderness areas for 4 to 10 weeks. In the 6- to 9-month approach, a base camp is established by the youths for the majority of the experience.

Both approaches emphasize using the group to help resolve problems. Group problem-solving sessions most typically occur when a youth or group of youths is creating a discipline problem. Such sessions occur immediately when the problem arises—before breakfast, while cooking lunch, during a hike, or when gathering wood. Anyone can call for a group session and all group members are expected to attend. The therapeutic aspect comes in as the entire group attempts to focus in on the particular youth's problem.

The positive aspect of the group sessions is that the leaders, who are familiar with the youth's prior delinquency history, try to tie his or her present problems in with the past problems. A negative aspect is that the youth participants in the group are given equal status with the adult leaders, while not having had similar training. In fact, there are no attempts to even teach the rudiments of problem-solving or peer helping skills to the group. As a result, the problem-solving sessions frequently break down into a kind of encounter group, with considerable frustration and shouting. Any resolution that occurs is that proposed by the leader in the end.

An aspect of therapeutic camping that has the most appeal is the survival mission or "solo." In this case, one of the youths is put in a challenging situation with nature in which he must succeed or be injured. Theoretically, it is the experience of conquering the formidable challenges that result in the development of a positive self-concept. In most programs, the youths are not trained for the survival confrontations. Collingwood (1975) has surmised that one value of such experiences is that the potential danger is so frightening that the adult leaders can for the first time get the attention of the youth. Obviously, in any rehabilitation approach, the most basic step is to get the client's attention.

## Review of the Research

The main study of therapeutic camping that will be reviewed is Kelly's (1974) report on Outward Bound. During the 10-year period from 1964 to 1974, approximately 1500 Massachusetts delinquent youths participated in the Outward Bound program. The research design involved an intensive evaluation of 120 of those youths.

The youths in the study were teenage boys 15½ to 17 years of age. The 120 boys were placed in two matched groups of 60 boys each. The matching criteria were: (1) IQ, (2) race, (3) religion, (4) offense, (5) area of residence, and (6) number of prior commitments. Youths who volunteered were selected only if they had no history of violence.

The boys assigned to the treatment group participated in the 26-day Outward Bound program and were then paroled. The control group attended the traditional training school program for 9 to 12 months and were then paroled. The treatment program was described as follows:

Outward Bound Schools expose the adolescent to severe physical challenge. The object is to build physical stamina and to push each individual to his physical limit. Thus the adolescent is called upon to achieve beyond what he believed he was capable; to demonstrate his competence in the most meaningful way—by action (Kelly and Baer, 1968, p. 5).

The program had three separate components, Colorado mountain climbing, Minnesota canoeing and camping, and Maine whaleboat cruising.

The youths in the two groups were followed-up for five years. *No* significant difference was seen in the recidivism rate of the two groups after five years. In an earlier study by Kelly and Baer (1971), a significant difference had been reported, after one-year follow-up. However, at an earlier point, 9 months, there was *no* significant difference. Therefore, at two out of three of the measuring points, there was no significant difference; and at the long-term point, 5 years, there was no difference. The results indicate that the camping program was not significantly better than the traditional Massachusetts training school program.

A study reported in chapter 4 involved the comparison of a forestry camp program against traditional training schools in California (Molof, 1967). The forestry camp program is similar to the camping approach in that it involves "physical activity, often under dangerous conditions," in an outdoor setting with boys working together in small groups. The results of Molof's study, which involved the random assignment of 469 boys, were negative. There was no significant difference in the recidivism rate of the camp group and the institution group after 15 months of follow-up.

## Conclusions

The two studies reviewed do not support the use of therapeutic or wilderness camping for the reduction of delinquent behavior. However, because of its popularity, the possible sources of effectiveness will be drawn out. The problem with the approach is that, as a whole, the negative aspects outweigh the positive at this time.

There may be benefits from camping for delinquent youths. However, some of the value is the same for a delinquent as it would be for anyone—a chance to get off alone, a recreation experience, a time to think, and a time to have fun. But what about the benefit of resolving the challenges in survival camping? The delinquent youths feel good about themselves in overcoming such challenges.

There is value for some delinquent youths in getting to the point of being willing to *hope* for success in their lives. Such youths are those who are so withdrawn or distracted that they cannot benefit from an institutional or community program. If therapeutic camping can engender such hope, then for those selected youths it has value. However, if therapeutic camping does give youths hope and memories of a good experience, but then simply packs them off for home, this approach has done considerably more harm than good. If the youths have not been given the comparable instruction in *home* survival skills, then they will again fail. This time, however, it will be more painful than before, because someone held out hope.

Whatever skills were taught the youths for survival in the deep woods, similar ones must be taught for success in the ghetto and the suburb. Whatever planning skills were taught for the building of a campfire, comparable skills must be taught for planning a career. Whatever social skills were taught for group survival, similar listening and responding skills must be taught for family relationships. Whatever physical fitness was achieved through hiking and swimming must be maintained for success in job and school.

Research in learning psychology (Goldstein, Heller, and Sechrest, 1966) clearly indicates that generalization of a skill increases the more the skill is practiced. Since this is true, camping is the most irrelevant setting possible for teaching delinquents classroom or job survival skills. As one delinquent boy put it when interviewed in the deep woods at his base camp, "This is fun, but I would rather be learning something that would help me get a job when I return to Houston." Therefore, from the review of the literature and the preceding discussion, the following prediction can be made.

**Specific Prediction**: If therapeutic camping is the primary treatment utilized to rehabilitate juvenile delinquents, it will fail.

As was discussed above, the camping approaches may have some initial benefits for certain delinquent youths. Recommendations will now be made regarding specific youths and required conditions regarding the use of camping for anything other than recreation.

**Specific Recommendations—The Youths:** A camping setting may be useful to help youths who think they cannot do anything right to get started in a success pattern. The advantage of camping is that it helps these kinds of youths get almost immediate closure on new and challenging tasks. These youths can be identified by their extremely low self-esteem.

**Specific Recommendations—The Program:** For the youths described above, the following program is recommended against those which have been tried and have failed.

After an objective form of youth selection has occurred, each youth should be diagnosed on a comprehensive set of camping and physical fitness skills. Counselors should be selected who not only perform at the highest level of the skills themselves but have the teaching skills to deliver to the youths. Systematic programs for each individual and the group should then be developed. Differential reinforcement should be provided at the beginning to encourage the youths' gains. Daily activities should be provided that moderately push the youths in their development.

If these program ingredients are provided, the results will be a good camping program. However, such a program, in itself, will not reduce delinquency. The next step would be a transition institution or community program where the youths could learn those specific skills needed to succeed back home. Such a program would focus on the youths' educational, vocational, and daily living skills, and as such would eliminate subsequent delinquency. The lack of such follow-up and transition programs is the main reason for the failure of camping projects to reduce delinquency.

Some of the proponents of the camping approach have little concern for the program, almost as if they thought there was something inherent in the woods that would rehabilitate the youths. Such an assumption is false. There is nothing inherent in any physical surroundings that will rehabilitate delinquent youths. The physical environment can at best only be a support to the programs and staff.

**General Prediction:** Those programs which primarily rely on physical surroundings to rehabilitate will fail.

**General Recommendation:** Considerably more attention and funds should be devoted to staff and programs than has been in the past.

This recommendation is consistent with the folk wisdom that a master teacher can teach anywhere—under a tree or in a one-room school. To further document the prediction, Part II of this book will document the impact of community-based programs in terms of the influence of their settings.

## References

Collingwood, T. Personal communication. Youth Services Project, Dallas Police Department. Dallas, Texas, 1975.

Goldstein, A.P., K. Heller, and L.B. Sechrest. *Psychotherapy and the Psychology of Behavior Change.* New York: Wiley, 1966.

Kelly, F.J. Outward bound and delinquency. Paper presented at Conference on Experiential Education. Estes Park, Colorado, 1974.

Kelly, F.J., and D.J. Baer. *Outward Bound Schools as an Alternative to Institutionalization for Adolescent Delinquent Boys.* Boston: Fandel Press, 1968.

Kelly, F.J., and D.J. Baer. Physical challenge as a treatment for delinquency. *Crime and Delinquency* 17 (1971): 437-445.

Molof, M.J. Forestry camp study: Comparison of recidivism rates of camp-eligible boys randomly assigned to camp and to institutional programs. Research Report No. 53. California Youth Authority, 1967.

# 9

# The Ideal Program

## Introduction

The following story is presented to summarize how components identified by research and through inference might logically fit together. The specific ingredients supported by research are listed in table 9-4. The summary of all the principles is presented in table 9-2.

From a distance, Cathy, just recently 16 years old, appears to be an old woman, moving in a slow, stiff manner. Faded blue jeans and an old white blouse usually cover her five-and-a-half-foot body. Her facial features are somewhat attractive under her short brown hair. Her attempt to appear cool and confident is betrayed by her brown eyes, which either stare dully off into space or dart nervously from object to object, refusing to concentrate on one thing. Her trouble began four years earlier.

Her parents first realized there was a problem when Cathy's junior high school principal told them she was skipping school. Cathy was placed on restriction for five weeks. All she could do was go to school; the rest of the time she had to stay home and do housework or babysit. For the first few weeks it looked as if everything was going better. However, Cathy would stay off by herself and not talk to her parents.

One Thursday afternoon, Cathy's father got a call at work to come to the police station right away. When he arrived, he saw Cathy crying and sitting next to a dirty looking older boy wearing a motorcycle jacket. The Sergeant motioned him to come in to his glass-walled office. A man who was introduced as the manager of an exclusive downtown hotel then proceeded to tell the story of how Cathy and the boy she was with had broken into one of the vacant hotel rooms on the top floor. Everyday since last Monday, instead of going to school, Cathy and the boy had come and stayed in the room for an all day orgy. When they were discovered, they were running around in the completely destroyed room. Furniture was broken and the carpet was ruined.

Cathy's father first sat on the edge of his chair, wide-eyed and with a tight jaw. As the story went on, he gradually slumped further down into his chair. When it was over, he hung limply on the seat staring off into space.

Cathy's parents were crushed. They were told by the juvenile authorities that Cathy would have to be placed outside of their home, somewhere that could provide better supervision. Cathy was placed in a series of residential programs. Each time she would stay for a couple of weeks, appearing on the surface to cooperate, and then run away. While on escape status she became involved in shoplifting, prostitution, and the use of a variety of illegal drugs. At one point, she was placed in a mental hospital, where she was labeled emotionally disturbed. About this time she began to become extremely moody, completely withdrawing from other people for hours. While at the mental hospital, she became close friends with a psychiatrist. She liked him and could always talk to him, but she later reported he never would give her any help aside from just listening. He always said she had to solve her problems for herself. After two months, Cathy was discharged from the hospital to her parents as "cured."

The first week home Cathy ran away. About six weeks later she was caught with a gang of boys who were trying to break into a TV store. This time when Cathy went before the juvenile judge, he felt he had no choice but to commit her to the state training school.

Cathy arrived at the training school somewhat afraid, but generally indifferent to what was happening to her. Because of her poor diet "on the streets," her skin was covered with blemishes and her hair was course and brittle. Most of the day she was either very tired and withdrawn or walking around talking nervously with staff and students.

Cathy, because she was somewhat attractive and smart, had been able to manipulate the staff in previous programs. However, in this program the staff very quickly got her attention by saying "No" to one of her demands. She then withdrew from students and staff and began planning an escape. She was immediately placed in the security cottage.

At first she angrily denied that she was going to run away, and then, with honest amazement, she asked how the staff knew her plans. They responded that they could tell she was upset and thought she was probably going to try to leave. The treatment staff visited her frequently during the four days she was in the security program. Cathy was bothered by the fact that though she was being somewhat punished and ill-treated, she was still being visited by the staff, as if they really cared. She was confused, but this only served to get her attention further. Never before had she met staff who were strict, yet seemed to understand her when she talked to them.

The staff who worked with Cathy, from houseparents and cooks, to the superintendent, had been trained extensively in *responding skills*. They were basically good and decent people who liked young people, but who, before training, were unable to effectively intervene with many of the students committed to the school. After empathy skills training, they not only knew how to listen, but they *heard* what the youths were saying. Though staff members did not always agree with what the youth said, they could respond in a way that told the youths that, at least, their feelings were being understood.

It was during Cathy's first two weeks at the training school that her cottage counselor began getting input from her on how she saw her problems. In individual counseling sessions, using the empathy skills, the counselor began to get a picture of how Cathy saw her world. At first, Cathy began by blaming the judge and her parents for her commitment. For her part, she was surprised to notice that she gradually began freely confessing things that she had never told any adult. She revealed that the treatment staff in the other programs had all basically laid the blame for her behavior on her parents. Cathy broke down crying, saying that she loved her parents, but that they just did not understand her. She said that blaming her parents always made her mad, because the trouble she got into was her fault, not her parents. She stated that her biggest problem was "doing dope." Everytime she started feeling down, her feelings and thoughts hurt so bad she had to escape.

The counselor responded to all of Cathy's feelings—that she did feel all alone and afraid when other people hurt her by the things they said. The counselor told her that the program she was now in had helped other girls with similar problems, but before Cathy could start her individualized program, she needed to take some tests. The tests were not tests that were passed or failed, but ones that could objectively diagnose where Cathy was in relation to the skills she needed to succeed back home. Table 9-1 presents Cathy's test profile. As can be observed, Cathy was above average in intelligence but below minimally effective in all other areas.

With the test results in hand, the counselor sat down with Cathy and together they set *behavioral goals* for what skill levels could be expected of her before she would be allowed her first visit home. A goal of achieving at least minimal effectiveness in all eight areas was agreed upon. In the social skills area—below minimally effective meant that Cathy could not even restate what

**Table 9-1**
**Cathy's Test Profile**

| | | | Level | | |
|---|---|---|---|---|---|
| *Test* | *Very Ineffective* | *Ineffective* | *Minimally Effective* | *Effective* | *Superior* |
| Physicial fitness | x | | | | |
| Social skills | x | | | | |
| Problem solving | x | | | | |
| Educational achievement | | x | | | |
| Study skills | x | | | | |
| Intelligence | | | | x | |
| Career decision-making skills | x | | | | |
| Career advancement skills | x | | | | |

another person said to her in the pretest role-playing situation—she would have to be able to empathetically respond to another person. In addition to the general skill deficiencies, Cathy's specific problems were diagnosed. Her uniquely low tolerance for emotional pain and her lack of career goals were the major problems. A program of individual and group work was developed for Cathy based upon her specific problems and her general skill deficiencies.

Most of Cathy's program emphasized the learning of new behaviors and skills. Fortunately, all the staff, including the cooks and other ancillary staff, had been taught a set of *teaching* skills whose effectiveness had been documented in other programs for delinquent youths. The skills emphasized the following techniques and content, as well as empathetic responding:

1. Individualized diagnosis
2. Specific learning goals
3. Individualized programs based upon personally relevant material
4. Basic academic skills
5. Multisensory teaching
6. Sequential presentations—breaking complex skills into simple steps
7. Initially rewarding of attention and persistence
8. Differential reinforcement of learning performance

The other critical element in the skills program was practice. If you went around the training school campus at any time, you would see youths in groups or alone practicing new skills. The entire campus was a teaching center, and the entire thrust of the staff-student interactions was teaching. Cathy's houseparent used cottage clean-up time to teach her how to efficiently and simply clean her room and make her bed. The cook taught Cathy basic nutrition and how to properly prepare foods. The Principal's secretary taught Cathy how to answer the telephone in a business-like manner. Cathy's entire day was spent learning new skills.

In the educational program Cathy was taught study skills that could help her improve her academic functioning. Although she was intelligent and a good reader, Cathy had always failed any test she took in school. The study skills emphasized how to find out from the teacher what the test would cover and how to study for it. After six weeks in the program, Cathy was improving in all areas except the educational program, even after learning the study skills. The teachers reported that she was just not trying.

It was at this point that the counselor took Cathy aside for a progress review. Cathy admitted that she liked the daily living skills and the social skills. She reported she didn't even mind the physical fitness program, with the daily run around the campus and all the sit-ups. In fact, she found that the physical exercise was helping her sleep better and she wasn't as nervous as before. But she just did not like school—it was stupid and a waste of time!

After the conference, Cathy's counselor went to talk to the school principal. Together they agreed it was time to put Cathy in a career skills program. When the counselor told Cathy, she really seemed pleased. She asked which vocational class she was going to be in—was it hospital aide training? The counselor shook his head and explained that career skills were those broad skills of decision making and career advancement that would help Cathy in any job—that it was not specific vocational training, like learning how to be a secretary.

Cathy went to the career skills class in the afternoon and her other classes in the morning. She began by learning about career decision making. At first, she resisted the systematic and detailed process of making a good career decision, because she said she already knew what she wanted to do. She wanted to be a hospital aide. Her teacher, instead of fighting the idea, said fine and gave her the assignment of answering a list of questions about the job. Two of the questions asked were, what did hospital aides do and how much money did they make? Cathy was not sure; but she answered the questions anyway and turned them into the teacher. Without even looking at her answers, the teacher showed her some books that would help her check her answers.

After finding the answers, Cathy was shocked! Not only did the job involve more cleaning than nursing, but the pay was half what she thought it was. The job wasn't at all what she had expected. When the bell rang, Cathy left the classroom without saying anything to the teacher. The next day, however, at the beginning of class, she sheepishly went up to his desk and asked to be placed back in the career decision-making skills group.

After several weeks, Cathy's teachers reported improvement in her school performance. Cathy's counselor went to the career skills teacher to find out what had happened. The teacher revealed that after going through the career decision-making steps, Cathy found out that what she really wanted to be was a nurse. She also learned that to get into nursing school, she had to have a high school diploma and know something about math and science. This was what made her start working harder in school.

Throughout Cathy's program, she had received special rewards for improved performance in the different skills areas. When her academic performance improved, she moved to a higher group in her cottage. She was allowed more freedom and privileges. Placement in this group was contingent upon maintaining a weekly performance of gains in all areas of her program. Some group rewards were planned, like special outings; other rewards were developed especially for Cathy.

At the three-month progress review, the most recent scores of Cathy's performance were reviewed. In all areas the scores were at the minimally effective level or higher. It was decided that Cathy could participate in her first visit home, to allow her the opportunity to *practice* the skills she had learned back in some of her problem settings. The home visit was not the first time Cathy would be with her folks since being placed at the school. Her whole family, including her brother and sisters, had regularly visited since her arrival, and had participated in several sessions of family communication skills training.

When Cathy got home, she noticed that not only had she changed, but her family was different. At meal time, instead of everyone eating on their own or in front of the TV set, the family sat around the table and talked. And boy, did everyone talk! The discussion was lively and the interruptions were numerous, but Cathy's father made sure that everyone got equal time. Not only was the meal time used to discuss the day's events, but the family used the time to plan their weekend recreation and work schedule. During the weekend, everything did not come off exactly as planned, but the family did spend more time together than they ever had before.

Cathy returned to the training school after the weekend very enthused about returning home. The counselor decided it was time to try Cathy out in her other problem setting, public school. Arrangements were made with the local public school in the town near the training school for Cathy to attend regular high school classes. Cathy was very nervous. The first day went well, but the second day some of the other students teased her about being from the "prison." She ran out of the school. But this time, instead of running away, she called her counselor to come and help her. At first she was furious! She refused to consider ever going back to that "dumb old school." After a while, she broke down and cried, really hurt because the other students did not like her.

Cathy had always wanted to have friends who were "straight," but she never knew how to talk to them. Through the social skills training she learned that the first step was to smile and say "Hi." Cathy agreed to return to the school and practice some of the social skills she had learned. Over time, Cathy started making friends at school; and at the first grading period, she passed all of her subjects. She was really pleased with herself.

It was now time for Cathy to leave the training school, but her program was not over. Through a parole program, she received follow-up skill training and practice for a year. However, Cathy got most of her help from her family. Though there were still disagreements and fighting, her parents, to Cathy, seemed to be able to listen better when she went to them with problems. They did not always have the answers, but they showed their care and understanding. The skills training for her family had made them more effective counselors, and with their help, Cathy made it.

## Discussion and Summary

The story of Cathy was developed to exemplify all the approaches in the preceding chapters that succeeded in rehabilitating delinquent youths or had emerged as general propositions. The program described in the story was in an institutional setting, but all the effective components can easily occur in any community program. This program is, indeed, independent of setting or context. The effective program ingredients will be just as beneficial in any setting. Table 9-2 summarizes the basic principles for the rehabilitation of juvenile delinquents that can be concluded from the results of the preceding eight chapters.

The rehabilitation of juvenile delinquents should focus upon teaching them skills that have been documented as improving their subsequent community behavior. These skills are listed in table 9-2: communication skills; daily living and survival skills; educational advancement and study skills to obtain a diploma or certificate that supports career goals; and career skills, such as career decision making and career advancement. These skills represent general areas of rehabilitation content that can help all youths.

**Table 9-2**
**Principles of Rehabilitation**

1. Get the youths' attention

2. Obtain input using staff who have empathy

3. Objectively diagnose

4. Set behavioral goal

5. Teach youths new behaviors using effective teaching methods

    *a.* Individualized diagnosis

    *b.* Specific learning goal

    *c.* Individualized program based upon personally relevant material

    *d.* Teach basic academic skills

    *e.* Multisensory techniques

    *f.* Sequential presentation, breaking complex skills into simple steps

    *g.* Initially rewarding youths' attention and persistence

    *h.* Differential reinforcement of learning performance

6. Teach skills in the following areas

    *a.* Communication skills

    *b.* Daily living and survival skills

    *c.* Educational advancement and study skills that result in a diploma or certificate that supports career goals

    *d.* Career skills, such as career decision making and career advancement

7. Practice skills in problem settings

8. Differentially reinforce

9. Family training in communication, problem-solving, and disciplining skills

10. Follow-up skill training and reinforcement

However, throughout this book, the importance of the *principle of specificity* in rehabilitation has been documented. As such, the principle suggests that there are certain unique problems of every delinquent youth that contribute to his or her antisocial behavior. It is the task of the rehabilitation workers to get input, to diagnose, and to set concrete goals with regard to the specific problems. Such problems may involve conflicts or deficits in medical, dental, nutritional, physical, social, sexual, family, educational, vocational, or religious-philosophical areas. By talking to the youths and their families, by studying the youths' past histories, and through objective diagnoses, the *specific problems* can be identified.

The preferred method of rehabilitation is teaching the youths skills. Carkhuff and Berensen (1976) have identified the content area that is involved in effectively teaching a skill. That content includes teaching a person the facts and concepts concerning the skill and its substeps as well as teaching the principles of why a skill works and how it is useful. The skill itself is taught through modeling, didactic presentation, and practice. Finally, Carkhuff and Berenson emphasize that you need to give the person the check steps they can use to tell for themselves whether they are doing the skill correctly.

The teaching model of Carkhuff and Berenson has been developed for all youth and adult populations. However, it does have immediate applicability for delinquent youths. Teaching the youths why they need the different skills they lack is one relevant method of teaching them about ethics and lawful behavior. In any event, whether it is for general skill deficiencies or for the specific problems of the youths, the principles of rehabilitation are relevant.

Figure 9-1 diagrams the model of delinquency rehabilitation developed in the preceding pages. Each of the main methods will now be discussed. The first step—getting the youth's *attention*—is sometimes achieved through arrest, judicial proceedings, or incarceration. With other youths, empathetic responses by caring staff opens them up to help. Sometimes the anger, fear, or concern of a youth's family facilitates the youth's focus on his or her problems.

The next step—getting *input*—includes talking to the youths and their families. It has been emphasized that to obtain relevant and factual input, it is necessary to use staff who have been trained in empathetic responding. *Diagnosis* includes testing the youths with objective measures on all the general and specific problem areas. *Measurable goals* are then formulated to state the *needs* of the youths in clear and behaviorally observable manners. As with all these steps, *skill teaching* can occur in an institutional or community program, whichever placement has been determined as the most appropriate for the individual youths. Skill teaching utilizes the methods and content listed in table 9-1, for both specific and general problems.

*Practice in the problem setting* occurs after the youths have learned and practiced their skills in a safe and neutral environment. The problem setting could be the home, school, job, or recreation hangout. Throughout the program,

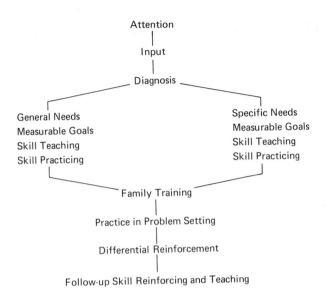

**Figure 9-1.** Model of Delinquency Rehabilitation

as the youths improve, they should receive *differential reinforcement.* Rewards contingent upon improved behavior have been found to help increase the frequency of the behavior, as long as the youths sufficiently know the behavior or skill to begin with. In this way, behavior modification's primary strength becomes a support to an eclectic model of rehabilitation.

*Training the family* can begin when the treatment is initiated. However, the family must have the improved communication, problem-solving, and disciplining skills before the youths, who have been placed out of the home, return. As with the youths, the program for the family includes getting their attention, obtaining input, and diagnosing, teaching the skills, providing differential reinforcement, and maintaining a follow-up. *Follow-up* help should be provided regardless of whether the youths have gone through the program while still living at home or have gone through it out of the home. For follow-up to be effective, the rehabilitation worker must observe the youths in their problem settings. This means eating with the families, visiting the classrooms, and observing the on-the-job interactions. The main task of the follow-up worker is to ensure that the youths can and do effectively apply the skills they learned in the rehabilitation program.

Before concluding this summary of the preceding eight chapters, the following two tables are presented. Table 9-3 is a summary of the rehabilitation methods reviewd in Part I that *failed.* The negative results notwithstanding, this

**Table 9-3**

**Summary of Approaches that Consistently Failed to Rehabilitate**

1. Casework

2. Direct services

3. Diagnosis and recommendations only

4. Diagnosis and referral only

5. Use of behavior modification for performance of complex behaviors (improving grades, reducing delinquent behavior)

6. Understanding teachers and discussion groups only

7. Manipulation of teacher expectancies

8. Affective educational approaches (Glasser-type discussion groups)

9. School attendance alone

10. Job placement

11. Vocational training

12. Occupational orientation

13. Field trips

14. Work programs

15. Group counseling

16. Individual psychotherapy

17. Family therapy

18. Therapeutic camping

book presented ways of upgrading these interventions. For example, a casework approach that is specific and utilizes teaching and behavior modification methods can be successful. Table 9-4 is a summary of those approaches which made statistically significant differences in the improvement of behavior. Table 9-4 was used to develop the rehabilitation model presented in figure 9-1. The model was developed in the following manner: a chapter-by-chapter review of what was effective; summaries of what succeeded and what failed; identification and organization of rehabilitation principles; and, finally, development of the delinquency rehabilitation model. The prediction is that if the model of rehabilitation is applied, there will be an increase in the favorable results of treatment programs for juvenile delinquents.

## A Personal Challenge to the Reader

To better understand and appreciate the preceding rehabilitation principles, it is time for the reader to act. The assignment can be as complex or as simple as

**Table 9-4**

**Summary of Approaches that Consistency Achieved Favorable Rehabilitation Results**

1. Behavior modification for simple behaviors
2. Contingency contracting involving the youths in setting their goals
3. Differential reinforcement
4. Specificity for rehabilitation goals
5. Education when it utilized
   a. Individualized diagnosis
   b. Specific learning goal
   c. Individualized program based upon relevant material
   d. Basic academic skills
   e. Multisensory teaching
   f. Sequential presentation, breaking complex skills into simpler ones
   g. Rewarding attention and persistence initially
   h. Differential reinforcement of learning performance
6. Job training with support educational training (G.E.D.)
7. Training in job advancement skills
8. Training in systematic career decision-making skills
9. Educational programs that culminate in a diploma or G.E.D.
10. Follow-up help after job placement
11. Group therapy with a teaching focus
12. Individual counseling that included the following ingredients:
    a. Counseling to get input from youths on problems
    b. Diagnose the problem and the problem setting
    c. Set behavioral goal
    d. Practice new behavior in the problem setting
    e. The staff member who provided the counseling directly observing the youths in the problem setting
    f. Evaluate and modify goals in subsequent counseling sessions
13. Family treatment that focused on improving the communication skills of the family
14. Parent training in problem-solving and disciplining skills

you desire. The one requirement is to spend time with a youth who is having trouble either with the law, with school, or in getting along with other people. The simplest task would be to try to teach a skill to the youth that he or she needs or wants to learn. Try to utilize as many of the previously enumerated steps as you can. However, rather than holding back until you are completely sure of all the steps, go ahead and try out what you understand, even if it only involves one or two steps.

To find a youth who needs help, contact any of the following organizations: Big Brother, Big Sister, YMCA or YWCA, the local juvenile probation department, the public school counselors, or any residential program that provides help to juvenile delinquents. All the preceding organizations rely on and utilize volunteer help and will provide some level of supervision to prevent any major difficulties. No matter how extensive a program you implement, the one requirements is to check back with the youth six months after your last contact. In this way, you can develop a method of evaluating your previous efforts. You know you have been effective if the youth is performing better in the area of his or her life that you focused upon, and you can be proud of yourself for the hard work it took and the fact that you did it.

Part II of this book will discuss the different levels of intervention offered by the juvenile justice system in its attempt to rehabilitate juvenile delinquents.

## Reference

Carkhuff, R.R., and B.G. Berenson. *Teaching as Treatment*. Amherst, Mass.: Human Resource Development Press, 1976.

**Part II:
System Interventions
as Treatment**

# 10 Diversion from the Juvenile Justice System

## Review of the Research

One of the first sets of system interventions to treat and reduce juvenile delinquency is *diversion*. The hope is that if the youths are treated at their earliest intrusion into the juvenile justice system, further involvement can be prevented. Juvenile diversion is not a new idea. The child guidance center movement in the 1930s was conceived as a way to divert youths from the correctional system. Many of the programs discussed in chapter 1 were developed as diversion projects, and, as we know, they failed.

A different approach was developed by Shulman (1945). Rather than utilizing counseling or casework, he developed what he termed a *controlled activity group*. The evaluation compared 50 problem boys matched into two equal-sized groups. The boys were 10 to 14 years of age.

The Group Guidance experiment conducted a new form of social group, the controlled activity group, set up within the structure of voluntary community recreation for normal children. Within the controlled activity group, problem and normal children mingled naturally in recreational activities (Shulman, 1945, p. 407).

The program met six hours a week over one school semester, and included games and classes in creative art, woodwork, metal, and leatherwork.

The regular school classroom behavior was measured using the Haggerty-Wickman-Olson behavior rating scales before and after treatment. No significant difference was seen in the behavior change between the treatment and control groups. Neither the activity group nor the positive association with normal teenagers made a significant difference in school classroom behavior. The negative results are unfortunately predictable because of the lack of logical relationship between the treatment—recreation and handicraft group—and the outcome—school classroom behavior.

Ahlstrom and Havighurst (1971) attempted a special school and work program for predelinquent boys. The 13- and 14-year-old boys were diagnosed as being both socially and educationally maladjusted. The boys were divided into a control group and a treatment group, with 200 youths each. The groups were comparable in that each boy met the criteria of average or below average intelligence, above average aggressive maladjustment scores, and below average classroom achievement.

117

The treatment consisted of the following special work and school program:

Experimental boys, beginning in the eighth grade received special attention through half days of classroom work geared to their abilities and their assumed needs, interests, and personal orientations and half days of supervised work experience; these boys had their own teachers and work supervisors (Ahlstrom and Havighurst, 1971, p. 5).

The work program focused upon "improving work habits and attitudes" through supervised work. The results were negative both for the school program and the work program. There was no significant difference between the treatment and control group in school adjustment. The authors reported that only one-fourth of the boys benefited from the work experience, and it was, therefore, declared a failure. Such a result is consistent with the findings reported in chapter 4, which concluded that there is nothing inherent in work that will rehabilitate delinquent youths.

The next two studies were implemented by the Sacramento Police Department (1972). The first study examined the effectiveness of having specially selected and trained police officers provide individual counseling for first offenders. There was a random assignment of 87 youths to the experimental group and 105 youths to the control group. The two groups included girls as well as boys. The treatment involved intensive counseling with the youths and their families.

Treatment was only initiated with those families who appeared to be cooperative. However, all the families were overwhelmingly favorable to participation, and no family asked to discontinue in the project. This favorable response by the families can possibly be attributed to the fact that they were asked to participate by police officers at a crisis point near the time of their child's arrest.

The results of the program were negative after approximately 8 months follow-up. There was no significant difference between the treatment group and the control group in their recidivism or rearrest. The unfavorable results are consistent with the demonstrated ineffectiveness of individual counseling already reported.

The second study (Sacramento Police Department, 1972) was similar, but this time involved previously identified predelinquent youths. The method used to diagnose the delinquent tendencies was to ask classroom teachers to rate habitual truants who were in their classes. Those youths scoring in the highest range of the scale were divided into two matched groups of 62 youths each. One group was selected at random to be the treatment group.

The treatment utilized was for a specially trained police officer to provide individual counseling to the identified youths at their school. The main counseling approach utilized was Reality Therapy. The results after three months of operation were unfavorable. No significant difference existed between the treatment group and the control group in rearrests. This study also received strong resistance from the school counselors and had to be delayed for four months. In any event, the results of individual counseling were again disappointing.

Pacoima Memorial Lutheran Hospital (1973) was responsible for a multiservice counseling and diversion project. One phase of the program involved a random assignment of 24 youths to one of the four following treatment groups.

1. Pickup and structured counseling
2. Pickup and unstructured counseling
3. No pickup and structured counseling
4. No pickup and unstructured counseling

The definition of structure and pickup were provided as follows:

(a) pick up youngsters at police station at time of referral
(b) do not pick up the youngster and leave the task of making contact to the juvenile and his family
(c) unstructured counseling (i.e., being available 24 hours a day, 7 days a week for *any* kind of counseling)
(d) structured counseling—only being available for counseling during office hours and specified appointment times (Pacoima Memorial Hospital, 1973, p. 41).

The results of the research were negative, since there was no significant difference between any of the four groups after 12 months follow-up. Neither picking the youth up immediately nor the fact that the counselor utilized an unstructured format made a significant difference.

Five delinquency diversion projects were evaluated in California, but only one of the programs met the research criteria by having a randomly selected control group (California, 1974). This project, the Alameda Delinquency Prevention Program, utilized 33 youths in the treatment group and 23 in the control group. The youths in both groups were male and female teenagers referred to the project because of an imminent possibility of their being turned over to the juvenile court.

The youths in the treatment group received intensive family counseling and casework once a week for approximately one year. The program emphasized direct casework with the family as a whole. The workers met with the families in their own homes at night and at other times that were conducive to the family's schedule. The project was concerned with not only the referred predelinquent youths, but with their entire families.

The results were disastrous. The youths in the treatment group did worse on almost every criteria. After 12 months of follow-up, the rearrest rate for the treated group was 22 percent higher. In terms of the number of youths arrested three or more times, the rate was almost double for the treatment group. This counseling and casework approach did more harm than doing nothing. It may be remembered from chapter 1 that a similar "intensive" program had the same unfavorable effect.

A project in Portland, Maine, was evaluated by Liedtke, Malbin, and Mech (1974). The youths participating in the project were boys and girls between 10 and 18 years of age. There were 57 youths randomly assigned to the treatment group and 40 youths randomly assigned to the control group. The youths were referred from the juvenile court to the youth diversion project. After 3 months follow-up, there was no significant difference between the two groups in their recidivism back to court. These findings make the seventh study in a row of diversion projects that achieved unfavorable results.

Unfortunately, the final project, this time conducted by the Seattle Police Department (1975), also obtained negative results. Two groups of 76 teenage boys and girls each participated in the study. The youths in the treatment group and their parents received interview and referral services from project social workers. Primary referral was to mental health agencies. After 12 months follow-up, no significant difference was seen in new offenses or in the seriousness of the new offenses for the two groups. The authors concluded that their approach was ineffective for the reduction of delinquency.

## Conclusions

Before making any conclusions about the eight studies reviewed in this chapter, additional information will be presented. Collingwood and Wilson (1976) surveyed 107 community diversion projects across the United States that were designed to divert juvenile delinquents out of the juvenile justice system. The results of the projects varied from positive to no significance to detrimental in terms of recidivism. However, most of the reported results were subjective impressions.

Because such a large majority of the projects were not systematically evaluated, the question arose, how can some kind of prediction be made about the effectiveness of the projects in the absence of controlled experiments? The answer was to look at the main service activity and review results on the effectiveness of that service activity. Table 10-1 presents the results of the survey in this area.

As can be observed, individual counseling was the dominant rehabilitation activity. It may be remembered from chapter 6 that this approach with delinquent youths is totally ineffective. The implication for those diversion projects in the United States which are relying on individual counseling is that *they will fail.* The second main approach reported was referral. From the studies reviewed in this chapter and in chapter 1, the prediction for projects using referral is that *they too will fail.*

**Table 10-1**
**Summary of Treatment Activities Provided by Diversion Projects**

| Type of Project | Number of Projects | Primary Main Service Reported | Primary Secondary Service Reported |
|---|---|---|---|
| Police diversion | 42 | Individual counseling | Referral |
| Police juvenile unit officer | 24 | Individual counseling | Referral |
| Community youth service bureau | 14 | Individual counseling | Parent counseling |
| Police school | 12 | Individual counseling | Referral |
| Probation diversion | 7 | Individual counseling | Referral |
| Police athletic league | 6 | Recreation | Individual counseling |
| Other police | 2 | Recreation | Lectures |
| Total | 107 | | |

Adapted from Collingwood and Wilson (1976).

This chapter reviewed eight studies of juvenile diversion projects involving 1095 youth. The results were uniformly negative. However, the results are predictable when one examines the primary treatment activities utilized: individual counseling, casework, and work experience. Should diversion be eliminated as a system intervention for delinquent youths? No, but it should have program standards that link it to the theory of specificity and to approaches that have achieved favorable effects.

**Specific Prediction:** Diversion projects will fail if they rely on counseling, casework, referral, or work experience to rehabilitate the youths.

**Specific Recommendation:** Diversion projects should be developed around teaching delivery strategies that will give the youths the skills they need to succeed in school, work, and home. Such approaches have a greater likelihood of success than what has been continually tried in the past.

Before leaving the diversion projects, a comment must be made concerning the reported cooperation obtained by the Sacramento Police Department (1972) utilizing a close identification with the local police department. Some would argue against a diversion project being placed in a police department or sheriff's office for various reasons. However, such an identification may be necessary to get the attention of the youths and their families as to the serious consequences of their behavior. Keve, Buchwalter, and Kirkpatrick (1973) reviewed a variety of diversion and Youth Service Bureau programs in Illinois. They concluded that there should be a more frequent use of the police department as a setting for such programs because of the potential for a more efficient referral and follow-up system, and because in their role as "peace officers" police are already engaged in considerable amounts of crisis intervention counseling. It must be reiterated, because of the negative results reviewed in this chapter, that there is nothing inherent in placing a diversion project in a law enforcement setting that will rehabilitate. The police setting might only facilitate the attainment of an effectively developed program.

The inferences that will be made in this chapter deal with the fact that even though it has been documented through previous studies that casework and individual counseling are ineffective with delinquent youths, recent diversion projects have been developed around those approaches. The hope was that even though they did not work with adjudicated delinquents, they might work with so-called predelinquents. However, this did not prove to be the case. Therefore, the following conclusions are warranted.

**General Prediction**: If a treatment approach has failed with delinquent youths in one segment of the juvenile justice system, it will probably fail in all other segments. If a treatment approach has succeeded in one part of the juvenile justice system, it will probably succeed in other segments.

**General Recommendation**: Treatment approaches that have succeeded with delinquent youths in one setting should be tried in other settings.

The above conclusions support the use of rehabilitation principles in a variety of settings, even though they may have been derived from one setting.

What should be utilized to obtain more successful results in diversion projects? It may be remembered from chapter 7 that many of the programs obtaining positive results were conducted as part of a diversion program. The specific ingredients contributing to the reduction of delinquent behavior were training programs that taught the family communication, problem-solving, and disciplining skills. Those programs would hold out considerable more hope for success than those approaches intensely reviewed in this chapter.

A diversion program that has achieved very favorable results, but that unfortunately did not involve a matched or randomly assigned control group, was recently reported by Collingwood, Williams, and Douds (1976). The project was part of the Dallas Police Department and dealt with youths referred for a variety of offenses who voluntarily participated. The main program ingredient was training the youths in interpersonal skills, problem-solving skills, and learning skills. There was also some work with the family and a school sign-in program. The youth workers were trained in empathetic counseling and systematic program development consistent with Carkhuff's Human Resource Development model (Carkhuff and Berenson, 1976).

Youth completing the program had only a 9.6 percent recidivism rate after 6 to 18 months follow-up. This was compared against comparable baseline recidivism rates of 45 to 50 percent. The reason for the positive results is that many of the favorable program ingredients emphasized in the previous chapters were combined in this one program. The success of this project and the programs reported in chapter 7 indicate under what qualitative conditions diversion will be effective. The quality factor is ensured when program ingredients that have obtained positive results in diversion as well as other settings are used. Table 10-2 presents this chapter's summary.

## References

Ahlstrom, W., and R. Havighurst. *Four Hundred Losers: Delinquent Boys in High School.* San Francisco: Jossey-Bass, 1971.

California Office of Criminal Justice Planning. *Cluster Evaluation of Five Diversion Projects: Final Report.* Sacramento, California: California Taxpayers' Association, 1974.

Carkhuff, R.R., and B.G. Berenson. *Teaching as Treatment.* Amherst, Mass.: Human Resource Development Press, 1976.

Collingwood, T.R., H. Williams, and A. Douds. An HRO approach to police diversion for juvenile offenders, *Personnel and Guidance Journal* (1976):435-437.

Collingwood, T. and R.D. Wilson. *National Survey of Diversion Projects.* Dallas Police Department. Dallas, Texas, 1976.

Keve, P.W., O.R. Buchwalter, and R.E. Kirkpatrick. *Report of Evaluation of Youth Service Bureaus.* American Technical Assistance Corporation, Washington, D.C., April 1973.

Liedtke, D., N. Malbin, and E.V. Mech. *Portland Youth Diversion Project*, Portland, Maine: Office of Youth Diversion Services, 1974.

Pacoima Memorial Lutheran Hospital. Multi-service approach to juvenile delinquency prevention. In F. Berkowitz, *Evaluation of Crime Control Programs in California: A Review.* Sacramento: California Council on Criminal Justice, 1973.

Sacramento Police Department. *The Delinquency Prevention Unit Project: Evaluation Report.* Sacramento: Sacramento Police Department, Youth Services Division, 1972.

Seattle Police Department. *Social Agency Referral: Project Evaluation.* Seattle, Wash.: Seattle Police Department, 1975.

Shulman, H.M. Delinquency treatment in the controlled activity group. *American Sociological Review* 10 (1945):405-414.

**Table 10-2**
**Juvenile Diversion Summary**

| Researcher | Number of Youths | | Intervention | Results | Follow-Up Results |
|---|---|---|---|---|---|
| | Experimental | Control | | | |
| Shulman (1945) | 25 | 25 | Controlled activity group | No significant difference in improved classroom behavior | |
| Ahlstrom and Havighurst (1971) | 200 | 200 | a. Special academic program b. Work experience program | No significant difference in school adjustment | |
| Sacramento Police Department (1972) | 87 | 105 | a. Individual counseling by specially trained police officers b. Family counseling | | No significant difference in recidivism after 8 months |
| Sacramento Police Department (1972) | 62 | 62 | a. Individual counseling of predelinquents b. Reality Therapy | No significant difference in offenses after 3 months operation | |
| Pacoima Memorial Lutheran Hospital (1973) | 12 | 12 | a. Picking the youths up at the police station b. Unstructured counseling | | No significant difference in recidivism after 12 months |
| California Office of Criminal Justice Planning (1974) | 33 | 23 | a. Family casework b. Family counseling | Treated youths had significantly higher arrest rates | |
| Liedtke, Malbin, and Mech (1974) | 57 | 40 | Youth diversion | | No significant difference in court record after 3 months |
| Seattle Police Department (1975) | 76 | 76 | Social work interview and referral program | | a. No significant difference in new offenses after 12 months b. No significant difference in seriousness of offenses |

# 11 Juvenile Probation

## Review of the Research

After a youth has broken the law and come to the attention of the police department, he or she is referred to local juvenile court. If the youth is found guilty of the alledged offense, he or she participates in a disposition hearing. For the majority of juvenile delinquents, the recommended disposition is juvenile probation. This chapter will review the different ways juvenile probation treatment has been evaluated, and present conclusions regarding the results of the studies.

Stuart Adams (1966), a correctional researcher whose studies have been discussed in other chapters, also investigated the effects of reduced probationer caseloads upon delinquency. The youths involved in the study were females assigned to the Los Angeles County Probation Department. The 62 girls were randomly assigned to participate in either the treatment group or the control group. The youths in the treatment group were assigned to officers with a reduced caseload of 15 subjects. Treatment also involved demonstration on the part of the probation officers of interest in the girls and their families, utilization of empathy in the relationships. The control group participated in the regular probation program, which involved infrequent contact and caseloads of one officer to 50 youths.

The results after five months of follow-up were mixed in their impact. No significant difference was seen in the two groups in terms of recidivism. However, the treatment group remained out of detention for longer amounts of time and, when locked up, they remained so for shorter periods. The treatment group also had to refer significantly fewer youths to the California Youth Authority for more intensive treatment. It cannot be concluded that the positive results are due solely to the reduced caseload because of the officer's utilization of empathy. As was reported in chapter 5, empathetic counselors are able to obtain positive follow-up behavior in their groups where others have failed.

The second Adams (1966) study on reduced probation caseloads involved delinquent boys. There were 239 boys on probation in Los Angeles County in the study. The boys were randomly assigned to either the treatment group, where the caseload size was 15, or to the control group, in which the caseload size was 75 boys. The probation officers with 15 boys were able to more frequently contact the boys, their families, and their teachers or employers. After over two years of follow-up, no apparent statistically significant difference

125

could be seen between the two groups in their recidivism. The treatment group redetention rate was 41.2 percent, while that of the control group was 44.2 percent, a difference of only 3 percent. This study questions the effectiveness of simply increasing the quantity of contact time between juvenile probation officers and their caseload.

Another study involving reduced or intensive probation caseloads was conducted by Feistman (1966). There was a random assignment of 38 youths to the treatment group and 29 youths to the control group. The youths were delinquent boys on probation in Los Angeles. The treatment group received intensive supervision in a caseload of one to 16. The caseload of the control group was 75 youths. In addition, the treatment group participated in "regular ongoing intensive counseling with the minor and his parent(s)." The program records documented that the treatment group had more frequent contacts with their probation officers. During the one-year operation of the program, there was no significant difference between the two groups in the number of unfavorable dismissals from probation. The treatment group's overall performance was no better than that of the control group.

Pilnick (1967) compared regular probation to a day treatment program for New Jersey delinquent boys. The 167 boys involved in the study were randomly assigned to one of three groups. Two of the groups were control groups, where the boys participated in the regular probation program. In the one treatment group, the boys attended an educational and counseling program for a half-day, five days a week, for four to seven months. The educational program involved teaching the regular high school curriculum on an individualized, remedial instruction basis. The boys also participated in regular, guided group interaction counseling sessions. Guided group interaction originated in New Jersey as a group treatment approach where the boys confronted each other about their negative behavior and tried to help each other with their problems. The group was also given the power to dispense rewards or punishments, such as when a boy could be released from the program.

The results of the intensive day treatment program were negative. During the program there was no significant difference in reading achievement gains between the control and treatment groups. Reading gains were not significant in comprehension, speed, or vocabulary, as measured by the Gates Reading Survey. The youths were also pretested and posttested on IQ test gains. On one test, a derivitive of the Wechsler Intelligence Scale, there was no significant difference. On a second test, the Otis Test of Mental Ability, there were significant gains in favor of the treatment group. After approximately one-half year on follow-up, no significant difference in favor of the treatment group in recidivism was reported.

The negative results certainly question the efficiency of day treatment with juvenile probationers. However, let us examine the treatment more closely. First, the goal of the program was to improve the youths' educational experiences. The procedure was an individualized remedial presentation of traditional high school courses. Success was then inappropriately measured in terms of reading skill gain, IQ gain, and recidivism. If the goal was to increase reading skills, then the program should have taught that. If the purpose was to reduce recidivism, then the skills to accomplish that aim should have been taught. Pilnick's (1967) study demonstrates how negative results can be obtained when there is no logical relationship between the rehabilitation goal—the rehabilitation program—and the measure selected to evaluate progress toward that goal.

After several negative studies, it is now pleasurable to report the outcome of an effective program presented by Hunter (1968). The unique ingredients of the program were that two aides, from the youths' neighborhood, participated on a team with a probation officer. The three team members were responsible for 30 boys. The treatment program ($N = 120$ boys) was compared to two control groups, on regular probation ($N = 32$ boys) and a probation camp program ($N = 44$ boys).

The experimental treatment program involved an initial comprehensive diagnosis of the youths' strengths and weaknesses in all areas of functioning. Then empathetic probation aides focused on one or two specific liabilities that were giving the youths trouble. For many of the youths, school and school attendance was a main problem. Therefore, the aides spent a majority of their time taking the youths to school each morning and helping to keep them there. The aides also transported the youths to and from job training programs. Families were also involved in the treatment process, and their support was solicited for the various programs.

The regular probation caseload involved one probation officer with approximately 75 boys. There was a random assignment of the youths to the three different groups. The results were favorable. The treatment group had a significantly lower rate of institutionalization compared to the regular probation control groups. Institutionalization was defined as commitment to a training school, probation camp, or detention in juvenile hall. The institutionalization rate of the treatment group, 25 percent, was half that of the regular probation group, 50 percent. There was no significant difference in the recidivism/commitment rate between the treatment group and the probation camp group. The results support the use of a treatment program with youths on probation versus the nonprogram of regular probation.

A series of comparisons of probation with other treatment approaches were made by Scarpitti and Stephenson (1968). New Jersey male delinquents between 16 and 18 years of age were involved in the studies. For purposes of experimental comparisons 44 boys were placed in each treatment group and matched with a like number of boys in the control group. The three matching variables were socioeconomic status, delinquency history, and race. The first comparison to be discussed involves a day treatment program similar to that evaluated by Pilnick (1967). The nonresidential day program involved youths coming from their homes during the day and participating in the combination work program and guided group interaction counseling activity. The control groups were youths receiving standard probation supervision.

The results were negative as far as the day treatment was concerned. No significant difference was apparent in the within-program failure rates. On the two-year follow-up measures of recidivism, the day treatment group did significantly worse than the probation group. These results, combined with those of Pilnick (1967), do not support the use of day treatment that emphasizes guided group interaction and educational or work programs.

The second comparison to be discussed from Scarpitti and Stephenson's (1968) study involves a residential group center program. Boys in this program were placed away from their families with a small group of other boys for approximately four months. The boys participated in a work program and guided group interaction on a daily basis. The results of the group center, when compared with the regular probation program, were negative. There was no significant difference in the within-program failure rate. The two-year follow-up assessment revealed that the matched youths in the group center program did significantly worse than the probationers.

The third comparison is between the regular probation program and youths committed to a New Jersey training school. The training school program was very restrictive, whereas the other programs allowed the youths more freedom. While assigned to the training school, the boys participated in school, work, and recreation programs. The average length of stay was nine months. Because of the restrictiveness of the program, there was a significantly lower within-program drop-out rate compared to day treatment, group center placement, and regular probation.

The two-year follow-up recidivism rate was significantly worse than that of the probation group. This result could be due to the fact that regardless of matching, more sophisticated delinquents are usually institutionalized. A much more interesting result is that the recidivism rate of the training school youths was not significantly greater than that of the youths in the two other community-based programs. In other words, neither the day treatment program nor the group home program did significantly better in terms of decreasing the youths' subsequent delinquency than traditional institutionalization. The so-called innovative, community-based programs were no more effective than the training school.

After considering these findings, one might ask the question, why not eliminate all programs for juvenile delinquents except probation? An additional finding by Scarpitti and Stephenson (1968) argues against that move. The recidivism rates of the within-program failure youths from the four groups were compared. The results were astonishing. The probation group, which had done so well on all comparisons, had a much greater recidivism rate than any of the other within-treatment failure groups. In other words, when a youth fails while in the probation program, he goes to subsequent crime at much higher rates than other delinquents in other programs. It is because of probation's failures that other alternatives must be available. Extrapolating from Scarpitti and Stephenson's (1968) results, 30 percent of the total number of youths on probation can be expected to need such alternatives. Coincidently, this figure compares closely with the average failure rate of 20 to 35 percent reported for 11 studies of probation effectiveness reviewed by England (1957).

Davies and Chapman (1969) researched the effects of changing a youth's probation officer. It was hypothesized that "probationers who have to make some kind of adjustment to more than one 'authority-figure' find it easier to come to terms with other forms of authority in the community" (Davies and Chapman, 1969, p. 250). Therefore, the study was designed to simply change the probation officer of 111 of the youths. These older teenage boys were compared to a matched group of 363 boys, both groups on probation in England.

The reconviction rates of the two groups were observed. No significant difference between the two group's subsequent offenses after 12 months was found. It is understandable that positive rehabilitation benefits would not accrue as a result of simply changing a youth's probation officer. However, why did worse results not occur as a result of the damaging effect of breaking up the casework relationship? The answer to that question is tied to the negative results of casework, which establish the fact that there are no positive benefits to begin with in a casework relationship with delinquent youths.

The next study is reported by the San Diego County Probation Department (1971). The study evaluated the effectiveness of a group counseling project with drug offenders. There was a random assignment of juvenile drug offenders to one of three groups. The treatment group had 250 boys and girls. The regular probation group had 125 boys and girls. The final group, 148 youths, was a control group where the youths' cases were closed after an initial interview, with no further intervention. The youths in the treatment group received six weeks of "group counseling and educational lectures which require[d] the participation of the minor and at least one of his parents."

After approximately 12 months of follow-up, the results in terms of recidivism were generally negative. No significant difference was seen in the recidivism rate of the three groups for drug offenses, nondrug offenses, and all offenses. There was no significant difference between the three groups in their offense rate per person for drug offenses. There was, however, a favorable difference between the treatment group and the two control groups in mean number of offenses per person for nondrug offenses. The generally negative results of the treatment for the youths who received group counseling is consistent with the unfavorable conclusions from chapter 5 of this book.

An experimental alternative to regular probation in Provo, Utah, was reported by Empey and Erickson (1972). There was a random assignment of boys to two different control conditions, 211 boys, and to an incarceration treatment program and a probation treatment approach, 115 boys. The treatment alternative to regular probation involved intensive guided group interaction and participation in a work program. The philosophy of the program was to get the youths involved with their peer group that was also in treatment. To this end, the staff attempted to make a boy confused and hostile so that he would turn to the group for help. The group meetings involved the youths in mutual problem solving and confrontation on various problems. The peer group also evaluated each boy's behavior and determined when a member was ready to leave the program. Typically, boys remained in the program from four to seven months. The control group participated in the regular probation supervision program.

The results were, on the whole, unfavorable. After four years of follow-up, there were no significant differences in the two groups' arrest statistics. When age was considered, younger boys in treatment had higher arrest statistics, while older treated youths (16 and above) had lower arrest rates. The senior author of the study, Empey, reported a year later in Ohlin (1973):

All subjects were followed in the study for four years after release, until most of all of them had reached the legal age of adulthood. In comparing the relative effectiveness of experimental and control groups, it was found that the intensive experimental program did not seem to be greatly superior to regular probation (Ohlin, 1973, p. 42).

The two main ingredients, a work program and guided group interaction, have been found less than useful in other studies. The negative results of this study validate the ineffectiveness of guided group interaction and the ineffectiveness of work programs as treatment for juvenile delinquents.

Venezia (1972) evaluated the effectiveness of unofficial probation. Male and female teenagers who were referred to the county juvenile probation department, usually for a first offense, were randomly assigned to the treatment group ($N = 65$) or the control group ($N = 58$). The treatment, unofficial probation, also known as "voluntary probation" or "informal probation" occurs when a youth admits his involvement and the probation staff does not file formal allegations. In addition, unofficial probation occurs:

With the consent of the minor and his parents.

For selected youngsters, those seen as in need of help but not yet requiring court intervention.

To provide these young people with services comparable to those afforded under formal probation supervision (Venezia, 1972, p. 150).

The main comparable service provided the youths was periodic supervision to ensure that they were staying out of trouble. Youths in the control group received no services after the intake unit determined their qualification for participation in the study.

The results after six months of follow-up were entirely negative in terms of the effectiveness of unofficial probation. There was no significant difference between the unofficial probation group's recidivism rate, 18.5 percent, and the control group's redicivism rate, 27.6 percent. Further, no significant differences existed between the two groups in length of time to referral, number of petitions filed, and reasons for referral. The results lead to the conclusions that unofficial probation is as ineffective as no treatment. The use of unofficial probation with first-time referrals is therefore seriously questioned.

Santa Clara County (1973*a*) reported the results of their day care treatment program. They developed a program alternative for status offenders, youths who had come to the attention of the juvenile court for a significant frequency of running away and truancy. Forty-three boys and girls were randomly assigned to the control group, where they were placed in a county ranch program. The youths in the day treatment program, 62 boys and girls, remained in their own homes and attended the day center. Day center treatment emphasized individual counseling based on each youth's diagnosed and prescribed differential treatment program.

The differential treatment approach utilized was the I-level system, based upon interpersonal maturity level. Youths participated in the program for four months. Due to the short length of operation of the program, only one of the main behavior indices of effectiveness was utilized—educational achievement gain. The results, unfortunately indicated no significant difference between the two groups in their educational achievement test score gains. This study represents the fourth day treatment program reviewed with probationers that obtained negative results.

The Santa Clara County Juvenile Probation Department conducted an additional study (1973*b*), this one involving first-time drug offenders. The youths were randomly assigned to one of three treatment groups or to the control group. The three treatment programs were an education-group therapy track, a transactional analysis counseling track, and a psychodrama track. The programs were described as follows:

The Education/Counseling Track was a short-term (six sessions) series of lectures and non-encounter group therapy sessions concerning drug abuse. Youths attended each session accompanied by at least one parent. The lecture portion of each meeting was conducted by a speaker from the police department, drug abuse prevention agencies and school and religious groups.

The Transactional Analysis Track was an application of the therapeutic techniques made famous by Eric Berne. Basic transactional analysis techniques involved application of intellectual and experimental activities within the group process which are directed toward perceptual elevation and increase of awareness of self and others. Specifically, these transactional analysis techniques were used to bring into the youth's awareness the self-defeating nature of his drug involvement.

The Psychodrama Track utilized therapeutic techniques which involve the youth in staging and acting out human situations, as a vehicle for understanding motivations for behavior, including drug abuse. This track consisted of eleven sessions (Sanat Clara County, 1973b, p. 21-22).

The control group participated in the regular probation program.

The results were negative. No significant differences were seen between the three treatment groups and the control group in their self-reported use of drugs or in the questionnaire scores of their family relationships and communication. The recidivism measure indicated a three-month and six-month difference in favor of the education/counseling group. However, after nine months of follow-up, that positive result had washed out. After nine months, there was no significant difference in the recidivism of the four groups. The results question the usefulness of education/counseling, transactional analysis, and psychodrama, as provided in the preceding study.

Kraus (1974) compared the effectiveness of monetary fines imposed upon juvenile delinquents versus regular probation in Australia. There were 65 male offenders carefully matched with a control group having a like number of boys. The youths in the treatment group were simply fined a certain amount of money. The average was $14.30 Australian currency. The youths were compared with boys on regular probation for approximately 12 months. Probation involved the youths receiving home visits from their probation officers once a month.

Across the different age groups and categories of offenses, there was no significant difference in the number of offenses committed after five years for the two groups. However, when offense history was broken out, it was found that first offenders who received such fines instead of probation had significantly fewer offenses. Youths who had engaged in stealing did better on probation than with fines in terms of subsequent commitment to detention. The main effect was that monetary fines were as good as probation. In fact, with first offenders, fines were better. The implication is that a much cheaper and more effective treatment than probation is available, at least for first offenders. The author stressed, however, that the youths should pay the fines themselves.

If youths should pay off their fines themselves, what about those youths who have no money or means to earn money. In an earlier chapter it was reported how FitzGerald (1974) induced youths on probation to work off their probation fines. He found that contingency contracts that resulted in some type of reward attractive to the youths motivated them to work at high levels of performance. The reward with the most substantial effect was a combination of time off probation and weekly group activities. The activities were chosen by the youths and included attendance at professional basketball games, ice hockey games, and the movies. It can be concluded that requiring first-offender juveniles to pay off or work off a fine is possible, and that such treatment has a high likelihood of being effective.

The use of community volunteers with juveniles on probation was extensively evaluated by Berger *et al.* (1975). There was a random assignment process utilized with the youths. Youths on regular probation were compared with youths on probation who in addition received services provided by volunteers. The volunteers functioned as tutors, as group counselors with the youths and their families, and even as volunteer probation officers. The results were unfavorable. After six months of follow-up, there was no significant difference between the treatment group and the control group in their rate of contact with the police. This study raises considerable doubts on the usefulness of volunteer programs as an effective rehabilitation approach.

## Conclusions

Seventeen studies involving over 2600 delinquents in various juvenile probation programs have been discussed. The purpose of this chapter is to discover what works with these youths who have come to the attention of the police enough times that they warranted referral to the juvenile probation and court system. Table 11-1 presents the chapter summary.

First, the negative findings will be summarized. Many of the various innovations, including day treatment, residential programs, reduced caseloads, intensive treatment, and group counseling, were matched up against regular juvenile probation. In most instances, probation was as effective if not more effective than many of the more expensive approaches. Because of the lack of beneficial results, the following programs should not be relied upon to rehabilitate juvenile delinquents on probation:

1. Reduced Caseloads
2. Intensive probation supervision
3. Day treatment
4. Guided group interaction
5. Residential group homes
6. Youth and parent lectures
7. Differential treatment emphasizing individual counseling
8. Transactional analysis
9. Psychodrama
10. Volunteer programs

Three of the studies reviewed cast doubt on the effectiveness of probation itself. The San Diego County (1971) study found no significant difference in probation's effectiveness compared to closing the case after an initial interview. The study, however, involved mild drug offenders only. Venezia (1972) determined through his research that unofficial probation services were no more effective than closing the case after an initial interview. Venezia's study generally

**Table 11-1**
**Juvenile Probation Summary**

| Researchers | Number of Youths | | Type of Program | Results | Follow-up Results |
|---|---|---|---|---|---|
| | Experimental | Control | | | |
| Adams (1966) | 62 | | a. Reduced caseload load from 50 to 15 b. Relationship oriented casework by probation officers | | a. No significant difference in redetention rate b. Shorter time in detention c. Smaller number went on to California Youth Authority |
| Adams (1966) | 239 | | a. Reduced caseload from 75 to 15 b. More frequent supervision contacts by probation officer | | No apparent significant difference in redetention rate |
| Feistman (1966) | 38 | 29 | a. Reduced caseload from 75 to 16 b. Family counseling c. More frequent contacts | No significant difference in unfavorable dismissal from probation | No |
| Pilnick *et al.* (1967) | 167 | | a. Day treatment with educational program b. Guided group interaction counseling | a. No significant difference in reading achievement b. Contradictory results on 2 IQ tests | No significant difference in recidivism |
| Hunter (1968) | 120 | 76 | a. Reduced caseloads from 75 to 30 for 1 officer and 2 indigenous probation aides b. Comprehensive treatment program | | Less institutionalization of treatment group compared to regular probation |
| Scarpitti and Stephenson (1968) | 44 | 44 | a. Day treatment program b. Guided group interaction | No significant difference in the within-program failure rate | Worse recidivism than regular probation group |
| Scarpitti and Stephenson (1968) | 44 | 44 | a. Residential group home program b. Guided group interaction | No significant difference in the within-program failure rate | Worse recidivism than regular probation group |
| Scarpitti and Stephenson (1968) | 44 | 44 | Training school program compared against probation | Significantly lower within-program failure rate | Worse recidivism than regular probation group |

**Table 11-1.** (cont.)

| Researchers | Number of Youths | | Type of Program | Results | Follow-up Results |
|---|---|---|---|---|---|
| | *Experimental* | *Control* | | | |
| Davies and Chapman (1969) | 111 | 363 | Changing the youths' probation officers | | No significant difference in subsequent offenses |
| San Diego County (1971) | 250 | 273 | *a.* Group counseling with parent lectures and informal probation <br> *b.* Formal probation | | *a.* No significant difference in recidivism rate <br> *b.* No significant difference in offenses per person for drug offenses <br> *c.* Fewer offenses per person for non-drug offenses |
| Empey and Erickson (1972) | 115 | 211 | *a.* Day treatment <br> *b.* Intensive guided group interaction <br> *c.* Work program | | *a.* No significant difference in arrest rate <br> *b.* Younger boys had higher arrest rate <br> *c.* Older boys, 16 and older had lower arrest rate |
| Venezia (1972) | 65 | 58 | Unofficial probation | | *a.* No significant difference in recidivism <br> *b.* No significant difference in length of time to recidivism |
| Santa Clara County (1973*a*) | 62 | 43 | *a.* Day treatment <br> *b.* Differential treatment based upon 1-level | No significant difference in educational achievement gain | No |
| Santa Clara County (1973*b*) | NS | | *a.* Group counseling <br> *b.* Transactional analysis <br> *c.* Psychodrama | *a.* No significant difference in self-reported use of drugs <br> *b.* No significant difference in family relationships and communication | No significant difference in recidivism after 9 months |
| Kraus (1974) | 65 | 65 | Monetary fines | | *a.* No significant difference in offenses after 5 years <br> *b.* First offenders had significantly fewer offenses |

**Table 11-1.** (cont.)

| Researchers | Number of Youths | | Type of Program | Results | Follow-up Results |
|---|---|---|---|---|---|
| | Experimental | Control | | | |
| FitzGerald (1974) | 15 | 5 | Weekly activities as reinforcement for working off probation fines | Increased work performance | No |
| Berger and Gold (1975) | NS | | Juvenile court volunteers as counselors and tutors | No significant difference in academic performance | No significant difference in police contacts |

involved first offenders or mild offenders. Kraus (1974) learned that monetary fines were more effective in reducing subsequent delinquency than probation with first offenders.

The first two studies indicate that with first offenders or mild drug offenders, closing the case is as effective as probation supervision. Should such offenders therefore be ignored? No! The youths in those studies were all brought before the probation department. The youths and their parents went through the initial intake. Then the cases for some of the youths were closed. I believe that, perhaps, if only for shock value, such initial intake and disposition is useful. For a great majority of first offenders, who are basically well-adjusted youths, there is a need not for rehabilitation, but for a sufficiently forceful encounter with the juvenile justice system that they learn that breaking certain laws will not be tolerated by society.

For first offenders, the use of monetary fines was found to be more effective than regular probation. The use of fines can provide a more just punishment, since the court can individualize the amount of the fine in proportion to the cost of the youth's damages. An additional advantage of fines is that they can provide some level of victim compensation. For fines to work with first offenders, the youths themselves must earn the money to pay for the fines. The potential for such a program is defeated if the parents pay the fines for the youths.

Should all first offenders simply go through intake, be fined, and then released? No! The purpose of probation intake services should be to diagnose the youths and their families to determine if and what treatment may be necessary. However, for the majority of first offenders, a monetary fine after intake may be sufficient.

Multiple offenders need additional services, including some form of probation supervision. Hunter (1968) utilized an extremely efficient and effective method of treatment. It may be remembered that in his study two probation aides from the local neighborhoods of the youths were assigned to assist each probation officer. The advantage of such a team is that the probation officer can provide the legal supervision and surveillance, while the probation aides under his or her direction are free to provide treatment. Contrastingly, in the other reduced caseload studies, there was increased probation officer supervision and surveillance through the increased contact. Comprehensive diagnosis, specific goal setting, and an intensive school attendance program were found to be effective in reducing delinquency when provided by the team. The use of such a high-quality treatment program for youths on probation is therefore recommended. Other forms of treatment recommended in earlier chapters are also applicable in the probation service setting. Below are the summary prediction and recommendation for this chapter.

**Specific Prediction**: Simply ignoring youth crime or providing ineffective services for youths will result in increased crime.

**Specific Recommendation**: Youths who break the law should go through at least the sequence indicated in figure 11-1.

The sequence illustrated in figure 11-1 does not recognize utilization of unofficial probation or informal probations as such, because it was found to be no more effective than closing the case. It was pointed out earlier that Hunter's (1968) program clearly increased the program quality, as well as the quantity of probation officer contracts. The major elements of Hunter's program included:

1. Use of indigenous probation aides
2. Empathetic staff
3. Comprehensive behavioral diagnosis
4. Goal setting
5. Individual treatment plans
6. Use of aides to control as well as monitor important youth behaviors, such as school attendance
7. Involvement of the family
8. Active solicitation of community and family support
9. Individual counseling
10. Variety of treatment approaches

Such an increase in quality and specificity of treatment did result in decreased delinquency compared to the nonprogram, regular probation.

In each chapter, general predictions and recommendations have been articulated to extend the knowledge gained to a broader range of situations. The particular finding from this chapter involves the quantity of probation officer contact and its ineffectiveness. This result is related to the theory of specificity.

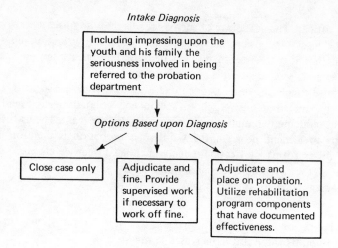

*Intake Diagnosis*

Including impressing upon the youth and his family the seriousness involved in being referred to the probation department

*Options Based upon Diagnosis*

| Close case only | Adjudicate and fine. Provide supervised work if necessary to work off fine. | Adjudicate and place on probation. Utilize rehabilitation program components that have documented effectiveness. |

**Figure 11-1.** Sequence of Options for Youthful Lawbreakers Based on Intake Diagnosis

**General Prediction**: Rehabilitation and educational programs will fail regardless of increased contact with the client or student if no delivery of relevant help is provided. Quantity of services and increased time, whether hours, days, months, or years, are in and of themselves irrelevant.

**General Recommendation**: Program administrators should focus on the quality of their programs in terms of relevance and behavioral change. *Relevance* can be assessed in terms of programs that are logically linked to diagnosed needs of the clients. *Behavioral change* can be evaluated through measured changes from initial diagnosis to follow-up behavior in the youth or clients at the conclusion of a program.

## References

Adams, S., Development of a program research service in probation. Los Angeles County Probation Department. Research Report Number 27. Los Angeles, 1966.

Berger, R.J., J.E. Crowley, M. Gold, J. Gray, and M.S. Arnold. *A Study of a Program of Volunteers Working with Juvenile Probationers*. Ann Arbor, Michigan: Institute for Social Research, 1975.

Davies, M., and B. Chapman. The relationship between change of supervising officer and the commission of an offense by probationers. *Case Conference* 16 (1969):250-253.

Empey, L., and M. Erickson. *The Provo Experiment.* Lexington, Mass.: Lexington Books, D.C. Heath, 1972.

England, R. What is responsible for satisfactory probation and post-probation outcome? *Journal of Criminal Law, Criminology and Police Science* 47 (1957):667-674.

Feistmen, E.G. Comparative analysis of the Willowbrook-Harbor Intensive Services Program. Los Angeles County Probation Department. Research Report Number 28. Los Angeles, 1966.

FitzGerald, T.J. Contingency contracting with juvenile offenders. *Criminology: An Interdisciplinary Journal* 12 (1974):241-248.

Hunter, E.F. Reduction of delinquency through expansion of opportunity. Los Angeles County Probation Department. Research Report Number 30. Los Angeles, 1968.

Kraus, J. The deterrent effect of fines and probation on male juvenile offenders. *Australian and New Zealand Journal of Criminology* 7 (1974):231-240.

Ohlin, L.E. *Prisoners in America.* Englewood Cliffs, New Jersey: Prentice Hall, 1973.

Pilnick, S. *et al. Collegefields: From Delinquency to Freedom.* Newark, New Jersey: Newark State College, 1967.

Santa Clara County. Santa Clara County juvenile probation day care program. In F. Berkowitz, *Evaluation of Crime Control Programs in California: A Review.* Sacramento: California Council on Criminal Justice, April 1973*a*.

Santa Clara County. Santa Clara County juvenile probation drug abuse prevention project. In F. Berkowitz, *Evaluation of Crime Control Programs in California: A Review.* Sacramento: California Council on Criminal Justice, April 1973*b*.

San Diego County Probation Department. *Research and Evaluation of the First Year of Operations of the San Diego County Juvenile Narcotics Project.* San Diego: San Diego County Probation Department, 1971.

Scarpitti, F., and R. Stephenson. A study of probation effectiveness. *The Journal of Criminal Law, Criminology and Police Science* 59 (1968):361-369.

Venezia, P. Unofficial probation: An evaluation of its effectiveness. *The Journal of Research in Crime and Delinquency* 9 (1972):149-170.

# 12  California's Probation Subsidy Program

## Introduction

A rather recent system intervention that has received considerable publicity as a useful community-based program for delinquent youths is California's Probation Subsidy Program. The program will be described, along with its history. Data will then be presented regarding its effectiveness.

The Probation Subsidy Program in California was based upon the following stated assumption:

> Modern correctional theory takes the position that the most effective correctional service should and must be offered at the local level if it is to achieve the greatest rehabilitative impact on the offender. The circumstances leading to delinquency and criminal behavior are the product of life in the community, and the resolution of these problems must be found in the community.... Probation is viewed by the state as a community service and the keystone to an effective total correctional system (California Board of Corrections, 1965, p. 3).

Therefore, recognizing that California views its system of local probation as being of crucial importance, how did the present system of state financial subsidy develop?

The roots for a subsidy system in California go back as far as 1948 and 1957 when different evaluation studies concluded that there were great discrepancies in the utilization of probation services from county to county. The 1957 study (Adams and Burdman, 1957) gathered extensive data documenting the poor quality of services in many of the counties. Rather than undiplomatically stating that fact, the study concluded that services varied from county to county and there needed to be more congruence between actual services and recognized professional standards.

The major recommendation was that the state should provide financial subsidies to fund the upgrading of the county probation departments. The study, along with its recommendations, was placed before the California State Assembly. The recommendations failed to gain approval.

A more recent study by the California Board of Corrections (1965) used the data of the previous reports and gathered further information. The probation subsidy recommendation of this report was endorsed and funded by the State Assembly. Two reasons can be given for the successful passage of this legislation. First, an important ingredient in the 1965 study was the direct involvement of over 80 professional and lay individuals concerned with probation in California. This involvement facilitated the generation of political support, especially on the part of the chief juvenile probation officers.

The second element contributing to legislative passage was the development of the concept of matching subsidy payments with corresponding reductions in county commitment rates to state programs. A variable formula was proposed to pay counties for reduced commitments. The appeal of this concept was that state funding for state programs could be reduced and the ensuing surplus of funds could pay for the new program. The subsidy program would emphasize the use of state funds to reduce caseloads of probation officers.

The recommendations that were part of this 1965 legislative package included several program proposals. The major one, which was a recommendation that was second in importance only to the subsidy proposal itself, was that,

the state, through the Department of the California Youth Authority, should assume the major responsibility and cost for *training* and *certification* of personnel working in probation (California Board of Corrections, 1965, p. 12).

Unfortunately, there was not enough legislative support for this recommendation, and it failed to gain passage. The Chairman of the Board of Corrections, in the study's cover letter to the Governor and the Assembly, reminded them that even though he was thankful for the passage of some of the recommendations,

there remains, however, legislative action for the second most significant recommendation of the study—that the state should assume the major responsibility for the training of probation personnel. The need for this undertaking is thoroughly developed and documented in the following report which the Board respectfully submits to you (California Board of Corrections, 1965, p. VI).

The training recommendation was based on the major assumption that money alone would not improve the California county probation programs. The report quoted one individual who in effect asked what good does it do to give probation departments money to reduce caseloads, "if the people who are carrying them don't know what to do with the reduced caseloads." Figure 12-1 summarizes the basic plan of probation subsidy. However, it should be remembered that all the plan was implemented except for the training of probation officers. Another weakness of the probation subsidy plan was that no funds were allocated for evaluation. For this reason, the program was in full operation for over seven years before knowledge of its effects was available. The next section of this chapter will report the results that have recently become available.

### Review of the Research

For the first seven years of probation subsidy in California, the only data that were provided were quarterly reports of the number of counties participating

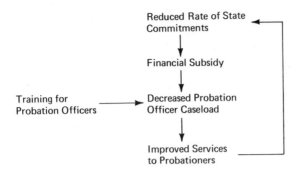

**Figure 12-1.** The Basic Probation Subsidy Plan

and the number of probationers served. The program was designed to divert both juveniles and adults from state commitments from all 58 counties in California. However, because participation in the program by a county was and is voluntary, not all the counties are involved in the program. The participation has increased from 31 counties to the present number of 47 (California Youth Authority, 1975).

The program served 22,000 adult and juvenile probationers in FY 1973-1974. Over half were juvenile court cases. There were approximately 1700 probation staff involved in special subsidy programs with the above probationers for the same period of time. The average caseload in the subsidy programs was reduced to about 30 youths per probation officer.

The California Youth Authority (1975) has reported increased juvenile commitment reductions by participating counties of from 460 in FY 1967 to 3431 in FY 1973. However, in a report by the California Department of Justice (1973), a decrease in juvenile court caseloads was reported for both regular and subsidy caseloads. The reported reasons for this downward trend are:

(1) The lowering of the age of adulthood to 18 years of age,
(2) The decline in the rate of increase in the California population of persons aged 10 through 15, and
(3) The increased use and acceptance of local community program alternatives that divert youth away from court processes (California Department of Justice, 1973, p. 2).

Therefore, if there were less juveniles coming before the juvenile court, some part of the decrease in commitments would be due to the reduced number of probationers.

The first evaluation of the probation subsidy plan was published almost eight years after the inception of the program (California Youth Authority,

1974). The report presented the status of the program with regard to its four major goals. The four goals for California were:

(1) To increase the protection afforded the citizens of this state,
(2) To permit a more even administration of justice,
(3) To rehabilitate offenders,
(4) To reduce the necessity for commitment of persons to state correctional institutions (California Youth Authority, 1974, pp. 2-3).

The main method for reaching the goals was for the state to provide funds to the local counties. The funds were allocated to reduce the probation caseload and to upgrade the services of the probation department.

The improvement of local probation department services was related to seven standards developed by the Youth Authority in cooperation with local officials. The standards included improved personnel standards, decreased probation officer caseloads, decreased supervisor caseloads, development of a classification system based upon the individual needs of the probationers, improved clerical support, increased funds for support services, and finally, funds for evaluation and research. It was thought that the implementation of the above standards would lead to the attainment of the program's goals.

The results of the data analysis will now be discussed in relation to the four goals. With regard to an increased protection of citizens, it was found that California's crime rate *increased* rather than decreased. The authors of the study argued that because subsidy caseloads constituted less than 10 percent of the total active caseload in 1972, the effects upon crime for the whole state would be and were negligible. In any event, the first goal has not been obtained.

The next goal dealt with trying to get a more even administration of justice. This aim was operationally defined as a reduction in the discrepancy in commitment rates from the various counties. Prior to the implementation of the subsidy program, the difference in the county commitment rates ranged from a low of 22 to a high of 119 per 100,000 population. By FY 1973, the range was only from a low of 8 to a high of 66, for a reduction in the statewide discrepancy of 44 percent. It can be concluded, therefore, that this goal has been successfully met.

The third goal was concerned with the effective rehabilitation of the probationers. Up to this point, the data analysis and results have been reported for both adults and juvenile offenders combined. The assessment of the program's rehabilitation results will now be discussed for the juvenile delinquents in the study. The procedure involved selecting a random sample of 843 juvenile probationers in the subsidy program. They were then matched with 1313 regular juvenile probationers. Both groups were largely represented with more serious offenders.

The results were negative. There was no significant difference in the number of arrests for the two groups after 12 months of supervision. There was also no significant difference between the subsidy group and the regular group in the number of findings of culpability for felonies or misdemeanors. The authors concluded,

Initial indications are that Subsidy Probation does not appear to be substantially more effective than regular probation with regard to the rehabilitation of a comparable group of more serious juvenile offenders (California Youth Authority, 1974, p. 39).

These results question the effectiveness of the probation program standards that were developed. The more intensive and costly subsidy program was no more effective than the regular probation program.

The final goal of probation subsidy was the reduction in the commitment of offenders to state institutions. The overall statewide commitment rate decreased from 67.5 per 100,000 prior to subsidy to 34.0 commitments per 100,000 in FY 1973. The proportion of juveniles committed to state institutions decreased from 18 percent in 1965 to 5.5 percent in 1972. There was also no ensuing increase in the use of local incarceration facilities for juveniles. The average daily population in local county camps and schools was 2669 in FY 1966 and 2612 in FY 1973. It can therefore be concluded that the goal of reducing statewide commitments to institutions was successfully achieved.

In 1975 the California Youth Authority reported the results of a more extensive evaluation of the rehabilitation efforts of probation subsidy. The study presented the results of the effectiveness of probation subsidy by comparing it with regular probation. There was also an attempt to compare subsidy probationers with youths who were on parole after several months of placement in a California Youth Authority institution. However, because of the reported incompatability of the samples on parole and in subsidy and the variance in criteria used to measure success, those results will not be presented.

One question the research attempted to answer was whether the youths in the subsidy program received improved supervision. There were 836 subsidy youths matched with 1290 regular probation youths. The results indicated that subsidy cases had significantly more contacts with their adult supervisors than the regular probationers. The subsidy group averaged one contact per month more than the regular probation group.

Additional data supported the fact that subsidy youths received more services. Significantly more of the subsidy group received typological classification and diagnosis services. Significantly more of the subsidy youths (41.5 percent) had a recorded treatment plan than the regular probation group (24.1 percent). These results document the fact that probation subsidy did provide a greater quantity of services. However, whether a higher quantity resulted in improved services is questioned by the following data.

The final set of results from the 1975 study were concerned with the question of probation subsidy's effectiveness. The study compared 859 subsidy youths with 1347 regular probationers. All the youths were male between 7 and 20 years of age. The authors discussed their hypothesis regarding the treatment effectiveness of probation subsidy:

The assumption here is that if "subsidy probation" utilizes improved supervision techniques, then the recidivism rates of probationers on its caseloads should be lower than the recidivism rates of similar probationers on ordinary probation caseloads (California Youth Authority, 1975, p. 22).

Unfortunately, the results were far from supportive. Not only was there no significant difference between the two groups' recidivism rate for the older boys (17 to 20 years of age), but the younger subsidy boys (7 to 16 years) did significantly worse than those younger boys on regular probation. The younger boys who were in the subsidy program also did significantly worse in the number who received a count finding for a felony offense. In summary, the results did not support the effectiveness of probation subsidy. In fact, for younger youths, the results argue against probation subsidy because of their performance.

Allen Breed, the Director of the California Youth Authority, made the following observations in his cover letter accompanying the 1975 report:

The study suggests that there is no difference between regular and special probation supervision in relation to recidivism. If this is true, we need to reexamine existing practices to determine if there are more effective ways to use state subsidy dollars. The Youth Authority is currently in the process of reformulating the Statewide Standards as part of this process. . . .

Finally, the results of the present study point to the great difficulty encountered in attempting to design and conduct effective rehabilitation programs, whether in institutions or in community settings. A greater percentage of our efforts and resources should be focused on delinquency prevention and diversion programs as potentially viable alternative means of achieving our goals of reducing crime and increasing the safety of our citizens (California Youth Authority, 1975, pp. 1-2).

**Conclusions**

The results of two major studies on California's Probation Subsidy Program have been presented. The conclusions will be discussed both in terms of those which are related to the program as a system intervention and those concerned with probation subsidy as a rehabilitation program intervention.

The preceding results document the fact that probation subsidy was not effective as a program intervention. The negative results that were obtained are consistent with those reported in preceding chapters—reduced caseloads were ineffective in other probation studies and more intensive casework results in worse delinquency. Therefore, the following can be concluded.

**Specific Prediction on Subsidy as a Program Intervention**: Probation subsidy programs will fail if they are built around reduced caseloads and more intensive casework services.

**General Prediction on Subsidy as a Program Intervention**: If subsidy funds are utilized in programs that have consistently proven negative (for example, casework, individual counseling, work programs, etc.), then the subsidy will have been wasted, because the programs will fail.

**Recommendations on Subsidy as a Program Intervention**: If subsidy is to be utilized, programs should be developed only around those programs which have proven effective.

The California Probation Subsidy Program will now be discussed in terms of its system interventions. It may be remembered that in addition to the goal of rehabilitation, three other main purposes were presented. Two of the three goals were positively affected by probation subsidy. There was a reduction in commitments to the state juvenile institutions, and there was a decrease in the discrepancy of county commitment rates to those state institutions. However, the third and most important goal—a reduction in crime and the ensuing protection of the community—was not reached. The crime rate increased substantially rather than being reduced.

The reason given for the lack of impact upon the statewide crime rate was that probation subsidy was only reaching 10 percent of those on probation. The recommendation is that subsidy can decrease the crime rate, as well as reduce state commitments, if the funds are utilized for the entire probation population. Since it has been clearly documented that the use of subsidy funds on reduced caseloads is no more effective than the cheaper regular program, funds can be used in other ways.

It was discovered in Texas that most juvenile probation officers were underpaid (Romig, 1976). As a result, those individuals in juvenile probation positions were either underqualified or were young men and women with little experience. In order for a subsidy program to impact the whole juvenile probation system, it must find a way to upgrade the caliber of individuals selected as juvenile probation officers. One technique proposed during the Texas Master Plan Project (Romig, 1976) was salary supplements. Another was to have a program specialist on each county's staff who would train the officers in those program principles which have proven effective in rehabilitation (specific treatment, G.E.D., career advancement skills, etc.). With higher salaries and subsequent training and program support, juvenile probation officers could be held accountable for the successes or failures of the youths on their caseload. The preceding discussion points to the following prediction and recommendation regarding probation subsidy as a system intervention.

**Prediction on Subsidy as a System Intervention**: If the goal of subsidy is to impact statewide crime rate and only a small percent of the individuals involved receive contact, then the intervention will fail.

**Specific Recommendation on Specificity in System Intervention**: The key elements of any system are the staff and programs. If probation subsidy is to affect the entire system, then all the staff and programs must be substantially improved.

Before leaving this topic, it must be pointed out that what is being offered here is a principle of specificity with regard to system intervention. Results are only obtained proportional to the degree that the system is acted upon. If you desire only a partial and specific change in the system, then only those elements in which change is desired should be affected. If you desire change in the entire system, then some element or program that affects the entire system must be sufficiently implemented.

### References

Adams, S., and M. Burdman. *Probation in California*. Sacramento: Special Study Commission on Correctional Facilities and Services, 1957.

California Board of Corrections. *Probation Study: Final Report*. Sacramento: Youth and Adult Corrections Agency, The Board of Corrections, 1965.

California Department of Justice. *Superior and Juvenile Court Probation Cases Active During 1972*. California Department of Justice, Division of Law Enforcement, Bureau of Criminal Statistics, 1973.

California Youth Authority. California's probation subsidy program. *A Progress Report to the Legislature, 1966-1973*. Sacramento, 1974.

California Youth Authority. California's probation subsidy program. *A Progress Report to the Legislature, Report No. 2*. Sacramento, 1975.

Romig, D. Texas juvenile corrections master plan. Unpublished manuscript. Austin, 1976.

# 13 Community Residential Programs

## Review of the Research

In 1975 the National Assessment of Juvenile Corrections Project published their report on residential programs and deinstitutionalization (Vinter, Downs, and Hall, 1975). They opened the chapter on community-based corrections by observing that since the failure of institutions was documented, maybe there was hope that community programs would be more successful in the task of rehabilitation. In the preceding three chapters, we have seen how many of the nonresidential community programs have obtained negative results. A close look will now be given to the residential community programs to determine how well they have worked.

Group homes, halfway houses, and residential centers are very similar, even though they are called by different names. The chief similarity is that the youths live and sleep at the program site. A group home differs from the others mainly in that it involves a smaller group of residents (4 to 6 only) and is staffed by a husband-and-wife team. The different community residential programs vary in the degree of programming that is directly provided versus that which the youths participate in with community youths. Reed (1967) reported the results of a vocational residential center program. One hundred and eleven male delinquent youths were divided into two matched groups. The boys averaged 15 1/2 years of age.

Both the treatment and the control group participated in a vocational program. The control group, however, was on parole, living at home. The treatment group lived in a residential program where they were allowed weekend visits to their homes. The program also included group counseling and family group counseling. The youths averaged three to four months in the program.

The results were negative. After six months of follow-up, the treatment group had a significantly higher failure rate, as measured by return to the institution. There was no significant difference reported in the family support provided during follow-up. A positive result was that the treatment group was more favorably involved in training and/or employment than the control group. However, this fact supports stated conclusions in earlier chapters—there is nothing inherent in a delinquent youth's participation in an educational or work program that prevents his or her subsequent delinquency. The findings of this study were that even though the residential project did better in terms of keeping the youths in training or on a job, it did worse in terms of preventing delinquent behavior.

149

In chapter 11, the study by Scarpitti and Stephenson (1968) was discussed. A portion of that study involved a comparison of a residential group home project with a training school program and regular probation. There were 44 boys matched with two other groups with the same number of boys. The boys in the residential group center were placed away from their homes with a small group of similarly delinquent youths. Placement lasted approximately four months. The boys participated in a guided group interaction program and a work program.

The boys in the residential program were compared with the two control groups, one of youths who were on regular probation and the other, a group of boys who had attended a state training school. Compared with the boys on probation, the treatment youths fared worse in a two-year follow-up of their recidivism rate. There was no significant difference in the two groups' within-program failure rate. In the comparison with the training school group, the youths in the residential program did not perform significantly better. The within-program failure rate was significantly lower for the training school group, where there was more structure. These results indicate that the community residential program was no more effective than a so-called institutional program. When compared with a cheaper, less intense community program—probation—the residential program was worse.

Foster homes have been held out as a form of residential treatment that retain most of the elements of normal home life. McCord, McCord, and Thurber (1968) conducted a 12-year follow-up study of a group of 19 delinquent boys who had been placed in foster homes. The boys subsequent criminal behavior was compared with a matched group of 19 delinquent youths not placed in foster homes. The foster home boys had significantly worse deviant behavior over the 12-year follow-up period. These results do not support the use of foster homes for the prevention of delinquent and criminal behavior.

Empey and Lubeck (1971) reported the results of their thorough investigation of the effects of a community-based group home. Teenage boys between 16 and 18 years of age were randomly assigned to the treatment and control groups. There were 141 boys in the treatment group and 121 in the control group. The treatment group boys attended regular public school and participated in guided group interaction with the other boys after school. They were compared with a similar group of boys who were assigned to a relatively open and treatment-oriented institution in a rural area.

Both groups had a high number of in-program failures and runaways, approximately 50 percent. There were no significant differences between the two groups in their in-program failures or the subsequent recidivism rates and their reduction in offenses. The one positive measure for the youths in the treatment group was in the less seriousness of their offenses. The main conclusions concerning the effectiveness of the community-based residential program must be negative due to the lack of a favorable difference in three out of four of the outcome criteria.

The use of group homes for youths referred to the California Youth Authority was reported on by Palmer (1972). Using very restrictive ad hoc analytical criteria, he was able to compare an experimental group of 12 boys with a control group of 74 boys. All the youths were participating in the community treatment project, which involved community placement in lieu of assignment to a training school. The group homes were staffed by nonprofessionally trained husband-and-wife teams who were responsible for the youths on a 24-hour basis. In addition, the youths' parole offices provided differential treatment based upon their levels of interpersonal functioning.

The youths in the treatment group were assigned to the group home, while the boys in the control group remained with their families. The results were negative, since no significant difference was seen in parole failure for the two groups. Whereas Empey and Lubeck's study did not support the superiority of community residential treatment compared to institutions, the present study establishes no superiority of group homes compared to the youths' own homes.

Collingwood (1972) described the results of a skills training approach that was part of a short-term residential treatment program in Arkansas. In the study, 48 delinquent boys and girls were randomly assigned to one of four treatment groups or to one of four control groups. The approximate age of the youths was 17. The author described the eight groups as follows.

*Systematic Physical Training Group* (P.T.) Subjects in this group received one hour of physical training a day, four days a week for four consecutive weeks for a total of 15 hours. Each hour was broken down into a 10 minute lecture and a 50 minute workout period in a gymnasium. Lecture content focused upon the principles of rest, hygiene, diet and exercise as a means to increase physical functioning. The gymnasium workout consisted of endurance/cardiovascular work such as distance running and sprints, strength conditioning (calisthenics) and agility drills. All subjects were coached to break their individual exercise and activity records every day. The physical training was systematically devised to facilitate successive improvements in performance and fitness level.

*Systematic Goal Setting Training Group* (G.S.) Subjects in this group received one hour of training a day, four days a week for four consecutive weeks for a total of 15 hours. A didactic-experiential approach was used whereby subjects were didactically taught how to choose a goal and develop a systematic program to obtain the goal. Experientially, they developed personal goal programs for themselves within the training process. Subjects were systematically trained on the use of Carkhuff and Friels' (1971) principles of program development which consist of nine basic steps: (1) choose a goal, (2) explain why it is important, (3) define and break down goal into observable behavioral steps, (4) rank steps in terms of degree of difficulty, (5) begin with the least difficult, (6) repeat each step until it is mastered, (7) review each step before advancing, (8) advance to next step after completion of less difficult step, (9) conclude program only when last step is mastered. Subjects worked through each step and outlined step-wise programs to follow in order to reach personal goals.

*Systematic Interpersonal Skills Training Group* (I.P.S.) Subjects in this group also received fifteen (15) hours of training. A modified didactic-experiential training approach outlined by Pierce and Drasgow (1969) was employed to shape subjects' responses to represent those of higher levels of the core facilitative conditions of empathy, respect, genuineness and concreteness. Using taped client stimuli expressions, subjects were first trained to identify feeling expressions, then to formulate one sentence responses reflecting feeling content. Subjects were then differentially reinforced to shape two and three sentence interactions with each other during role playing experiences.

*Systematic Physical, Intellectual and Emotional Training Group* (P.I.E.) Subjects in this group received all three systematic physical, intellectual and emotional-interpersonal training programs for a total of 45 hours.

*Therapeutic Recreation Activity Control Group* (R.) Subjects in this group participated in various recreation activities for approximately 15 hours over a four week period. Subjects were able to choose to participate in any of over 16 physical activities offered by the Center's recreation service over the time period. The activities were semi-structured to allow participants to participate at their own pace and involvement regardless of activity. This served as an unsystematic physical program.

*Personal and Work Adjustment Training Control Group* (P.W.T.) Subjects in this group received the rehabilitation Center's existing personal adjustment training program one hour a day, five days a week for three weeks for a total of 15 hours. The basic content of the program was oriented toward teaching subjects the basic facts relevant to understanding the world of work (job seeking, job retention) and money management. This served as an unsystematic intellectual program.

*Group Counseling Control Group* (G.C.) Subjects in this group received one hour of counseling, one hour a day, five days a week for three weeks for a total of 15 hours. The content of this group focused upon the subjects' understanding interpersonal effects upon one another. A non-directive approach was utilized. This served as an unsystematic emotional-interpersonal program.

*Control-Control Group* (C.) Subjects in this group did not receive any special treatment except for normal rehabilitation services (vocational training, individual counseling). They received a pre-post assessment for a 4 week time interval (Collingwood, 1972, pp. 2-5).

All subjects were pretested and posttested on their physical, emotional, and intellectual functioning. The following results were positive for the four treatment groups, where the difference was significant beyond the .001 level of confidence. The systematic physical training group increased in their physical functioning. The systematic goal setting group increased in their intellectual functioning, while the systematic interpersonal skills training group increased in their emotional functioning. The treatment group receiving training in all three of the above areas increased in all of the corresponding areas of functioning.

This study well represents the theory of specificity applied to treatment. In those areas where the youth offenders received systematic instruction, they improved. In those other areas where no training was provided, there were no improvements. None of the control groups came close in comparison to the gains of the treatment groups. A minimally significant gain was recorded in the group counseling control group. The major drawback of the study was a lack of any follow-up investigations. As it stands, what can be concluded is that systematic training in the physical, emotional, or intellectual aspects of a delinquent's life can lead to improved functioning in the corresponding area. Similarly, a comprehensive program focusing on all three areas can result in combined benefits.

Handler (1975) reported the results of an evaluation of three separate community-based programs. However, only two of the studies utilized experimentally valid control groups. The programs could each handle between 20 and 50 youngsters, and had a board of directors composed of local citizens from each of three different Midwest communities.

They encourage the youngsters to participate in community activities that range from going to local events with a staff escort, to attending public schools regularly, to spending weekends at home and elsewhere. Local volunteers augment services of all the programs by befriending individual youngsters, providing transportation and recreation . . . (Handler, 1975, p. 217).

The programs also attempted to individualize treatment built around the individual youth's problems. A point system was used in each program, where the youths earned different levels of freedom and privileges.

In the first program, Children's Center, the average length of stay was between three and four months. In the evaluation, 53 boys and girls were compared with 42 similar youths. Baseline comparisons revealed no initial difference between the groups on 13 relevant variables. The youths in the treatment group participated in a community residential center that emphasized a behavior modification system as treatment. The delinquent youths in the control group lived at home. The nine-month follow-up results were negative. No significant differences were seen in school grades, tardiness, suspension from school, criminal contacts, placement changes, and family placements. The treatment group did worse in terms of school attendance, juvenile and criminal contacts, and institutional placement. The clearly unfavorable results question the use of a residential center that emphasizes behavior modification.

Handler (1975) presented the evaluation of the second community residential center. In this study, 33 youths, predominantly 15-year-old boys, were matched with 33 youths in a control group. The youths in the treatment group resided at the center approximately five months. The center program included school attendance and utilization of staff interpersonal relationships to bring about change. While the treatment group resided at the center, the control group remained at home and received normal juvenile probation services.

There was a significant positive reduction in delinquent behavior on the part of the treatment group after six months of follow-up. However, there was an even greater reduction on the part of the control group, a significantly greater reduction. The results, first of all, do not support the use of community residential centers for youths on juvenile probation. According to this study, remaining at home would have more favorable benefits. The second observation is that this study unequivocally demonstrates the value of using an appropriately selected control group. The fact that we knew the control group's behavior improved significantly more than the treatment group's protected us from the false conclusion that this residential group home was effective.

## Conclusions

This chapter has presented the results of eight studies involving almost 800 delinquent youths in community residential programs. The follow-up results of all the programs, whether halfway houses, group homes, foster homes, or residential centers, were negative. There was either no significant difference or, as was the case in five of the eight programs, the community residential group did worse. The only program that reported any success was Collingwood's rehabilitation center program, which was based upon the Carkhuff model of systematic skill development in the physical, emotional, and intellectual areas. However, that program did not provide a follow-up evaluation. Table 13-1 presents the summaries.

In the opening quotation of this chapter, rehabilitation promise was held out for delinquent youths through community programs. As we have seen, such a promise did not materialize through community residential programs. To answer the question of why such a failure occurred, the programs that were provided in the community residential setting will be examined. In addition to the community setting, the major program elements were group counseling, family group counseling, guided group interaction, differential treatment, behavior modification, and emphasis on positive interpersonal relationships with the staff. Throughout this book, all these approaches have consistently failed as rehabilitative influences, except for behavior modification. And with behavior modification, success occurred only when the behavior to be changed was simple, specifically identified, and reinforced. Behavior modification also did not succeed in terms of reducing delinquent behavior. The negative results of the studies in this chapter indicate that there is nothing inherent in a community-based setting that will offset an ineffective program.

Vinter (1976) reported the results of a national survey of juvenile corrections programs. The treatment approaches in 10 community residential homes and in 9 community day treatment programs were examined. The dominant approaches in those community programs were: individual counseling, group counseling, Reality Therapy, and behavior modification. The most frequently

**Table 13-1**
**Community Residential Programs Summary**

| Researcher | Number of Youths | | Intervention | Results | Follow-up Results |
|---|---|---|---|---|---|
| | *Experimental* | *Control* | | | |
| Reed (1967) | 111 | | *a.* Halfway house<br>*b.* Group counseling<br>*c.* Family group counseling | | *a.* Treatment group had higher failure rate<br>*b.* Treatment group more involved in training and/or employment |
| Scarpitti and Stephenson (1969) | 44 | 44 | *a.* Residential group home program<br>*b.* Guided group interaction | No significant difference in the within program failure rate | *a.* Worse recidivism than regular probation group<br>*b.* No significant difference in recidivism compared to institutional program |
| McCord, McCord, and Thurber (1968) | 19 | 19 | Foster home | | Higher rate of criminal involvement after 12 years |
| Empey and Lubeck (1971) | 141 | 121 | *a.* Halfway house<br>*b.* Guided group interaction | Fewer program graduates | *a.* No significant difference in recidivism<br>*b.* No significant difference in reduction in offenses<br>*c.* Less serious offenses |
| Palmer (1971) | 12 | 74 | *a.* Group home<br>*b.* Differential treatment | | No significant difference in parole revocation |
| Collingwood (1972) | 24 | 24 | *a.* Rehabilitation center<br>*b.* Systematic physical training<br>*c.* Systematic interpersonal skills training<br>*d.* Systematic goal setting training | Improved physical, emotional, and intellectual functioning | |
| Handler (1975) Children's Center | 53 | 42 | *a.* Community residential center<br>*b.* Behavior modification system | | *a.* No significant difference in school grades, tardiness, suspension from school, criminal contacts, placement changes, and family placements |

**Table 13-1.** (cont.)

| Researcher | Number of Youths | | Intervention | Results | Follow-up Results |
| | Experimental | Control | | | |
| --- | --- | --- | --- | --- | --- |
| | | | | | b. Worse perform-ance in school at-tendance, juvenile contacts, criminal contacts, and in-stitutional place-ment |
| Handler (1975) Teen Place | 33 | 33 | a. Community residential center b. Staff interper-sonal relationships | | Less reduction in delinquent be-havior after 6 months follow-up |

used method was individual counseling. It may be remembered from preceding chapters that all these approaches have proven unsuccessful in improving the community behavior of delinquent youths. The above findings lead to the following prediction.

**Specific Prediction**: Community residential programs will fail as long as the internal program is composed of approaches that have failed in other settings.

In other words, there is nothing inherent in a community program that will rehabilitate delinquent youths. If such a program is to succeed, it must be composed of effective staff and programs.

**Specific Recommendation**: Community residential programs should include the program elements of effective programs.

Those program ingredients have been summarized in chapter 9.

Is this an *anti*-community services chapter? No! Community programs are needed that treat delinquent behavior at its earliest onset—diversion programs. Community programs are needed that provide intensive and ongoing treatment—probation programs. Residential programs are needed that provide temporary care while the youths receive more intensive training. Residential programs are needed for youths whose delinquent behavior does not warrant the custody and security of a training school. Community programs, both residential and nonresidential, are needed for youths who need transition and follow-up help as they return to their communities from a training school. The key point, though, is that in all these contexts, an effective rehabilitation program must be developed beyond that which is inherent in the setting. The youths must be diagnosed on their specific interpersonal, educational, and vocational needs; provided with systematic instruction and practice in the skills needed; reinforced for success; and given appropriate transitional opportunities to practice the new behavior in the setting where the problems arose in the first place.

This chapter does suggest that there is an ideal community setting—*the family*. In five of the preceding studies, youths placed with their own families did as well or better than similar youths placed in alternate settings. The issue is how to get the youths and the family working together positively. Chapter 7 described methods that emphasized improving family communication skills. The first alternative to unsatisfactory living situations should be the provision of communication skills training. The next alternative is that in some instances the youths may have to be placed with relatives other than their parents. While family skills training is in process, either with the parents or the alternate relatives, the youths should be worked with to change whatever behavior is causing the disruption.

If the youths continue to break the law, it may be the fault of the youths, the families, or their interaction. At this point, other residential options should be explored. If, after placement, while receiving rehabilitation skills help, youths still violate the law, then a structured institution is needed. Such an institution can be large or small, in the community or in a rural setting. The primary ingredient is a secure setting that prevents the youths from further illegal behavior.

Whether the youths are institutionalized or placed in an alternative community residential setting, the goal for the majority of the youths should be to provide the shortest length of stay necessary so that they can continue training back in their own homes. To facilitate such a program, the families should be continually involved throughout the youths' absences. This should be the preferred course of action for the majority of delinquent youths. There may be, however, certain youths who will never succeed with any of their family relatives. These situations are in the minority; but when they occur, a trained foster family or a long-term residential program can be used until the youths are old enough to live on their own.

**General Prediction**: The greater the positive involvement of the families in the rehabilitation programs, the greater the likelihood of success. This involvement of the families, however, should be along the lines of training in improved problem-solving, communication, and discipline techniques.

**General Recommendation**: The families should be involved in the rehabilitation programs through

1.  Getting input on what the problems are
2.  Diagnosing the youths and the families' needs
3.  Teaching the families improved interaction patterns
4.  Teaching the parents how they can teach their children the skills they need to succeed

5.  Training the families in reward and punishment techniques
6.  Receiving praise and rewards themselves as the youths improve

The real inherent value of so-called community-based programs is that they allow for the possibility of a greater quantity of contact between the youths and their families. However, there is no guarantee that the increased contact will occur. As was pointed out in chapter 11, increased contact between the youths and their probation officers did not make a difference—quantity did not ensure quality. It is the responsibility of the rehabilitation workers to train the youths and their families for an increase in the quality of interaction.

## References

Collingwood, T.R. The effects of systematic physical, intellectual and emotional personal adjustment programs. Research Report. Hot Springs, Arkansas: Rehabilitation Research and Training Center, State of Arkansas, 1972.

Empey, L.T., and S.G. Lubeck. *The Silverlake Experiment: Testing Delinquency Theory and Community Intervention.* Chicago: Aldine-Atherton, 1971.

Handler, E. Residential Treatment Programs for Juvenile Delinquents. *Social Work* 20 (1975):217-222.

McCord, J., W. McCord, and E. Thurber. The effect of foster home placement in the prevention of adult antisocial behavior. In Stratton, J.R., and R. Terry, *Prevention of Delinquency.* New York: Macmillan, 1968.

Palmer, T.B. The group home project. Differential placement of delinquents in group homes. California Youth Authority and National Institute of Mental Health, 1972.

Reed, A. *The MacLaren Vocational Center.* MacLaren School for Boys. Woodburn, Oregon, 1967.

Scarpitti, F.R., and R.M. Stephenson. Essexfields: A Non-Residential Experiment in Group Centered Rehabilitation of Delinquents *Americal Journal of Correction* 31 (1969):12-18.

Vinter, R.D. *Time Out. A National Study of Juvenile Correctional Programs.* National Assessment of Juvenile Corrections. Univ. of Michigan, 1976.

Vinter, R.D., G. Downs, J. Hall. Juvenile corrections in the states: Residential programs and deinstitutionalization, A preliminary report. National Assessment of Juvenile Corrections. Univ. of Michigan, 1975.

# 14 Institutional Programs

## Review of the Research

Institutional treatment, as opposed to the other components of the juvenile justice system, is viewed as the treatment of last resort. Typically, a delinquent youth who comes before a juvenile court for a delinquency hearing is not committed to the state's institutional programs. Romig and Saddler (1976) have documented in Texas that less than 3 percent of the entire juvenile court delinquency referrals were committed to the state's training schools during 1972, 1973, or 1974.

Institutional placement by the juvenile judge generally occurs only after community resources and programs have failed. At a Texas training school, Romig (1973) discovered that all but 6 percent of the youths in residence had participated in some form of community program prior to being placed at the training school. About two-thirds of the youths studied, 67 percent, were involved in at least a juvenile probation program and one other service (group home, foster home, or special counseling program). It can be concluded for those youths that institutional placement occurred only after community programs had been tried and failed in reducing the illegal behavior.

This chapter will present the results of a variety of institutional approaches aimed at reducing delinquent behavior. Levinson and Kitchener (1964) compared the results of a milieu therapy institutional program with regular institutional activities. The youths were older teenage boys committed to the old National Training School in Washington, D.C. There was a combination of 225 boys who had committed federal or state offenses assigned to either the treatment or the control group. The youths in the milieu treatment group received group and individual counseling. Their treatment was also typified by more informal and therapeutic staff-inmate contacts than the control group.

The results were negative in terms of a significant difference between the two groups in misconduct reports while at the training school. However, the boys in the special treatment program reported less for sick call. After approximately 15 months of follow-up, there was no significant difference in the community adjustment of the two groups as measured by failure on parole. The treatment group, however, committed fewer serious offenses. The results of the study indicate that, on two of the criteria, there were positive benefits reported for the treatment, while no difference was found for the other two criteria.

Craft, Stephenson, and Granger (1965) examined the effects of a self-

159

government milieu therapy approach with delinquent youths in England. The institution this time, however, was a mental hospital. Fifty male delinquents from 13 to 25 years of age were alternately assigned to one of two programs. The treatment group participated in the following self-government approach and were told upon admission,

that the villa belonged to them; and that because each had something to contribute, each had a seat together with staff on the ward council, which ran the ward (Craft, Stephenson, and Granger, 1965, p. 546).

The ward council met two to three times weekly, as did the group therapy. Staff were specially "chosen from within the hospital for their tolerance and desire to participate."

The control group participated in an authoritarian-disciplinary program with some individual treatment. Both groups participated in a work program that involved rewards for good performance. The results of the follow-up study, performed after 14 months, were very negative. The treatment group committed significantly more offenses since discharge than the control group. There was no significant difference in the jobs held by the two groups. The authors concluded that the relatively disciplined work program was better than the more permissive group therapy, milieu approach.

The effects of different approaches in assigning boys at the National Training School to their counselors was examined by Levinson and Kitchener (1966). Three hundred boys were randomly assigned to one of four treatment groups. The only difference in the four groups was the method used to assign the boys to their cottage counselors. The first treatment group involved a boy being assigned to a counselor based upon similarity in self-perceived personality needs. The second method was that the counselor simply picked those boys he thought he could work with. The third treatment group involved boys selecting other groups of boys that they wanted to be with. The final method was a control group where the boys were assigned to their cottage group on a random basis.

The criteria of performance that were monitored for a five-month period were:

a. academic school grades
b. vocational work grades
c. cottage adjustment grades
d. number of minor misconduct reports
e. number of major misconduct reports
f. number of different boys receiving major reports
g. number of boys paroled and
h. number of boys transferred for failure to adjust (Levinson and Kitchener, 1966, p. 364).

All groups were basically the same in their improvement on most of the criteria. All groups did decrease in minor misconduct reports and transfers, but there was no significant difference in the improvement. The one piece of data that indicated that the personality matching technique was favorable was in a comparison of mean ranks on the different criteria. However, because of the other nonsignificant differences, the conclusions concerning the importance of counselor-student matching must remain tentative.

Seckel (1967) reported the results of an experiment comparing an intensive short-term treatment approach with the regular California training school program. There was a random assignment of 75 boys to the treatment group and 54 boys to the control group. The average age of both groups of boys was 17 years. The three main elements of the treatment program were a five-month determinant length of stay, self-government among the boys, and more intensive individual or group therapy than the control group.

An important element of the Fremont Program consisted of weekly living unit meetings to discuss problems of group living and any other matters of concern. The meetings were conducted mainly by the wards themselves as student council forums; staff had little or no direct involvement (Seckel, 1967, p. 27).

The educational program also emphasized counseling and discussion groups.

Contrary to the expectations of the proponents of the program, who wanted the program to be established as a model, there was no significant difference in the follow-up performance of the two groups. The recidivism rates at both the 15- and 24-month follow-up points were similar. The recidivism failure rate for the treatment group was 44 percent after 24 months, almost half. The negative results of a self-government, counseling approach have now been documented by two studies.

Knight (1970) presented the results of two different studies of the Marshall Program, a therapeutic community approach to institutional programming. Both studies involved teenage boys committed to the California Youth Authority. The main program components were the use of guided group interaction and a short term, 90-day program:

In this intensive treatment and rehabilitation effort, the Marshall Program strives to apply the concepts of the "therapeutic community," in which the wards share in the responsibility for their own treatment and are involved in decisions relating to their own treatment. On Marshall, this approach includes small group counseling meetings, a daily community counseling meeting attended by all wards and Marshall staff, and weekly group counseling with parents (Knight, 1970, p. 2).

The approach emphasized youths confronting each other in their group meetings, much as guided group interaction does.

The first study involved 109 boys in the treatment group compared with 209 similar youths. The boys in the treatment group were specially selected for their ability to make a favorable community adjustment without prolonged institutionalization. The within-program failure rate of the treatment group was 16 percent and included those youths who had to be transferred because of poor adjustment. The treatment group boys were compared with youths participating in a regular training school program. There was no significant difference between the two groups in their parole revocation rate after 15 months of follow-up.

The second study utilized 123 boys in the treatment group matched with the same number of boys in the control group. This time the results of 15 months of follow-up were even more negative. The treatment group had a significantly worse parole performance. The author did report differentially positive effects for older boys who had committed offenses with two or more other boys. However, for the majority of delinquent youths, it can be concluded that a therapeutic community approach involving confrontation as a major therapeutic technique is ineffective.

An innovative program for psychopathic delinquents was researched by Ingram, Gerard, Quay, and Levinson (1970). The youths involved in the study were delinquent boys committed to the National Training School, an old unit of the Federal Bureau of Prisons in Washington, D.C. Twenty treatment subjects were matched with 21 similar boys who were committed to the institution at the same time. The matching criteria were race, IQ, personality test classification, and type of commitment. Data concerning two control groups involving youths who were committed to the training school prior to the start of the treatment are excluded because of the lack of comparability in time and history with the treatment group.

The authors were concerned with developing an alternative to the traditional verbal and counseling approaches usually, tried with delinquent youths. Their approach emphasized program novelty and excitement. There were special tournaments, excursions, and field trips, along with nightly recreation and athletic competition against the staff:

A seven-days-a-week program was designed for the evening hours and weekends. Because for these youth, boredom quickly builds under routine conditions, all program elements were selected to emphasize novelty and excitement (Ingram et al., 1970, p. 25).

Psychodrama was the therapeutic approach of choice because of its emphasis on action.

The results were negative in a comparison of the treatment group with their contemporary control group. There were no significant differences in the three measures of institutional performance: days spent in the security or segregation unit, the number of assaultive offenses, and the number of youths showing unsatisfactory institutional releases. No follow-up results were presented. The authors are to be praised for their attempts to produce an alternative to the clearly documented failure of casework and counseling. I agree that we have to move toward more active therapy approaches. However, this highly novel program did not focus therapeutically on the boys' problems. All it did was keep them constructively busy 24 hours a day. In the end its effects were no different than the regular institutional program for the psychopathic delinquents.

Jesness (1971) evaluated the effectiveness of a differential treatment program upon delinquent youths committed to the Preston Training School in California. The study involved the random assignment of 655 boys to the treatment condition and 515 boys to the control group, which participated in the regular institutional program. The differential treatment approach utilized was based upon the California developed, I-level classification scheme. In the I-level method, boys are assigned to different interpersonal maturity and integration levels based upon diagnostic tests and interviews. The youths in the Preston study were diagnosed into the three main I-levels and nine delinquent subtypes shown in table 14-1. The higher the level, the more socially appropriate the behavior and the attitudes.

Management staff received 70 hours training, while the group supervisors and youth counselors received 34 hours training in I-level and the differential treatment methodology. After the youths were diagnosed, they were placed in cottages with youths in the same subtype classification, and with staff who were matched with the youths in terms of personality, interests, and working style. Each of the cottages developed a unique counseling, educational, and vocational program based upon the diagnosed subtype of the youths.

The results of the 15- and 24-month follow-up studies were negative in each

**Table 14-1**
**I-Levels and Subtypes of the Youths in the Preston Study**

| I-Level | Code Name | Subtype | Proportion in Preston Sample |
|---------|-----------|---------|------------------------------|
| 2 | Aa | Unsocialized, Aggressive | 2.6% |
| 2 | Ap | Unsocialized, Passive | 9.6% |
| 2 | Cfc | Conformist, Immature | 23.8% |
| 3 | Cfm | Conformist, Cultural | 13.6% |
| 3 | Mp | Manipulator | 18.6% |
| 3 | Na | Neurotic, Acting-Out | 13.8% |
| 3 | Nx | Neurotic, Anxious | 15.2% |
| 4 | Se | Situational Emotional Reaction | 1.9% |
| 4. | Ci | Cultural Identifier | 1.0% |

Adapted from Jesness (1971), p. 40.

case. There was no significant difference between the treatment and control groups in their parole revocation rates at the two follow-up points. The negative results of differential treatment and staff-student matching are somewhat understandable when one examines that on the differential treatment cottages; even though the style of presentation was individualized, the same unsuccessful treatment methods used elsewhere were dominant: work program, individual counseling, group discussions, token economy, and group counseling. The results of this study do not support such differential treatment.

Many studies have been undertaken to prove the advantages of small 20- to 25-bed living units compared to larger living units. The one study to date that involved a random assignment of youths to either a 50-bed unit or to a 20-bed unit was conducted by Jesness (1972). The experiment involved 95 boys randomly assigned to the treatment group and 186 boys assigned to the control. The study occurred at the Fricot Ranch School, a facility of the California Youth Authority. The researchers attempted to control the study in such a way that the only difference between the two groups was the living-unit size—20 beds for the treatment group and 50 beds for the control group.

The results were mixed in their support of the smaller living unit. Youths in the treatment group received almost five times more staff time than youths in the larger cottages. In the 1957 to 1959 phase of the study, after 12 months of follow-up, there was no significant difference between the two groups. In the 1960 to 1964 phase of the research, the treatment group did better at 12 months. However, after 24 months of follow-up, the superior parole performance dissipated. There was no significant difference after 36 and 60 months of follow-up. One positive benefit for the treatment group was the less time spent in lock-up. The conclusion is that there is nothing inherent in a smaller living unit that will rehabilitate delinquent youths. The fact that there was a higher quantity of staff-student contact in the smaller cottage did not necessarily translate into a higher quality of interaction.

Before leaving the study, a comment made by Jesness should be included:

Although it is doubtful that increasing the staff-to-boy ratios can directly lead to better outcomes, these programs with base survival-level staff-to-boy ratios can probably not do effective treatment regardless of the treatment theory used or the technical expertness of staff (Jesness, 1974, p. 24).

Having a small staff-student ratio is not a sufficient condition, in and of itself, to rehabilitate delinquent youths. However, in order to have the time to appropriately train and teach the youths in methods this book is recommending, the staff-student ratio cannot be as it was in the 50-bed living units. Fortunately, it has been documented by Knight (1971) that in a nationwide survey, "over 90 percent of the total new and planned units in state institutions have capacities of 30 or below." However, it must be reemphasized that there is nothing inherent in the smaller cottages that will improve the rehabilitation of delinquent youths.

Tupker and Pointer (1975) evaluated the effectiveness of a differential treatment approach at the Iowa Training School for Boys. The method was based upon the factor analytic classification system developed by Herbert Quay and the Federal Bureau of Prisons. At the Iowa School, 143 boys were randomly assigned to the treatment group, while 129 were similarly placed in the control group. The average age of both groups was 16 years. The boys in the experimental (E) group were assigned to their cottages through homogeneous behavior category classification. The control group boys were placed in cottages according to their age.

The Quay classification system is based upon the following four primary groups:

BC-1: Immature, inadequate youth
BC-2: Neurotic, emotionally disturbed youth
BC-3: Psychopathic, aggressive youth
BC-4: Gang delinquent youth

The boys in the experimental cottages were diagnosed in all the above types except for the BC-2 category, which had no youths. The following describes the three programs put into effect.

The E BC-1 program was designed to deal more effectively with, among other things, the very high dependency needs, the immaturity, and the low self-esteem of the BC-1 Ss, e.g., by providing large amounts of individual counseling. The E BC-3 program was designed to cope more effectively with the more aggressive, manipulative and power-oriented individuals assigned to it by developing, for example, a program with a relatively high level of structure and with direct, immediate feedback concerning progress in school. The E BC-4 program was patterned, to a large extent, after Reality Therapy. Treatment in this case, was geared to the needs and the problems of the socialized and group-oriented individuals assigned to it. The program was designed to deal more effectively with minimizing the effects of the delinquent peer group as a reinforcer and to the development of individual responsibility (Tupker and Pointer, 1974, p. 92).

The control group participated in the regular institutional program.

The results were *not* favorable. There was no significant difference in the two groups' institutional adjustments, as measured by the number of times in detention, the number of days in detention, the number of times AWOL from the institution, and the number of transfers to more secure units. Only with the BC-3 experimental group was there a positive result, with their having significantly more special leaves than their control group. However, there was no significant difference between any of the experimental groups and the control group in their recidivism rate. Once again, differential treatment and homogeneous grouping of delinquents in an institutional program was not effective.

The effects of a therapeutic community approach with drug offenders was reported by Seckel (1975). The experiment compared 40 boys who participated in the project with a matched control group of 34 similar youths. The treatment involved the development of a therapeutic community called the Family Program on the gounds of the Preston School of Industry, a training school of the California Youth Authority.

The goals of treatment are to give members a better understanding of their own behaviors and interpersonal relations, and to improve their social skills to cope with pressures relating to drug abuse and delinquent tendencies after release to parole. Treatment includes the use of verbal confrontation methods, role playing, encounters and related techniques, and supportive interaction (Seckel, 1975, p. 2).

The boys in the control group participated in the regular training school program.

The main follow-up measures revealed no significant difference in the parole failure rate of the two groups after 12 months. There was also no significant difference in the number of arrests for drug abuse. Cost effectiveness analysis revealed that the treatment program was not more cost-effective. As with all therapeutic community approaches, this program failed in terms of demonstrating more effectiveness than regular institutional programs.

In the final study to be reported in this section, Maskin (1976) evaluated the effectiveness of a family communication skills approach compared with a work-oriented program. Thirty first-commitment boys at the work-oriented ranch program were matched against 30 similar boys at the family treatment program ranch. The boys were between 15 and 17 years of age. The treatment program,

emphasize[d] a "parent-child" interaction through individual and group counseling in order to provide the parents and youth an opportunity to learn better communication skills (Maskin, 1976, p. 432).

The youths received four months of follow-up help following release from the institution. The youth's in the control group participated in a ranch work program that also included recreational and sports activities.

The results were positive. There was significantly better institutional behavior for the family skills group. The family skills group also had a significantly lower follow-up recidivism rate. The author concluded, "Improvement of family and social relations appears to influence directly the lower recidivism rates observed in this study (Maskin, 1976, p. 433). The favorable results of a skills approach designed to improve parent-child communication is consistent with research reported in previous chapters.

## Conclusions

Twelve studies on the effects of various forms of institutional treatment with over 3000 juvenile delinquent youths have been discussed in the preceding section. Of the 12 studies, only one obtained completely positive results—Maskin's research on family communication skills. The one study of milieu therapy obtained partially favorable results compared with the regular institutional program. One study that utilized staff and student matching had a partially favorable improvement in institutional behavior. However, the second of the two matching studies reported no significant difference in follow-up parole performance. For milieu therapy and matching as institutional intervention, it can be concluded that they are partially effective.

The majority of the studies in this chapter obtained negative results (see table 14-2). The following approaches were tried in at least 2 of the 12 projects and found ineffective or no more effective than the regular programs: self-government, shorter lengths of stay, therapeutic community, confrontive forms of therapy, and differential treatment. The one study of a smaller unit size obtained a nonsignificant difference when compared to the regular unit size. The Federal Bureau of Prisons study of a highly novel and exciting program for psychopathic delinquents achieved nonsignificant results also. When trying to answer why the programs failed, it is useful to look at their specific program components. When this was done, it was found that the main program elements were group counseling, individual counseling, work programs, guided group interaction, and intensive casework, all programs whose failures have been documented throughout this book.

**Specific Prediction**: So-called innovative programs, such as self-government, shorter lengths of stay, therapeutic communities, confrontation therapy, and differential treatment, will all fail, as long as their dominant ingredients are combinations of ineffective rehabilitation methods.

**Specific Recommendation**: The differential treatment approach should utilize specificity and the teaching of skills to the youths and their families rather than the ineffective methods tried to date.

The goal of the rehabilitation of delinquent youths is furthered through individual and specific treatment. Differential treatment, as a concept, is clearly a move in the right direction. However, since the concept was implemented, the same ineffective treatment approaches (individual counseling, group counseling, and intensive staff casework) have been used and only varied in their intensity and style of presentation. The main recommendation is in fact to *go beyond* differential treatment to truly individualized treatment.

**Table 14-2**
**Institutional Programs Summary**

| Researcher | Number of Youths | | Intervention | Results | Follow-up Results |
|---|---|---|---|---|---|
| | Experimental | Control | | | |
| Levinson and Kitchener (1964) | 225 | | a. Milieu therapy b. Staff team approach | a. Fewer youth sick b. No significant difference in misconduct reports | a. No significant difference in parole failure b. Fewer serious offenses |
| Craft, Stephenson, and Granger (1965) | 25 | 25 | a. Self government b. Group therapy | | a. Greater number of offenses b. No significant difference in number of jobs held |
| Levinson and Kitchener (1966) | 300 | | a. Matching counselors with youths b. Boys picking boys c. Counselors picking boys | a. No significant difference in improvement in the four groups b. Matching group did somewhat better in overall institutional performance | |
| Seckel (1967) | 75 | 54 | a. Five month determinant length of stay b. Self-government among the youths c. Intensive individual or group therapy | | No significant difference in recidivism rate at either 15 or 24 months |
| Knight (1970) | 209 | 209 | a. Therapeutic community b. Short-term 90-day program c. Confrontation therapy | High within-program failure rate | No significant difference in parole follow-up performance after 15 months |
| Knight (1970) | 123 | 123 | a. Therapeutic community b. Short-term 90-day program c. Confrontation therapy | | Worse parole performance for treatment group |
| Ingram, Gerard, Quay, and Levinson (1970) | 20 | 21 | a. Emphasis on program novelty and excitement b. Nightly organized recreation c. Psychodrama | No significant difference in days a. Days spent in security b. Number of assaultive offenses c. Unsatisfactory institutional release | |

**Table 14-2. (cont.)**

| Researcher | Number of Youths | | Intervention | Results | Follow-up Results |
|---|---|---|---|---|---|
| | Experimental | Control | | | |
| Jesness (1971) | 655 | 515 | *a.* Matched staff and students *b.* Differential treatment program for each subtype of offender | | No significant difference in parole failure rate at 15 and 24 months |
| Jesness (1972) | 95 | 186 | Assignment to a 20-boy unit | | *a.* No significant difference in parole revocations after 36 and 60 months *b.* Less time in lock-up |
| Tupker and Pointer (1975) | 143 | 129 | Differential treatment based upon Quay classification | No significant difference in *a.* Number of days or times in detention *b.* Number of times AWOL from the institution *c.* Number of transfers | No significant difference in recidivism |
| Seckel (1975) | 40 | 34 | *a.* Confrontive therapy *b.* Therapeutic community | | *a.* No significant difference in parole failure rate after 12 months *b.* No significant difference in drug abuse *c.* Less cost-effective |
| Maskin (1976) | 30 | 30 | Family communication skills | Less use of the detention unit | Less recidivism |

The self-government, therapeutic communities, and guided group interaction approaches always fail. A major flaw in these methods is the assumption that the group can make better treatment judgments regarding individual youths than can the staff or the youths themselves. That assumption is incorrect. Neither the group nor the youths, initially, can make accurate judgments regarding present or future treatment needs. If the youths could make those kinds of discriminations, they would not have been incarcerated in the first place. It is for this same reason that solely relying on the youths input to develop a treatment plan is inappropriate.

It is my judgment that the movement toward wanting delinquents to have a bigger say in their treatment was designed to combat what was perceived as arbitrary decision making by uncaring staff. Without conceding whether institutional staff are arbitrary or not, it would be useful for all parties involved to move toward criteria of treatment decision making that are *objective*. Such criteria will not be evaluated subjectively by staff, the youths themselves, or the peer group. Objective criteria can be observed, measured, and recorded. The youths will be able to know at each point in their institutional stays what they need to learn and how far they must go. Finally, objective measures of treatment needs and progress are consistent with an approach to delinquency rehabilitation that emphasizes treatment specificity and skills. In fact, such an approach requires objective measures as a feedback mechanism to modify or improve the treatment process.

**General Prediction**: Whenever treatment decision making is based upon subjective criteria, whether of the youths, the staff, or the group, such judgments will be less accurate than decisions based upon objective measurements of behavior.

**General Recommendation**: Treatment diagnosis, placement, progress, release, and follow-up should all be based upon measurements of rehabilitation skills that reduce the likelihood of further delinquency.

Though such objective criteria of progress are needed in all aspects of the juvenile justice system, they are *most critical* in situations where institutional placement is depriving youths of physical and social liberty and freedom.

## References

Craft, M., G. Stephenson, and C. Granger. A controlled trial of authoritarian and self-governing regimes with adolescent psychopaths. *American Journal of Orthopsychiatry* 34 (1965):543-554.

Ingram, G.L., R.E. Gerard, H.C. Quay, R.B. Levinson. An experimental program for the psychopathic delinquents: Looking in the "correctional waste-basket." *Journal of Research in Crime and Delinquency* 7 (1970):24-30.

Jesness, C.F. Comparative effectiveness of two institutional treatment programs for delinquents: The Fricot project. In *A Review of Accumulated Research in the California Youth Authority,* Keith Griffiths, ed. Sacramento: California Youth Authority, 1974.

Jesness, C.F. Comparative effectiveness of two institutional treatment programs for delinquents. *Child Care Quarterly* 1 (Winter, 1972):119-130.

Jesness, C.F. The Preston typology study, an experiment with differential treatment in an institution. *Journal of Research in Crime and Delinquency* 8 (1971):38-52.

Knight, D. The Marshall Program, Assessment of a Short-Term Institutional Treatment Program. Part II: Amenability to Confrontive Peer-Group Treatment. Research Report No. 59. Sacramento: California Youth Authority, 1970.

Knight, D. The Impact of Living-Unit Size in Youth Training Schools. Sacramento: California Youth Authority, 1971.

Levinson, R.B., and H.L. Kitchener. *Demonstration Counseling Project*. Washington, D.C.: National Training School for Boys, 1964.

Levinson, R.B., and H.L. Kitchener. Treatment of delinquents: Comparison of four methods for assigning inmates to counselors. *Journal of Consulting Psychology* 30 (1966):364.

Maskin, M.B. The differential impact of work-oriented vs. communication-oriented juvenile correction programs upon recidivism rates in delinquent males. *Journal of Clinical Psychology* 32 (1976):432-433.

Romig, D.A. *Use of Community Services Prior to Commitment*. Brownwood, Texas: Brownwood State Home and School, 1973.

Romig, D.A., and C. Saddler. *Texas Juvenile Court Statistics for 1974*. Texas Youth Council. Austin, Texas, 1976.

Seckel, J. The Fremont Experiment: Assessment of Residential Treatment at a Youth Authority Reception Center. Research Report No. 50. Sacramento: California Youth Authority, 1967.

Seckel, J. Assessment of Preston Family Drug Treatment Project. Sacramento: California Youth Authority, 1975.

Tupker, H.E., and J.C. Pointer. *The Iowa Differential Classification and Treatment Project*. Eldora, Iowa: Iowa Training School for Boys, 1975.

# 15

# Massachusetts' Deinstitutionalization Project

## Introduction

For almost three years, from 1973 to 1975, the juvenile corrections world was bombarded with publicity concerning a new truly effective way of dealing with chronic juvenile offenders who required institutional placement. This innovative approach was to release all the youth from the institution and close the institution. The project was called the Massachusetts Experiment in Deinstitutionalization. Early reports of success, from a criminal justice study conducted by the Harvard University, provided all that was needed for radical reformers in other states to urge the closing down of all juvenile correctional institutions.

## History of the Project

Prior to 1969, the Division of Youth Services in Massachusetts was characterized as having overcrowded institutions with poor educational and rehabilitation programs. The administration was viewed as authoritarian and closed to new ideas. In fairness to this administration, people do admit that there was no brutality, that the institutions were clean and open, that the food was good, and that structured recreation was provided. The main problems were the lack of training or rehabilitation; the recidivism rate was high, and the citizens wanted change. The director at this time was asked to resign, and the agency was reorganized.

After a nationwide search, a new commissioner, Dr. Jerome Miller, was appointed to head up the new Department of Youth Services (DYS) in October 1969. He took over with a strong mandate of support from the governor, the juvenile judges, and the public to develop an effective rehabilitation program. Through 1969 and 1970, consistent with everyone's desires, Dr. Miller attempted to implement a rehabilitation program in the state's training schools. He utilized the expertise of Dr. Maxwell Jones from England and Harry Vorrath of the positive peer culture approach to implement the therapeutic community approach. Dr. Jones provided less than a week's training at one of the institutions in the beginning of 1970. Mr. Vorrath, later in 1970, provided a three-day training session on positive peer culture, a variant of guided group interaction.

Based on that training, Dr. Miller began the changeover to a therapeutic community style of treatment. As a result, the youths spent large parts of the day in bed or watching TV, discipline became lax, and the living units reportedly became filthy. Gradually the institutions became more and more out of control. There were mass runaways, fires, and extensive vandalism (Serrill, 1975).

Miller felt blocked in terms of trying to change the staff or the programs in the existing training schools. The citizens of Massachusetts were supportive of his attempts to improve the institutions, but they were impatient to see the promised changes. Many of his early supporters began questioning his reform programs after visiting the institutions and observing the negative results (Poitrast, 1976). Miller needed to demonstrate positive action. Miller and Leavey were discussing the institutions late one evening when someone suggested, at first jokingly, to close them all down. The idea was discussed and the decision was made to close all the facilities. At first, there was no clear plan on what was going to happen to the youths (Leavey, 1976).

A four-month timetable was developed by Leavey and his staff, but it was cut to four weeks by Miller. He felt he had to begin closing the institutions while the legislature was not in session during their January 1972 recess, because he knew that they would fight and block his plan. In a two-month period, all the youth committed to the state's institutions were released and placed elsewhere, except for 20 girls (Serrill, 1975). Federal funds were requested to build small facilities across the state to fill the gap. However, the money did not arrive in time. Line item budget funds were shifted without legislative authorization to purchase the services of private programs. Many new private corporations sprang up to accommodate the need. Some of them utilized the grounds and buildings of the old institutions that DYS had only recently evacuated. In fact, Miller was allowing the use of the old institutional buildings, grounds, and rural locations, which is inconsistent with the concept of community-based treatment. There is some agreement that the early private programs had difficulties. Recidivism and escape rates were high.

From the beginning, the biggest problem was what to do with youths who needed secure programs. Several private programs were contracted with to meet this need. However, they were unable to stop the high escape rates. In fact, it was the Department of Youth Services policy that even the secure program should be "open." The result was that no secure programs existed. The juvenile judges became disenchanted. Where earlier they had supported Miller, they then became frustrated and finally irate. As Miller's support began to drop, he resigned in January 1973 to go to Illinois. There he was initially supported, but after a year and a half he was asked to resign.

Joseph Leavey took over as the new Commissioner of the Department of Youth Services. Leavey wanted to carry on in the Miller tradition, keeping all the institutions closed and not developing any secure programs. He was left with an administrative nightmare. Funds had been committed where no funds were available. Private vendors were promised money, and there was no mechanism to provide regular payment. There were no administrative mechanisms to conduct program reviews and evaluations. Leavey was called before the Massachusetts Legislature's Joint Committee on Post Audit and Oversight to answer charges of gross mismanagement. The Post Audit and Oversight Bureau documented many financial and program problems and concluded:

The legacy left to the Commonwealth by Commissioner Miller upon his departure for the State of Illinois is closed departmental institutions to be sure. He has also bequeathed, however, insufficient maximum security settings for that number of juvenile offenders which the great majority of individuals dealing with the problem agree are necessary, a demoralized department, and an ill-supervised private placement program which has resulted in increased runaways, escapes, deaths, and other attendant consequences (Management Audit of the Department of Youth Services, p. 260).

Leavey worked on improving the purchase of services program. Nonresidential programs were developed that have proven effective with some youths. However, he felt trapped with regard to his agency's use of existing institutions. He had received permission to delete 300 state positions, contingent on the fact that his new programs would not need houseparents, caseworkers, maintenance men, cooks, and so on in state-operated programs. However, if he opened even one state program that used any of the staff in the above classifications, he would have been required to reestablish all the positions in that job classification. He felt, therefore, that he could use only private programs; and unfortunately, they just could not deliver adequately secure programs.

Through 1975, newspapers and television covered the recent failures of the deinstitutionalization of the Department of Youth Services. In particular, Channel 5 TV, outside of Boston, ran a series of broadcasts that resulted in a citizen request for Leavey's resignation as head of the Department of Youth Services. The main charge was that the lack of secure programs was causing increased crime on the streets and increased recidivism of youths. Toward the latter part of 1975, Commissioner Leavey was forced to resign.

The future of services for delinquent youths in Massachusetts is uncertain. The state is polarized and emotionally aroused concerning the experience of the past few years. It is difficult for representatives of the different viewpoints to rationally sit down and plot a positive course for the department. It remains to be seen if the bad will that has built up in so many quarters of the state can be worked through toward a favorable outcome.

The new Commissioner, Jack Calhoun, was interviewed the first week in February 1976. He stated that he felt the Massachusetts programs were at day one, almost as if nothing had been done. His point was that Miller, and even Leavey, did not have a set of programs and policies based upon any kind of systematic planning. At best, they had only one goal—close the institutions. Calhoun has determined that his agency needs a master plan that will move activities from management by reflex to management that moves in the direction of long-range goals. It is his mission to develop a balanced program that utilizes community resources to the maximum extent, but has secure programs for those who need it (Calhoun, 1976). Future studies will determine the effectiveness of his program. However, data have been generated concerning the experiment initiated by Miller and will be discussed in the next section.

### Analysis of the Data

The data concerning the effectiveness of the Massachusetts experience in deinstitutionalization will be presented from three separate sources. Unfortunately, none of the three studies, including the one conducted by the Harvard Law School, utilized matched or randomly assigned control groups. However, since the studies that will be cited are used by the proponents of the Massachusetts approach to deinstitutionalization, it will serve our purpose to know the content of those studies.

In 1974 the Post Audit and Oversight Bureau conducted a management audit of the Department of Youth Services (Joint Committee on Post Audit and Oversight, 1974). In the study, data regarding a substantial increase in the runaway rate of juveniles committed to the Department of Youth Services (DYS) were reported. In FY 1969, prior to deinstitutionalization, 449 runaways were reported; and during FY 1973, there were 989 runaways reported at comparable facilities. Deaths of youths committed to the DYS were also found to have increased:

During the three years prior to reorganization, eight youths in the care of the Department died, two of these appearing to be from natural causes. Since October, 1969, at least thirty-seven youths have died while under the Department's care, only two of whom died of natural causes (Joint Committee on Post Audit and Oversight, 1974, p. 234).

The increase in deaths was from 2 a year to 7.5 a year, almost a 400 percent increase. As with all the data presented in the Management Audit, the Department of Youth Services was given the opportunity to refute or comment on the findings. In each case, DYS, while remarking that the increased runaways and deaths were unfortunate, did not dispute the data.

One justification for the closing of the institutions and the placement of youths in community-based programs was that the youths would be able to more favorably identify with, and get involved in, the community programs. It could be concluded that if youths were more positive about their community placement, one would expect a decrease in runaway rate. The logic would be that if a youth could see that the program was helping him or, at least, was better than previously restrictive programs, he would stay and participate in the program. To the contrary, the data indicate that the runaway rate, rather than declining, increased over 120 percent.

The report also included court recidivism rates for six Suffolk County (Boston) courts for 1971 and data on the East Boston District Court for 1972:

A survey in six Suffolk county courts relative to East Boston recidivism among parolees from the Youth Services Board in the year 1971 shows the following [table 15-1] (Joint Committee on Post Audit and Oversight, 1974, p. 265):

The recidivism data shown in table 15-1 establishes the fact that many youths on parole from the Department of Youth Services were committing serious enough offenses to require reappearances before the juvenile court; in some cases, twice within one year. The high recidivism rates indicate that the community-based emphasis was ineffective with a majority of delinquent youths committed from an urban environment.

The authors of the report concluded:

The establishment of the Department of Youth Services, in 1969, was intended to be an extensive step forward in the treatment of juvenile offenders. It presaged an era of expectation and hope that new methods of supervision and rehabilitation would be discovered resulting in the delivery of greater quality of service to youths at less cost to the Commonwealth. This enactment envisioned the development of modernized procedures of placement and mandated the development of alternatives to institutionalization for subsequent implementation. It envisioned a well planned, well monitored, and legislatively sanctioned approach to progressive forms of treatment. Unfortunately, this did not materialize. The administration of the new Department has been marked by disregard of statutory provisions and administrative procedures, amounting at time to misfeasance and nonfeasance, as well as inefficiency, mismanagement and waste (Joint Committee on Post Audit and Oversight, 1974, p. S-1).

The authors also took issue with the statement that regardless of all the problems and ensuing difficulties, at least deinstitutionalization was more

**Table 15-1**
**Recidivism Among Parolees from the Youth Services Board for Suffolk County and East Boston Courts for 1971**

| Court | Committed | Repeaters | Recidivism |
|-------|-----------|-----------|------------|
| Boston Juvenile | 105 | 96 | 91.4% |
| East Boston | 25 | 24 | 96.0% |
| Chelsea | 26 | 24 | 92.0% |
| Charlestown | 8 | 6 | 75.0% |
| West Roxbury | 42 | 39 | 92.8% |
| Brighton | 11 | 8 | 72.7% |

Adapted from Joint Committee on Post Audit and Oversight (1974), p. 265.

humane. From their viewpoint, no data had been presented substantiating the "humaneness" of the deinstitutionalized approach. In conclusion, the overall impression gained and presented by the legislative committee was of an ineffective organization whose financial control was as mismanaged as its control of the youths under its care.

A second study of deinstitutionalization and recidivism was conducted by Harvard University. The studies are part of a seven-year program of evaluation of the Massachusetts Department of Youth Services begun in 1970 by Dr. Lloyd Ohlin. The initial recidivism data (Ohlin, Miller, and Coates, 1974) were presented as part of a review of previous data on Massachusetts state delinquency programs. The comparisons were made against groups of youths released at different times who were *not* randomly assigned or matched with comparable youths.

The results comparing the six-month recidivism rate for girls, as measured by the percent of girls reappearing in court, indicated an *increase* in the recidivism rate. The six-month rate prior to deinstitutionalization was 13 to 27 percent. The rate of the girls released during the massive closing of the institutions was 20 percent. However, the rate reported for the girls participating fully in the new community-based programs was up to 30 percent. The authors concluded, along with the Department of Youth Services, that some special program revisions were necessary for the youthful female offenders, since the deinstitutionalized program was not effective.

With boys, the 1974 report had more favorable results, but they were results that were later found to be in error. Table 15-2 presents a comparison of the six-month recidivism data for boys. Recidivism in each case is the percent of youths in the study group with a court reappearance. As can be seen, the rate for three of the four time periods is very similar, around 50 percent. The final rate, however, for the youths participating in the new community-based programs is dramatically less, 25 percent. It was these findings that prompted the Department of Youth Services to call press conferences and go before national

**Table 15-2**

**Comparison of Six-Month Recidivism of Boys Committed to the Department of Youth Services**

| Year | Number | Court Reappearance |
|------|--------|--------------------|
| 1962 | 88 | 49% |
| 1971-1972 | 94 | 48-61% |
| 1972 | 74 | 50% |
| 1973-1974 | 117 | 25%* |

Adapted from Ohlin, Miller, and Coates (1974).

*Later discovered that this figure was in error. Actual figure is 49 percent.

audiences to declare the results of the experiment in deinstitutionalization a success.

However, their jubilation was premature and in error. It was later found that the 25 percent figure was not the correct rate. The actual rate was 49 percent. What 25 percent represented was the number of youths placed on formal probation or adjudicated delinquents, while 49 percent was the comparable rate of youths who had appeared before the court.

The increased figure of 49 percent for the six-month rate is consistent with what has been subsequently published (Coates, Miller, and Ohlin, 1975; and Serrill, 1975). The recent reports have also published the 12-month recidivism rate for court reappearance and the 6- and 12-month recidivism rates for probation or commitment. In each instance, the total recidivism rates are only for the four Western and Northern regions of Massachusetts. The regions including Boston and the Southeast regions do not have data available at this time from the Harvard study. However, such data were previously reported in the report of the Joint Committee on Post Audit and Oversight. These regions are less urban than those in the first study.

Table 15-3 presents the comparisons for 6 and 12 months. For boys there are no major differences in the recidivism rates either for court appearance or probation or commitment. With girls the community-based sample had higher recidivism rates in each case. The girls' rate of probation or commitment is twice

**Table 15-3**
**Comparison of Recidivism Rates of a 1968 Institution Group and a 1974 Community Group** (for Regions I through IV)

| | After 6 Months | After 12 Months |
|---|---|---|
| *Boys* | | |
| 1. Reappearance in Court | | |
| a. 1968 | 49% | 62% |
| b. 1974 | 49% | 68% |
| 2. Probation or Commitment | | |
| a. 1968 | 30% | 42% |
| b. 1974 | 29% | 41% |
| *Girls* | | |
| 1. Reappearance in Court | | |
| a. 1968 | 13% | 26% |
| b. 1974 | 19% | 35% |
| 2. Probation or Commitment | | |
| a. 1968 | 8% | 8% |
| b. 1974 | 12% | 16% |

Adapted from Coates, Miller, and Ohlin (1975).

as high for the community-based group as for the institutional group. It can not be concluded from the recidivism data provided by the Harvard study that the community-based, deinstitutionalized program is any more effective than the previous program.

Another source of data that will be discussed is that provided by the Commissioner of Probation for the Commonwealth of Massachusetts. The recividism rate for a sample of 103 committed juveniles was reported (Commissioner of Probation, 1975). The 12-month recidivism rate, as measured by reappearance in court, was 71 percent for the sample. The 71 percent recidivism rate is very similar to the 68 percent rate reported by the Harvard study. Foley (1976) of the Commissioner of Probation's office also reported the data in table 15-4 on youths bound over to the criminal court. As can be observed, after deinstitutionalization began in 1972, the rate of criminal proceedings instituted increased over 270 percent. Except for a small decrease in 1974, the rate has remained at the higher level for four years. The increase in the number of youths bound over for criminal prosecution is an indication of the lack of confidence by the judicial system in the Massachusetts Department of Youth Services' ability to handle serious offenders. In this instance, it is the youths who suffer—moving from the juvenile system, where rehabilitation is the overriding purpose, to the adult system, where punishment, retribution, and the protection of the community, are the priority goals.

### Conclusions

The negative results of the Massachusetts experiment in deinstitutionalization were predictable. Increases in runaway rates, deaths of youths, higher recidivism rates with girls, increases in the institution of criminal proceedings, and the high recidivism rate of Boston youths have all been reported. At best, the data on the four Western and Northern regions for boys reveals no significant difference in

**Table 15-4**
**Juveniles Bound Over to Criminal Court (Delinquency Complaints Dismissed)**

| Year | Number |
| --- | --- |
| 1970 | 35 |
| 1971 | 35 |
| 1972 | 135 |
| 1973 | 129 |
| 1974 | 76 |
| 1975 | 126 |

Adapted from Foley (1976).

the recidivism rate of boys participating in the community programs compared to boys in the old institutional programs. However, it must be remembered that one of the overriding mandates for change in the old institutional system was its high rate of recidivism. After putting the state, the youths, and the staff through the turmoil of the drastic changes in closing down the state's training schools, we find that, at best, the new approach with boys is no better in terms of rehabilitation outcome than the system it condemned. With girls the recidivism rates of the community-based programs are higher.

**Specific Prediction**: Closing training schools and placing youths summarily in hastily developed community programs will fail as a rehabilitation approach.

**Specific Recommendation**: A truly effective juvenile correctional system should have quality institutional programs for youths who need them *and* quality community-based programs for youths whose objective diagnosis indicates such placement.

The Massachusetts experiment has taught us that institutional programs cannot be closed across the board and the youths placed back in the communities without first changing the communities in some way. Initially, it was because of problems in the community that the youths were sent to institutions. Specific ways in which the community can be helped to create programs wherein the youths can succeed are to work with the youth's family and to upgrade the community-based programs according to recommendations presented in earlier chapters. If both the youths and their community resources are worked with simultaneously and improved, then the likelihood of success is increased.

The documentation of the failures of the Massachusetts experience led to the conclusion that as a system intervention, such methods are ineffective. At best, Jerome Miller had a one-step program—close the institutions. True system intervention, on the other hand, requires detailed planning and program implementation. Romig (1972*a*; 1972*b*; and 1976) has documented the effectiveness of more systematic intervention methods in juvenile justice program development. The following represents an outline of the major steps:

1. Determine top management's overall goals
2. Needs assessment based upon degree of goal attainment
   Assess:
   a. Youth
   b. Staff
   c. Programs
   d. Outcomes (follow-up)
3. Staff and citizen interviews
4. Develop new objectives based upon documented deficits

5. Develop and implement new programs to reach objectives
6. Utilize extensive staff training as a method to give staff the ability to reach the new objectives
7. Develop objective measurement criteria to provide feedback on progress

In his major system intervention at the Rhode Island Boys Training School, Carkhuff (1974) emphasized many of these methods and the importance of a "theme" around which the program or intervention could revolve. The use of a *central theme or mission* by an agency facilitates the attainment of goals by allowing staff to more clearly identify their programs. The use of the preceding systematic intervention methods will enable administrators to bring about the changes they want in ways that will ensure success rather than chaos.

Before leaving Massachusetts and the experiment in deinstitutionalization, a final word should be said. The goal of system intervention in juvenile corrections was misplaced in Massachusetts. The goal of the juvenile justice system is not the closing of juvenile training schools—the goal is to close the *adult* prisons and *adult* jails and *adult* probation departments. The goal of the juvenile justice system is to intervene so successfully with the offenders as juveniles that when they become adults, they will be productive citizens rather than chronic offenders. A state or a country that is closing juvenile training schools while building more adult prisons and jails has in some way reversed its priorities. The major policy objective for the United States of America should not center, as it now does, on where rehabilitation of juvenile delinquents should occur—institutions or community programs—but on *how* to so effectively rehabilitate youthful offenders that as adults they become law-abiding citizens.

## References

Calhoun, J. Personal communication. February 1976.

Carkhuff, R.R. *Cry Twice.* Amherst, Mass.: Human Resource Development Press, 1974.

Coates, R.B., A.D. Miller, and L.E. Ohlin. Exploratory Analysis of Recidivism and Cohort Data on the Massachusetts Youth Correctional System. Center for Criminal Justice. Harvard Law School, July 1975.

Foley, J.P. Personal Communication and Study Concerning Certain Juveniles Committed for Minority to Department of Youth Services in June and September 1974. Deputy Commissioner of Massachusetts, 1976.

Leavey, J. Personal communication. February 1976.

Management Audit of the Department of Youth Services. Joint Committee on Post Audit and Oversight. Post Audit and Oversight Bureau. Massachusetts General Court 1974.

Ohlin, L.E., A.D. Miller, and R.B. Coates. Quarterly Report of the DYS Project Center for Criminal Justice. Harvard Law School, July 1974.

Poitrast, F. Personal communication. February 1976.

Romig, D.A. *Needs Assessment and Evaluation of the Brownwood State Home and School.* Brownwood, Texas: Brownwood State Home and School, 1972*a*.

Romig, D.A. *Needs Assessment and Evaluation of the Gainesville State School for Girls.* Brownwood, Texas: Brownwood State Home and School, 1972*b*.

Romig, D.A. Texas Juvenile Corrections Master Plan. (in press) 1976.

Serrill, M. Juvenile Corrections in Massachusetts. *Corrections Magazine* 2 (1975):3-40.

# 16 Parole

## Review of the Research

Parole is the final system intervention in the juvenile justice system. Parole is similar to probation in that they both are community-based programs that involve professional adult supervision. The main difference is that probation is one of the first interventions utilized after a youth is judged delinquent, whereas parole most typically occurs after a youth has spent some time in a state institution and has been released. *Parole* originally developed as a method of treatment in the adult correctional system that allowed inmates from prison who had performed well to be released early under professional supervision. Additional uses of parole were soon documented:

Parole is the service that aids the released prisoner to bridge the gap between the relatively abnormal environment of the prison and the environment of the community. By providing supervision and guidance during the critical early months of parole, reversion to crime may be prevented. Secondly, parole provides a period in the life of the offender when he can be removed from society as soon as he shows indications of dangerous behavior without waiting until he commits a new crime. Thirdly, it provides legal authority to compel a former offender to live up to certain accepted standards of conduct. Fourthly, it provides for the former offender a period of supervision under normal social conditions, a testing period, before he is completely free (Giardini, 1959, p. 19).

These purposes can apply equally to the juvenile parole system.

The four purposes can be divided into two categories: follow-up treatment and legal supervision. Though the two roles may not be incompatible, the skills and programs involved are certainly distinct and different. Various approaches in reconciling the differences and obtaining a better parole performance from the youths will now be discussed.

The first study was one by Johnson (1965) that involved comparing the effects of two different parole caseloads. Youths on parole from the California Youth Authority back to their home in Alameda County were subjects in the study. There was a random assignment of 360 youths to the control group. Youths in the treatment group were assigned to 37-parolee caseloads and received more intensive parole supervision. The control group youths were assigned to 72-youth caseloads.

The results were negative. Those youths in the smaller caseload had a significantly greater number of unfavorable discharges from parole. There was also no significant difference in the number of parole violations and the severity of offenses committed by the two groups after 18 months on parole. The reduced caseload did not make a significant reduction in the youths' subsequent delinquent behaviors back in the community. It was hypothesized that this lack of impact occurred because the reduced caseload usually meant increased surveillance rather than increased treatment.

A study was conducted by the Training Center in Youth Development at Boston University (1966), where reduced caseload was defined as increased treatment. There was an after-the-fact random selection of treatment and control youths. To control for the possible differences in the two groups, the recidivism results were reported also controlling for the major characteristics in the youths' backgrounds. All the youths were boys between 14 and 15 years of age. The treatment group participated in a reduced caseload of 25 boys and received educational counseling from specially trained college graduate counselors. The boys in the treatment group also received some group counseling. The control group youths participated in the regular 75-boy caseload parole supervision program.

The results did not support the special parole program. The results after six months of special treatment indicated no significant difference in recidivism for the two groups. These results were computed controlling for age, IQ, delinquency history, and age of first incarceration. The negative effects of the reduced caseload are consistent with the previous study and the research reported in chapter 11. The fact that the special treatment program—educational counseling and group counseling—did not make a difference has also been documented in previous chapters.

Jones (1969) reported the results of a similar program in New York City. All the youths had been sent to a training school. The primary commitment offenses were theft, burglary, and school problems. Thirty-four youths were in the experimental group, while 24 were in the appropriately selected control group. The treatment program was entitled the New York City Reintegration Project and involved providing the youths with casework services and family counseling on small caseloads. The goals of the program were to help ease the youths' transitions back home by providing jobs and school placement services as well as individual counseling. The youths in the control group participated in the standard parole program.

There was no significant difference between the two groups in their recidivism rates. Both groups had a recidivism rate near 41 percent. The authors pointed out that employment was difficult to obtain, except for low-paying jobs. This program, as with the previous ones, had no built-in reward system to reinforce positive behavior. The fact that the only jobs that were available were ones that were low paying probably served more as punishment and discouragement to the youths. Once again, though a special attempt was made to help the youths, the more intensive program did not demonstrate any measurable superiority over the regular nonprogram.

The effects of two different parole programs were presented by Pond (1970). In both programs, culturally deprived delinquent boys, primarily from urban inner-city neighborhoods, were placed in an intensive parole program in lieu of institutionalization and subsequent regular parole. The youths in the first program were boys between 13 and 18 years of age from the Watts unit in South Central Los Angeles. There were 102 boys randomly assigned to the treatment group and 70 boys to the control group. The boys in the treatment program participated entirely in the community-based program in a caseload that involved one Community Delinquency Control Project worker to 25 youths. The program also involved matching of the youths and project worker based upon the I-level system discussed in chapter 14. A main method of treatment was confrontive group counseling.

The youths in the control group went through the regular institutional and parole programs. The results of the arrest and parole revocation data after 15 months of parole were unfavorable for the treatment group. They had no significant difference in their parole revocation rate, but had a significantly greater number of youths who were arrested two or more times when compared with the control group. The arrest rate for the treatment group was 80.4 percent, while the control group had a 77.1 percent rate—both very unsatisfactory. The conclusion is that both programs were not effective, and that the special treatment was, in fact, somewhat worse.

The second study by Pond (1970) was similar. Teenage delinquent boys from the same type of background, but this time from the Jefferson unit of Los Angeles, participated in a variation of the Community Delinquency Control Project. There was a random assignment of 78 boys to the treatment group and 51 boys to the control group. The program involved three of the previous study's ingredients: intensive parole program, a reduced caseload, and staff matched with youths based upon I-level classification. The additional program element was intensive individual counseling. The control group participated in regular institutional program and subsequent parole program.

After 15 months of participation in the parole programs, the revocation and arrest records of the two groups were compared. Once again the results were unfavorable for the treatment group. There was no significant difference in their revocation history, while their arrest records revealed that significantly more treatment group boys were arrested two or more times. In fact, over twice as many treatment youths had been arrested two or more times. The two preceding programs were developed not only as alternatives to the regular parole programs but also as substitutes for institutional treatment. In terms of the arrest statistics, even though both the new and the old programs did poorly, it would have to be concluded that the traditional institutional and parole programs were better.

These studies have mainly been concerned with the results of innovative approaches to the parole process. A study by Hudson (1973) directly questioned the effectiveness of parole itself. The youths in the study were boys and girls from two Minnesota training schools who were categorized as having a low risk for parole failure. Behaviorally, *low risk* meant: (1) returning to their own home, (2) not diagnosed as severely emotionally disturbed, (3) low incidence of physical assaults, and (4) no officially known involvement in rape or arson. After qualifying in the low-risk category, 120 boys and girls were randomly assigned to the experimental treatment group, while 114 were similarly assigned to the control group. The control group was released from the institution on regular parole supervision. The treatment group in turn was released to the community under the conditions of no formal parole supervision.

The results were surprising. Rather than doing worse without the parole supervision, the treatment group did at least as well in some instances and better on one criteria. After 10 months of community placement, the data on both groups were examined. There was no significant difference in the arrest statistics of the two groups. There was no significant difference in the number of parole revocations for the two groups of girls. The boys who had no supervision had significantly fewer parole revocations. However, when the treatment boys were revoked, it was generally for significantly more serious offenses than the control group. The conclusion of this phase of the study is that for certain low-risk youths, parole is generally no more effective than no parole.

The author reported some additional data that has some relevance to improving rehabilitation programs for delinquent youths. When the youths were asked "to rank the relative seriousness of difficulty experienced around key areas, a high degree of agreement was obtained" (Hudson, 1973, p. 12). The three most serious problems in order of difficulty were: (1) family, (2) school, and (3) work. This ranking really sets the priority for the content of rehabilitation programs for delinquent youths. They need skills to succeed with their families, with school, and on a job.

The youths were also asked with whom they would discuss their problems. The mothers and fathers were rated highest, their friends, sisters, and brothers next. Hudson also examined, for both groups, who they went to for help. Both groups went to their families. Neither the control group on parole nor the treatment group not on parole contacted their parole officer or other professional helping agencies. This data explains why all the studies focusing on improving the communication and problem-solving skills of the family were so successful. Increasing the skills of the delinquent youths' mothers, fathers, sisters, and brothers improved the degree and quality of help that the youths were likely to receive when they went to their families with their problems. The conclusion is clear: all delinquency rehabilitation programs should focus upon giving the family helping skills—not necessarily because the family is the cause of the delinquency, but because it is to the family that the youths turn in times of crisis.

Palmer (1974*b*) summarized the results of the decade-long research by the California Youth Authority of their Community Treatment Project. The program involved the random assignment of low-risk youths to either the usual institutional and parole program or to a special community-based treatment program involving intensive parole supervision. The low-risk criteria for program participation involved first offenders, youths who had not committed offenses like armed robbery, assault with a deadly weapon, or forcible rape. The study involved both males and females from approximately 9 to 19 years of age. There were 686 youths assigned to the treatment group and 328 assigned to the control group.

The treatment program utilized the I-level differential treatment approach, with youths being placed in homogeneous groups with matched parole officers. The treatment program was individualized for the youths, but the main elements included individual and group counseling, a special day treatment center, and alternate home placement when required. The caseload was 10 to 12 youths per worker. The performance of the treatment group was compared with youths who participated in the regular institutional and parole program.

The results were partially favorable. The boys in the treatment group had a significantly lower per month arrest rate. The recidivism rate was also significantly lower after 24 months of parole follow-up, 44 percent versus 63 percent for the control group boys. One major negative result for the treatment group boys was that the control group males who were favorably discharged performed 15 percent better than the comparable group of experimental youths after four years of post-California Youth Authority follow-up. Within the I-level classification, several categories of boys performed significantly better in the institutional program. The girls of both groups had no significant difference in their follow-up behavior. Because of the mixed results of the study, a clear conclusion concerning this phase of the Community Treatment Project cannot be made.

Palmer (1974a) presented the results of Phase III of the project that investigated the effects of appropriate initial placement, as diagnosed in the reception center, compared with inappropriate placement. The two initial placement choices were either community treatment or a small minimum security residential program housing 23 to 25 youths. Prior to placement, the youths were diagnosed according to their interests, motivations, and limitations as to which was the preferred initial placement. After the diagnosis was completed and documented, the youths—boys between 13 and 21 years of age—were randomly assigned to one of four groups:

1. Appropriately placed—residential
2. Appropriately placed—community
3. Inappropriately placed—residential
4. Inappropriately placed—community

The results of the analysis of the recidivism data clearly favored appropriate placement of the youths, especially for youths who needed the residential placement. This study supports the fact that community-based placement with nonviolent first offenders can be either for better or worse depending upon the youths' needs. This conclusion establishes the critical importance of the use of diagnostic processes in determining youth placement. The placement decision, whether residential or community-based, is in some ways dependent upon how much initial structure the youths need in their programming.

## Conclusions

This chapter has reviewed 8 studies involving over 2300 youths, all concerned with the effectiveness of the juvenile parole program. Of the eight studies, six were concerned with reduced caseloads and more intensive treatment or supervision. The treatment usually consisted of casework and/or individual or group counseling. In not one of the studies were the results overwhelmingly favorable. In five of the six projects, the results were considerably more negative in terms of the success of the reduced caseload, intensive treatment approach. Table 16-1 presents this chapter's summaries.

The study by Hudson (1973) questioned whether parole itself was effective. In the project, low-risk youths were simply released back into the community without any follow-up supervision or parole treatment. Their performance was as good as youths who had parole supervision. An additional finding of Hudson's study was that the youths who were on parole did not voluntarily go to their parole officers when they needed help. Instead they went to their families with their problems.

Palmer (1974a) reported results concerning the importance of appropriate placement in either a residential or community-based program. The results were clear: for some youths, residential placement was the best choice for initial treatment. The results of Palmer's Community Treatment Project support the conclusion that some delinquent youths perform better in community-based programs, while for other youths, institutional treatment is an unequivocal necessity. The negative results of parole and the various innovative approaches lead to the following prediction.

**Specific Prediction**: Parole programs in which treatment consists of casework, individual counseling, or group counseling will fail in their efforts to help youths successfully reintegrate into the community.

Since most juvenile parole programs provide, at best, the preceding three approaches, the best guess is that they will fail. Should parole, therefore, be abolished as a system intervention. No! It should not be discontinued. But it should be radically revised.

Since the recommendations throughout this book have emphasized teaching delinquent youths skills in the family, social, educational, and vocational areas, parole should take its place in ensuring that the skills learned in an institution

**Table 16-1**
**Parole Summary**

| Researchers | Number of Youths | | Intervention | Results | Follow-up Results |
|---|---|---|---|---|---|
| | Experimental | Control | | | |
| Johnson (1965) | 360 | 360 | Reduced parole caseload size | a. Significantly more unfavorable discharges b. No significant difference in parole violations c. No significant difference in severity of offenses | |
| Boston University Training Center in Youth Development (1966) | | | a. Educational counselors b. Reduced parole caseload | No significant difference in recidivism | |
| Jones (1969) | 34 | 24 | a. Reduced caseload b. Family counseling c. Casework | | No significant difference in recidivism |
| Pond (1970) | 102 | 70 | a. Intensive parole program b. Reduced caseload c. Matching staff and youths d. Confrontive group counseling | After 15 months parole a. More arrests for treated youths b. No significant difference in parole revocations | |
| Pond (1970) | 78 | 51 | a. Intensive parole program b. Reduced caseload c. Matching staff with youths d. Individual counseling | After 15 months parole a. More arrests for treated youths b. No significant difference in parole revocations | |
| Hudson (1973) | 120 | 114 | Placement of low-risk youths on parole without formal supervision | After 10 months a. No significant difference in arrest statistics b. No significant difference in girls' parole revocations c. Boys in experimental group had fewer parole revocations but were committed for more serious offenses | |

**Table 16-1.** (cont.)

| Researchers | Number of Youths | | Intervention | Results | Follow-up Results |
|---|---|---|---|---|---|
| | Experimental | Control | | | |
| Palmer (1974) | 686 | 328 | *a.* Differential treatment including appropriate placement *b.* Matching of staff and youths *c.* Day treatment program *d.* Reduced caseloads | | *a.* Significantly fewer offenses and recidivism for boys *b.* No significant difference in community performance for girls |
| Palmer (1974) | | | Appropriate placement in community or institution | Significantly lower recidivism rate for appropriately placed youths | |

effectively assist the youths when they return to the community. In an institution, the skills can be taught and even practiced in role-playing situations. The real test, however, is when the youths are back home, where all the problems occurred in the first place. The parole officer in this model becomes a teacher who is with his students on the firing line to observe the success or failure of the new behaviors and skills the youths try out. The parole officer/teacher can then differentially reward the youths for succeeding or failing and provide extra skill training if necessary.

**Specific Recommendation**: Parole programs should become teaching-oriented programs, emphasizing the skills needed for success in the community.

The content of the parole teaching programs has been implied in previous chapters. The fact that what is taught should be an extension of previous programs, whether institutional or community-based, will be discussed in detail in the next chapter. Certain content or skills are suggested from findings reported by Mahan and Andre (1971):

Feedback from parole and public school personnel strongly indicates that California Youth Authority wards fail or drop out of school because of affective rather than cognitive difficulties. The wards do not appear to see the personal relevancy of subject matter because their real concerns are in the area of interpersonal relationships (Mahan and Andre, 1971, p. 1).

This conclusion is similar to that reported in chapter 4, that the reasons the youths were fired from their jobs or quit were more the result of interpersonal factors than the technical requirements of the jobs themselves. This need for an emphasis upon interpersonal skill training for delinquent youths cuts across all programs, because ultimately the youths will have to make it back in the community on their own. Interpersonal skills clearly are related to family communication skills, whose success in various programs has been reported throughout this book. Because of these facts, the following prediction and recommendation are warranted.

**General Prediction**: Those programs for delinquent youths which emphasize teaching the youths interpersonal skills, as well as intellectual skills, will succeed.

**General Recommendation**: All delinquency rehabilitation programs should focus upon teaching the youths interpersonal skills. The teaching should include specific training and practice on each subskill. The real-life use of the skills in the community should be built in as a program requirement.

It seems logical that one very important function of parole would be to provide the assistance to institutional programs in such real-life skills use and follow-up. The importance of an integrated juvenile justice system for all rehabilitation program objectives will be discussed in the next chapter.

**References**

Boston University Training Center in Youth Development. *Educational Counselors: Training for a New Definition of After-Care of Juvenile Parolees.* Boston: Boston Univ. Press, 1966.

Giardini, G. *The Parole Process.* Springfield, Ill.: Charles C. Thomas, 1959.

Hudson, C.H. Summary Report: An Experimental Study of the Differential Effects of Parole Supervision For A Group of Adolescent Boys and Girls. Minneapolis, Minnesota: Minnesota Dept. of Corrections, 1973.

Johnson, B.M. The "Failure" of a Parole Research Project. *California Youth Authority Quarterly* 18 (1965):35-39.

Jones, H. From reform school to society. In H. Weissman, ed., *Individual and Group Services in The Mobilization For Youth Experience.* New York: Associated Press, 1969.

Mahan, J., and C.R. Andre. Progress Report on the Differential Education Project Paso Robles School for Boys. Educational Research Series Report No. 2. Sacramento: California Youth Authority, 1971.

Palmer, T. The Community Treatment Project. In K. Griffiths, ed., *A Review of Accumulated Research in the California Youth Authority.* Sacramento: California Youth Authority, 1974*a*.

Palmer, T. The Youth Authority's Treatment Project. *Federal Probation* 38 (1974*b*):74-92.

Pond, E. The Los Angeles Community Delinquency Control Project: An

Experiment in the Rehabilitation of Delinquents in an urban community. Research Report No. 60. Sacramento: California Youth Authority, 1970.

# 17 The Ideal System

## Introduction

The preceding chapters have discussed studies and conclusions concerning the different components of the juvenile justice system of rehabilitation. The levels of intervention move from the least intense—diversion, probation, and community residential programs—to the most intense and structured—institutional programs—and back out to the less structured supervision of parole. Figure 17-1 illustrates the system of rehabilitation interventions.

At any point in the system of interventions, a youth can be so effectively dealt with through the provided programs that placement in further levels of the system is prevented. For example, if a youth is first placed in a diversion program that successfully helps the youth and his or her family, then participation in juvenile probation will not be necessary as long as the youth does not break the law again. To give you a better idea of the system as displayed in figure 17-1, each of the components will now be reviewed in light of the conclusions of the preceding chapters.

1. *Diversion Programs.* The first level of system intervention, diversion programs, was developed to provide services to the youths and families at the point of the initial contact with law enforcement agencies. The overriding premise was that if the youths could be treated at the first sign of their illegal behavior, then further involvement with the juvenile justice system could be prevented. In chapter 10, it was discovered that there was nothing inherent in a diversion program that caused youths to discontinue further illegal behavior. In fact, most of the diversion programs reported negative results.

Should diversion programs be discontinued? No! In fact, the director of the California Youth Authority, Allan Breed, after reporting some of the disappointing results of California's Probation Subsidy Program, thought that more attention should be given to diversion. When the ingredients of the programs that failed were examined, it was found that the dominant treatment approaches used were individual counseling, casework, and group counseling. Earlier chapters have documented the failure of those treatment modalities. In chapter 7, four studies involving diversion reported success when they focused on improving the communication skills of the family.

Successful program ingredients identified in previous chapters can and should be applied to improve juvenile diversion programs, such as teaching study skills and providing differential reinforcement for improved behavior. The Ideal

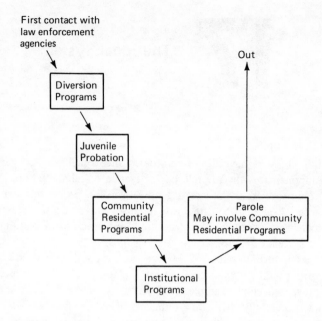

First contact with
law enforcement
agencies

Out

Diversion
Programs

Juvenile
Probation

Community
Residential
Programs

Parole
May involve Community
Residential Programs

Institutional
Programs

**Figure 17-1.** Juvenile Justice System of Rehabilitation

Rehabilitation Program presented in chapter 9 is applicable to diversion settings. A new emphasis on skills is preferred to the current approaches, which are no different than those developed during the 1930s under the name of child guidance centers.

In chapter 10, information was presented concerning the placement of such programs in a police setting. The primary rationale for such placement is that referral and follow-up feedback are facilitated because the primary source of referrals are from law enforcement agencies. The main recommendation to be made at this point is that diversion programs, if not directly under the supervision of police departments, should be closely allied with and mutually supportive of the local police programs.

Because of the potential threat of a diminished responsibility for juvenile probation programs if the diversion programs are effective, cooperation and involvement with the local probation department must be solicited. In one state, a minority of chief juvenile probation officers were able to effectively delay the development of a statewide diversion program because of what they perceived as a potential threat to their probation programs. Juvenile probation staff should also be involved in the development of diversion programs because of their past involvement with the delinquent youths in their respective communities. Diversion programs cooperating with the local law enforcement agencies and juvenile probation departments will create a combined system intervention that cannot fail.

2. *Probation Program.* Probation programs were the next level of system interventions to be evaluated. The most effective form of probation treatment utilized a rehabilitation team and provided specific intervention for specific problems. The team utilized paraprofessional staff from the youths' neighborhoods to provide treatment under the supervision of probation officers. In this model of probation, the paraprofessional rehabilitation aides are free to provide treatment, while the probation officers perform the supervision and surveillance of the youths' potentially illegal behavior. The thrust of the rehabilitation team approach is once again to give the youths and their families the skills needed to help the youths succeed socially, intellectually, and vocationally.

Some data were presented in chapter 11 that indicated that for certain youths release or monetary fines were as effective as probation supervision. Therefore, the model in figure 17-2 is presented. This model recognizes that some youths will be referred to juvenile court and probation who do not need treatment but who do need some form of punishment. Monetary fines the youths must pay off themselves provide a flexible form of punishment that, in itself for those youth so diagnosed, is the most effective form of treatment. Monetary fines also allow for some form of retribution and victim compensation.

The success of the model in figure 17-2 is dependent upon effective diagnosis utilizing objective test measurements. For youths who require rehabilitation services, the diagnostic tests become the baseline or pretests in which subsequent progress can be measured. Posttests and follow-up assessments should be utilized to document the success or failure of the various programs. In this way, administrators can learn which of their programs are most effective.

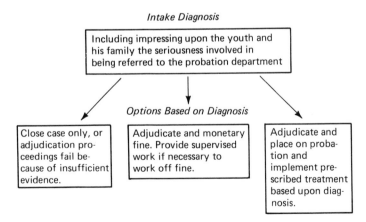

**Figure 17-2.** Treatment Options for Delinquents Based on Intake Diagnosis

California's Probation Subsidy Program is a system intervention that cuts across several levels of the juvenile justice system. The published results to date were discussed. Based upon the negative results of reduced probation officer caseloads and traditional treatment, new program standards were recommended. Probation subsidy and financial support should be contingent upon the utilization of program approaches with documented effectiveness.

As a system intervention, probation subsidy only impacted a small portion of the total system. If subsidy programs are desired that effect the entire population of juveniles on probation, then interventions should be built around staff training and comprehensive program revision. If the skills of probation officers and the programs they implement are improved, then all the youths coming in contact with those staff will be benefited. *Specificity* in system intervention was presented as a principle stating that if you desire specific results from certain geographic regions or programs, then the system interventions must impact those regions or programs. The need for a strong evaluation system is critical with probation subsidy in order to quickly document and communicate to others those programs which achieve the highest effectiveness.

3. *Community Residential Programs.* The main conclusion of chapter 13 is that there is nothing inherent in a community-based setting that will rehabilitate. Community residential settings, as with the previous levels of juvenile justice system interventions, need effective programs. Community residential programs are needed that provide social skills, educational skills that move the youths toward a diploma or certificate, career advancement and decision-making skills, and family communication skills. Such residential programs will help youths whose behavior has not warranted the more structured institutional programs or for youths returning to the community from training schools.

The ideal community-based program is the family. For a majority of youths, the goals of the residential programs should include preparation for return to their families. It was pointed out that in some cases a family placement might include relatives other than parents. In addition to receiving family communication skills, discipline skills, and problem-solving skills training, the family should be involved in all aspects of their youth's rehabilitation program. Input should be collected from them concerning how they see the problem, after their attention has been directed to the seriousness of the youth's behavior. Their difficulties should be diagnosed with specific solutions provided by skill training. They should practice the new skills in the problem settings, such as getting up on Monday mornings, eating meals together, and completing family weekend work projects. They should receive differential reinforcement as they succeed, and follow-up help should be provided after the youths have returned to their homes. Though complicated and laborious, these steps provide a greater assurance of an effective reintegration of the youths with their families after the use of alternative residential programs.

4. *Institutional Programs.* As with the other system interventions, certain

institutional programs consistently succeeded, while others consistently failed. One successful approach was structured programs, which achieved more favorable results than permissive approaches. The more permissive programs allowed the youths to have considerable control over their own discipline and level of supervision. Youths committed to institutions need a variety of levels of supervision imposed by the staff and programs, so that each youth is given only that amount of freedom that he or she can successfully handle. A levels system that allows youths to earn progressively higher degrees of freedom is consistent with the principles of effective behavior modification.

As with all programs, but most especially with institutional programs, objective measures of rehabilitation progress are needed. Such criteria allow the youths to know how they can have control over the amount of freedom they earn and when they are ready to return to the community. Prior to release, the youths should have had practice in performing successfully in the problem settings of family interaction, public school or work, and peer relationships. Whether an institution is in a rural or urban setting is irrelevant as long as the setting allows for practice in the problem settings and for, at least, monthly family contact between the youths, the families, and the rehabilitation workers. Institutional programs that focus upon improving the communication skills and interaction patterns of the family will be successful.

5. *Parole Programs.* Presently, most parole programs resemble current probation programs in that both emphasize supervision and surveillance of the youths. Parole, as a system intervention, lacks the ingredients for what could be one of the most impactful interventions of all—*follow-up*. Programs throughout this book that had follow-up help built in as a program ingredient achieved more favorable results than those programs lacking such assistance. The goal of parole as a system intervention should be to provide a transition for youths returning to their communities in the form of further instruction and practice in the same skills learned in the institutions.

If surveillance/supervision is to be retained as an additional goal of parole, then parole should incorporate the rehabilitation team approach developed for probation. The rehabilitation aides can provide the teaching programs and follow-up help. The parole officer then supervises the rehabilitation aides as well as providing the supervision/surveillance function for the youths. The development of more effective parole programs will favorably impact the entire juvenile justice system.

## Summary

The goal of the juvenile justice system is to so effectively deal with delinquent youths that they have the skills and desire to get what they want in ways that are within the boundary of the law. The other side of the goal is to reduce the number of prisons and jails that are needed for these youths when they become adults.

The way in which the different components of the juvenile justice system can mesh is through a focus on youth—on our children—on their specific problems and on their skill deficits. From diversion programs to parole programs, there can be a greater agreement on the rehabilitation goals for the youths. In this way, the different levels of system intervention support each other.

Seckel and Pops (1974) reported the disparaging lack of continuity in the number and types of goals for youths committed to the California Youth Authority. The goals of staff at the reception center were different from the goals at the institution, and both sets of goals for the same youths were different from those of the parole staff. From the resulting lack of agreement and support of rehabilitation goals, one could predict the failure of the total juvenile system to combat the rise in crime.

Methods that would increase the continuity of goals across all elements of the juvenile justice system include:

1. Development of statewide juvenile justice system themes or missions.
2. Staff training in a common rehabilitation approach, preferably an eclectic model based upon methods with documented success.
3. Utilization of similar diagnostic tests and methods that can be utilized as progress measures as given youths move throughout the system.
4. Development of a common language for describing behavior, problems, and success or failure in the rehabilitation program.

Continuity and consistency of rehabilitation goals will result in a more effective system.

The preceding chapters documented two approaches in system intervention that failed—the Massachusetts Experiment in Deinstitutionalization and some aspects of the California Probation Subsidy Program. As system interventions, neither specifically dealt with the youths in such a way as to give them new skills to succeed where before they had failed. The conclusion is that no matter how broad or sweeping the changes in a system are, there must be a check to be sure that those at the lowest level in the system—in this case the youths—are favorably affected.

Looking again at the entire system of interventions, the question can be asked, can any portion of the system be deleted or deemphasized? The answer is no. All aspects of the present system are needed, but they should be modified as recommended throughout this book. Should any level of the system receive more emphasis than the other parts? To answer that question, we must examine a finding reported by Massimo and Shore (1963):

The service was initiated at a crisis point when the subject was expelled from school or dropped out for reasons of his own. It was believed that even though the delinquent overtly rejected school, leaving it was still a crisis to him and made him more amenable to help (Massimo and Shore, 1963, p. 635).

Treatment initiated as close as possible to the point of crisis will be more effective. The reasons for this are that soon after the crisis, the youths and their parents are still experiencing it; it is more immediate; its effects can be seen and talked about. Because the intervention is close to the crisis, the program can more easily gain the attention of the youths and their families and implement activities that are more specifically and directly tied to the crisis.

The crisis can be expulsion from school, being picked up by the police, placement in detention, placement out of the home, or breaking any major law and getting caught. For a majority of youths, the first few delinquent acts are not serious enough for probation or institutional placement. However, it is at this initial crisis point that rehabilitation services could be the most cost-effective in terms of a little bit of help preventing a lot of subsequent more serious problems. It is to this end that diversion programs should devote themselves. The fact that such diversion programs should be initiated *immediately* after the youths have been picked up by the police emphasizes the importance of the required close relationship of law enforcement agencies with diversion programs. In terms of broad interventions, the juvenile justice system should turn more to creating effective diversion programs that pick up on the youths' problems at the earliest point.

### Conclusions

The purpose of this book has been to summarize those programs and interventions across the country which have succeeded, and to describe new standards for the treatment of juvenile delinquents. The present system is part of the problem. Youths and their families are initially promised hope through the countless existing programs. In the end, they come away disillusioned, angry, and hurt. Such feelings can be contrasted with the rich joy of youths who get the skills they need, who try them out, and who surprisingly see life begin to go their way. *Justice For Our Children* is about taking hostility and hurt and replacing it with confidence and hope.

### References

Massimo, J.L., and M.F. Shore. The effectiveness of a comprehensive vocationally oriented psychotherapeutic program for adolescent delinquent boys, *American Journal of Orthopsychiatry* 33 (1963):634-642.

Seckel, J.P., and S.M. Pops. *Case Review and Planning: A Study of Treatment Goal Emphasis and Consistency*. California Youth Authority, 1973.

# Index

# Index

academic education, 25-42

behavior modification, 11-24, 28, 29, 33, 36, 63, 92, 109, 111, 113, 154
behavioral goals, 21, 83, 109

California's Probation Subsidy Program, 141-148
camping, therapeutic, 44, 97-102, 112
career ladder, 45, 47, 51
casework, 3-10, 34, 112, 147, 156, 186, 196
community residential programs, 45, 149-158
control group, xv, xxiii
counseling, group, 5, 26, 44, 57-76, 112, 113, 190

deinstitutionalization, 149, 162
delinquency prevention, 7
diagnosis, 6, 7, 29, 36, 73, 74, 81, 84, 94, 109, 111, 112, 113, 136, 138, 163, 170, 197
differential treatment, 164-167 *passim*
direct services, 7
diversion, 7, 117-124, 195

education. *See* academic education
experimental group, xxiii

family therapy, 4, 87-96, 109, 111, 112, 118, 119, 157

G.E.D. (Graduate Equivalency Diploma), 33, 49, 51, 43, 109, 147

Haggerty-Olsen-Wickman ratings, 58, 60, 117
human resource development model, 122

individual counseling. *See* casework; individual psychotherapy
individualization, 94, 109, 113

individual psychotherapy, 44, 77-86, 112, 190
institutional programs, 7, 15, 26, 58, 67, 68, 78, 84, 128, 150, 156, 159-172, 175, 181, 195, 198

Massachusetts' Deinstitutionalization Project, 173-184
methods, xxii
monetary fines, 136

parole, 7, 62, 162, 166, 185-194, 199
probation, juvenile, 7, 16, 61, 67, 91, 114, 121, 125-140, 159, 195, 196, 197
problem solving, 26, 52

recidivism rate, xxv, 11, 44, 45, 47, 63, 81, 88, 120, 128, 129, 161, 166, 177, 181
recommendations, 7
referral, 6, 112, 121
rehabilitation, xv, xxii, xxvi, 44, 52, 73, 94, 98, 99, 129, 144, 156, 157
residential programs. *See* institutional programs
rewards. *See* behavior modification

social work. *See* casework
specificity, 14, 16, 21, 29, 44, 74, 84, 88, 91, 110, 112, 113, 137, 148, 198
statistically significant difference, xxv
subjects, xiii
system interventions, 115
system, the ideal, 195-202

treatment group, xxiii

vocational programs, 43-56, 84, 100, 109, 112, 113

work programs. *See* vocational programs

youth service bureaus, 7

205

# About the Author

**Dennis A. Romig** has worked in the field of child psychology and juvenile delinquent rehabilitation for the past eight years, serving as central office program director for the Texas Youth Council and as clinical director and chief psychologist at the Brownwood State Home and School, a facility of the Texas Youth Council. Dr. Romig has also worked with emotionally disturbed and visually handicapped youth populations in community and institutional programs.

Dr. Romig received the B.A. in basic science from Graceland College, and both the M.A. in counseling psychology and the Ph.D. in educational psychology from the University of Texas. He is a licensed psychologist, listed in *Who's Who in the South and Southwest*, and a consultant for the development of more effective state juvenile justice programs. He has written over forty articles and research publications and coauthored the *Review of Research on Delinquency in Texas* and the *Texas Juvenile Corrections Master Plan*.

## DATE DUE

| | | |
|---|---|---|
| APR 10 1980 | | |
| DEC 15 1995 | | |
| NOV 03 1996 | | |
| NOV 22 2000 | | |
| | | |
| | | |
| | | |
| | | |
| | | |
| | | |
| | | |
| | | |
| | | |
| | | |
| | | |
| | | |
| | | |
| | | |

IDEAL 3370 UNGUMMED, 3371 GUMMED   PRINTED IN U.S.A.